OLD TESTAMENT MESSAGE

A Biblical-Theological Commentary

Carroll Stuhlmueller, C.P. and Martin McNamara, M.S.C.
EDITORS

Old Testament Message, Volume 16

DANIEL, FIRST MACCABEES, SECOND MACCABEES

with an
Excursus on the Apocalyptic Genre

John J. Collins

Michael Glazier, Inc.
Wilmington, Delaware

First published in 1981 by:
MICHAEL GLAZIER, INC.
1723 Delaware Avenue
Wilmington, Delaware 19806

Distributed outside U.S., Canada & Philippines by:
GILL & MACMILLAN, LTD.
Goldenbridge, Inchicore
Dublin 8 Ireland

Library of Congress Catalog Card Number: 81–80825
International Standard Book Number
Old Testament Message series: 0-89453-235-9
DANIEL, FIRST MACCABEES, SECOND MACCABEES
With an Excursus on the Apocalyptic Genre:
0-89453-250-2 (Michael Glazier, Inc.)
7171-1180-6 (Gill & Macmillan, Ltd.)

Cover design by Lillian Brulc

Printed in the United States of America

Contents

Editors' Preface   xiii

Introduction

The historical setting   1
The historical critical method   4
Religion and society   5
History and theology   6

The Book of Daniel

INTRODUCTION   11
     The date   11
     The unity of the book   14
     The genres of Daniel   18

THE BOOK OF DANIEL: COMMENTARY

THE TALES   20
     Daniel Chap. 1: Jewish Youths at the Gentile Court   20
         Food and drink   23
     Daniel Chap. 2: Nebuchadnezzar's Dream   25
         The four kingdoms   31
         The significance of the dream   33
         The political attitude in Daniel 2   34

Daniel Chap. 3: The Fiery Furnace   36
   The significance of the story   45
   The prayer of Azariah   47
   The song of the three young men   48
Daniel Chap. 4: The Madness of Nebuchadnezzar   48
   The objection to gentile kings   54
   The perspective on political power   55
Daniel Chap. 5: The Writing on the Wall   55
   The judgment on the king   60
Daniel Chap. 6: The Lions' Den   61
   The note of vengeance   66
The Tales in Retrospect   67

THE VISIONS   69
Daniel Chap. 7: The Beasts from the Sea and
   "One like a Son of Man"   69
   The beasts from the sea   72
   The heavenly judgment   76
   The little horn   79
   The kingdom   80
   The impact of the vision   80
   The truth of the vision   82
   The relevance of the vision   83
Daniel Chap. 8: The Ram and the Goat   84
   The application of the vision   88
Daniel Chap. 9: The Seventy Weeks of Years   90
   The prayer of Daniel   92
   The angel's interpretation   93
   The truth of the prophecy   96
Daniel Chap. 10: The Battle in Heaven   97
Daniel Chap. 11: The Hellenistic Wars   102
   The career of Antiochus Epiphanes   105
   The conduct advocated by Daniel   106
   The characterization of the king   107

Daniel Chap. 12:1-3: The Resurrection 108
  The belief in resurrection 110
  The significance and value of the belief 111
Daniel Chap. 12:4-13: The Conclusion 113
The Visions in Retrospect 115

THE ADDITIONS TO THE BOOK OF DANIEL 118
  Susanna 118
    The wisdom of Daniel 123
  Bel and the Dragon 123
    Idolatry 129

Excursus on the Apocalyptic Genre

What is an apocalypse? 130
The earliest Jewish apocalypses 132
The Book of the Watchers as an illustration 133
The otherworldly journey 135
The Old Testament precedents 137
The extent of the apocalyptic literature 139
The Dead Sea Scrolls 140
The later apocalypses 141
The common perspective of the apocalypses 143
The significance of the apocalyptic world-view 144

First Maccabees

INTRODUCTION 149
  The date of composition 149
  The use of sources 150
  The theology of the book 151

FIRST MACCABEES: COMMENTARY

1 Mac 1:1-10: The Introduction   153

PART ONE: THE PERSECUTION   154
   1 Mac 1:11-40: The preliminary events   154
   1 Mac 1:41-64: The persecution   158
   1 Mac 2:1-28: The zeal of Mattathias   161
   The act of zeal   163
   1 Mac 2:29-38: The martyrs in the wilderness   164
   1 Mac 2:39-48: The reaction of Mattathias   166
   1 Mac 2:49-70: The testament of Mattathias   168

PART TWO: THE CAREER OF JUDAS   171
   1 Mac 3:1-9: The glory of his people   171
   1 Mac 3:10-26: Judas' initial victories   172
   1 Mac 3:27-4:35: The battles of Emmaus and Beth-zur   174
   The theology of victory   180
   1 Mac 4:36-60: The re-consecration of the temple   181
   1 Mac 5: Gathering in the scattered Jews   184
   1 Mac 6:1-17: The death of Antiochus Epiphanes   189
   1 Mac 6:18-63: The first defeat   191
   1 Mac 7:1-20: Alcimus and the Hasideans   196
   1 Mac 7:21-50: The defeat of Nicanor   199
   1 Mac 8: The treaty with Rome   202
   1 Mac 9:1-22: The death of Judas   208

PART THREE: THE CAREER OF JONATHAN   211
   1 Mac 9:23-73: The rise of Jonathan   211
   1 Mac 10: Jonathan and the Gentile kings   216
   1 Mac 11: The Jews and the dynastic struggles   222
   1 Mac 12:1-23: Jews and Spartans   227
   1 Mac 12: 24-53: The capture of Jonathan   231

PART FOUR: THE CAREER OF SIMON   233
1 Mac 13: The rise of Simon   233
1 Mac 14:1-15: Simon's reign as a messianic age   238
1 Mac 14:16-24: International recognition   241
1 Mac 14:25-49: The edict of the people   242
1 Mac 15:1-16:10: The renewed Syrian threat   245
1 Mac 16:11-24: The death of Simon   251
First Maccabees in Retrospect   253

Second Maccabees

INTRODUCTION   259
The composition of 2 Maccabees   259
The date of composition   261
Historical value   263
Theological and political perspective   264

SECOND MACCABEES: COMMENTARY

Introductory material   268
2 Mac 1:1-9: The first letter   268
The second letter   270
2 Mac 1:10-17: The death of Antiochus   270
2 Mac 1:18-2:18: The legend of the fire   271
2 Mac 2: 19-32: The abbreviator's preface   277

PART ONE: THE FIRST ASSAULT
   ON THE TEMPLE   279
2 Mac 3: The legend of Heliodorus   279

PART TWO: THE HELLENISTIC REFORM
   AND THE PERSECUTION   286
2 Mac 4: The corruption of the priesthood   286
The mission of Onias   291

Jason as high priest   291
Menelaus and the murder of Onias   293
2 Mac 5: The intervention of Antiochus   295
2 Mac 6:1-11: The religious persecution   299
2 Mac 6:12-17: The theology of persecution   302
2 Mac 6:18-31: The martyrdom of Eleazar   304
2 Mac 7: The seven brothers   306
The impact of the chapter   313
2 Mac 8: The Maccabean Revolt   314
2 Mac 9: The death of Antiochus Epiphanes   319
The conversion of Antiochus   323
2 Mac 10:1-9: The purification of the temple   324

PART THREE: THE SUCCESSORS OF
    EPIPHANES   326
A. THE REIGN OF ANTIOCHUS EUPATOR   326
2 Mac 10:10-38: Gorgias and Timothy   326
2 Mac 11:1-15: The defeat of Lysias   330
2 Mac 11:16-38: Four Letters   332
2 Mac 12:1-9: The massacre at Joppa   335
2 Mac 12:10-31: The campaign against Timothy   336
2 Mac 12:39-45: After the battle   340
2 Mac 13:1-8: The death of Menelaus   341
2 Mac 13:9-26: The failure of Eupator's attack   342

B. THE REIGN OF DEMETRIUS   345
2 Mac 14:1-10: The complaint of Alcimus   345
2 Mac 14:11-36: Judas and Nicanor   347
2 Mac 14:37-46: The suicide of Razis   350
2 Mac 15:1-5: The threatened attack on the sabbath   352
2 Mac 15:6-27: The motivation of the Jews   353
2 Mac 15:28-36: The death of Nicanor   356
2 Mac 15:37-39: The epilogue   358

SECOND MACCABEES IN RETROSPECT   358

FOR FURTHER READING 361

I	History of the Maccabean Period	361
II	Daniel	361
III	Apocalyptic Literature	362
IV	First and Second Maccabees	364

CHRONOLOGICAL TABLES 365
I	The Babylonian and Persian Periods	365
II	The Hellenistic Kingdoms	366
III	The Maccabean Period	366

MAPS 369
The Four Kingdoms	369
The Hellenistic Empires	370
Palestine in the Maccabean Period	371

Editors' Preface

Old Testament Message brings into our life and religion today the ancient word of God to Israel. This word, according to the book of the prophet Isaiah, had soaked the earth like "rain and snow coming gently down from heaven" and had returned to God fruitfully in all forms of human life (Isa 55:10). The authors of this series remain true to this ancient Israelite heritage and draw us into the home, the temple and the market place of God's chosen people. Although they rely upon the tools of modern scholarship to uncover the distant places and culture of the biblical world, yet they also refocus these insights in a language clear and understandable for any interested reader today. They enable us, even if this be our first acquaintance with the Old Testament, to become sister and brother, or at least good neighbor, to our religious ancestors. In this way we begin to hear God's word ever more forcefully in our own times and across our world, within our prayer and worship, in our secular needs and perplexing problems.

Because life is complex and our world includes, at times in a single large city, vastly different styles of living, we have much to learn from the Israelite Scriptures. The Old Testament spans forty-six biblical books and almost nineteen hundred years of life. It extends through desert, agricultural and urban ways of human existence. The literary style embraces a world of literature and human emotions. Its history began with Moses and the birth-pangs of a new people, it came of age politically and economically under David and Solomon, it reeled under the fiery threats of prophets like Amos and Jeremiah. The people despaired and yet were re-created with new hope during the Babylonian exile. Later reconstruction in the homeland and then the trauma of apocalyptic movements prepared for the revelation of "the mystery hidden for ages in God who created all things" (Eph 3:9).

While the Old Testament telescopes twelve to nineteen hundred years of human existence within the small country of Israel, any single moment of time today witnesses to the reenactment of this entire history across the wide expanse of planet earth. Each verse of the Old Testament is being relived somewhere in our world today. We need, therefore, the *entire* Old Testament and all twenty-three volumes of this new set, in order to be totally a "Bible person" within today's widely diverse society.

The subtitle of this series—"A Biblical-Theological Commentary"—clarifies what these twenty-three volumes intend to do.

Their *purpose* is theological: to feel the pulse of God's word for its *religious* impact and direction.

Their *method* is biblical: to establish the scriptural word firmly within the life and culture of ancient Israel.

Their *style* is commentary: not to explain verse by verse but to follow a presentation of the message that is easily understandable to any serious reader, even if this person is untrained in ancient history and biblical languages.

Old Testament Message—like its predecessor, *New Testament Message*—is aimed at the entire English-speaking world and so is a collaborative effort of an international team. The twenty-one contributors are women and men drawn from North America, Ireland, Britain and Australia. They are scholars who have published in scientific journals, but they have been chosen equally as well for their proven ability to communicate on a popular level. This twenty-three book set comes from Roman Catholic writers, yet, like the Bible itself, it reaches beyond interpretations restricted to an individual church and so enables men and women rooted in biblical faith to unite and so to appreciate their own traditions more fully and more adequately.

Most of all, through the word of God, we seek the blessedness and joy of those

who walk in the law of the Lord!...

who seek God with their whole heart (Ps. 119:1-2).

CARROLL STUHLMUELLER, C.P.   MARTIN McNAMARA, M.S.C.

INTRODUCTION

THE HISTORICAL SETTING

IN THE YEAR 167 B.C.E. King Antiochus IV Epiphanes of Syria made a systematic attempt to suppress the Jewish religion. The Jewish law was banned and copies of the law were burned. Distinctive Jewish practices such as circumcision were outlawed under penalty of death. The Jewish sacrificial cult was suppressed and a pagan altar was erected on top of the great altar of sacrifice in the temple, thus profaning the holy place in the eyes of the Jews.

Such outright persecution of a religion was highly unusual in antiquity, and scholars are divided as to the king's motivation in undertaking it. Some follow 1 Maccabees and suppose that the persecution was part of a cultural program on the part of the king, to unify his empire (1 Mac 1:41-42: "Then the king wrote to his whole kingdom that all should be one people and that each should give up his customs"). Others see the king as only taking sides in an inner-Jewish conflict. There is no doubt that Antiochus encouraged Hellenization or the acceptance of Greek ways. There is also no doubt that there was a Jewish party in Jerusalem which eagerly promoted the transformation of Jerusalem into a Greek city. Shortly after Antiochus became king in 175 B.C.E. he had been approached by Jason, brother of the high priest Onias, who "obtained the high priesthood by

1

corruption" offering to pay the king vast sums of money. In return, Jason was authorized to erect a gymnasium in Jerusalem to draw up a list of "Antiochenes in Jerusalem (2 Mac 4:7–17). So the initial attempt to transform Jerusalem into a Greek city and introduce a Hellenistic way of life was made on Jewish initiative or at least with considerable Jewish cooperation. Tension within the Jewish community was heightened when, about three years later, Jason was outbid for the high priesthood by a certain Menelaus, who had been sent to deliver the tribute to Antiochus. Jason subsequently recaptured Jerusalem by force but this provoked the intervention of Antiochus. In 169 B.C.E. the king conquered Jerusalem and plundered the temple and left behind an occupying force commanded by one Philip "in character more barbarous than the man who appointed him" (2 Mac 5:22). The subsequent escalation of events which led up to the persecution is not entirely clear. Antiochus was humiliated by the Romans in Egypt and his frustration may have influenced his attitude towards the Jews. Philip treated the people of Jerusalem harshly. A fortress called Akra was built near the temple as a Syrian stronghold in Jerusalem. It is possible that the attempt to suppress the Jewish law was suggested or encouraged by the Hellenizing Jews. It is also possible that the traditional Jews were already in revolt against Menelaus and the king before Antiochus intervened in 169 and that the rebellion flared up again after he departed. Either the king himself, or, more probably, the Hellenizing Jews, must have realized that the opposition they encountered was rooted in the very nature of the Jewish law and could only be overcome by suppression of that law. It is apparent, in any case, that the persecution was not simply a willful act on the part of the king, but was the culmination of a complicated build-up of tension over several years and involved a deep division within the Jewish community.

The events of 167 B.C.E. were fateful ones in Jewish history. Not only did they introduce the spectre of religious persecution to the pages of history. They also occasioned the Maccabean revolt, which has stood through the centuries as a striking paradigm for recourse to armed, violent revolution in the name of religion. The purification of the Jerusalem temple by Judas Maccabee in 164 B.C.E. is one of the great events of Jewish history and is still commemorated in the celebration of Hanukkah.

The persecution under Antiochus and the Maccabean revolt are the focal point for the three books discussed in this volume—Daniel and 1 and 2 Maccabees. The books of Maccabees are narrative accounts of the events which led up to and followed the persecution and the outbreak of revolt. They are not, however, simple historical documents, as we shall see. They are ideological documents which construe the events they report so as to convey specific (and different) interpretations. They are also religious and theological documents since they view the historical events not only in terms of human action but also in terms of divine providence, and, occasionally, supernatural causality. Our concern in this commentary is primarily with the religious perspective of these works, not with historical reconstruction for its own sake.

Both 1 and 2 Maccabees in their present form, were written forty or fifty years after the Maccabean revolt. The Book of Daniel originated in much greater immediacy to the crucial events of 169-164. The visions of Daniel were composed in precisely this period, and completed prior to the death of Antiochus Epiphanes in 164. Here again our concern in this volume is not to extract historical information for its own sake but to appreciate the particular, apocalyptic, perspective in which Daniel views the segment of history with which it is concerned.

The Book of Daniel also contains older material in chapters 1-6. These chapters are set in the Babylonian exile in the sixth century B.C.E. They are not historical documents, and are more likely to have been composed in the third century, although they incorporate traditional material which may be older. These chapters did not arise from the conflicts of the time of Antiochus Epiphanes although they were surely found relevant then. They do, however, provide further illustrations of the interaction of religion and politics. They reflect the problems confronting Jewish exiles in lands which were dominated by other religions, and the difficulty of correlating the kingdom of God with the temporal powers of the day.

The historical critical method

The crisis which led to the Maccabean revolt is the focal point for these three books in the sense that it was the occasion of their composition, and dominates their subject matter. This historical setting is of fundamental importance if we are to grasp the theological message of these books. It has been the great contribution of the historical-critical method of biblical scholarship to show clearly that the bible is not a timeless book of perennial philosophy or theology. The various books of the bible were written at specific junctures, in response to specific historical problems. The meaning and relevance of any document must vary with the problem to which it is applied. The message of the Maccabees or of Daniel is not a message for all seasons. The actions and beliefs manifested in those books were provoked by particular circumstances. Their justification and their efficacy can only be properly judged with these circumstances in mind.

This is not to say that these books are purely historical relics of antiquarian interest. The type of situation in which they were composed is one that recurs with some frequency. The problems to which they responded are problems that arise anew in analogous situations—the relation between politics and religion, the ethics of revolution, the ultimate nature of certain obligations which demand the sacrifice of life, the question of theodicy, or whether there is justice in the world which will prevail over the evil of the moment. These questions are ageless and have indeed taken on new relevance in our time in view of the horrors of the Holocaust. The specific ways in which these questions are formulated and then answered in the Books of Maccabees and Daniel are relative to the particular circumstances of the time and so limited. Yet these books are illuminating for other analogous situations. They provide case studies and specific examples. What they lose in universality they gain in concreteness and vividness.

Religion and society

Of all the questions raised by these books perhaps the most fundamental is the relation between religion and politics. Other questions, such as theodicy, or the justice of the power that rules the world, arise in the context of this fundamental problem. The reason that the justice of God is temporarily in doubt is that the political order is disrupted. The religion persecuted by Antiochus was very specifically the religion of the Jews. What was at issue was not only their cultic worship, but their very identity as a distinct people with a distinctive way of life. The question of theodicy appears in this context as the question of the vindication of the Jewish way of life in a hostile world.

It must be said at the outset that these books do not present a single uniform and normative conception of the Jewish way of life. There is of course extensive common ground between the three. Observance of the Jewish law is of basic importance in each case. Yet there are considerable differences between Daniel and 1 Maccabees in their overall conception of piety and of the conduct required of a faithful

Jew. The most conspicuous difference lies in Daniel's
avoidance of, and failure to endorse, the violent revolution
of the Maccabees. The conception of religion varies with the
view of Judaism. Daniel's visions are largely occupied with
the supernatural world. In 1 Maccabees the primary emphasis is on human actions (2 Maccabees is closer to Daniel
in this respect). These differences between the individual
works do not lessen the link between their views of religion
and of Jewish life, but rather accentuate it. 1 Maccabees
may rightly be viewed as the ideology of the Maccabees and
their descendents, the Hasmonean kings of Judea. Daniel
presents rather the ideology of a non-militant group, the
"wise teachers" or *maskilim*. The Jewish tradition permitted
more than one response to the crisis of the reign of Antiochus Epiphanes.

History and Theology

It should be obvious from the preceding pages that our
objective in this volume is not to extract theological doctrines from these books. The bible cannot be viewed as an
accumulation of revealed truths, each of which is per-
manently valid once it is manifested. Such a view results
when we attempt to read the bible as if it were from God's
point of view, without regard to the human circumstances
which shaped its composition. There is simply no way in
which human critics can profitably discuss the intentions of
a divine author. We can however discuss the method and
message of the human authors, and the differing perspectives of the individual books show the propriety and even
necessity of taking this approach. Any theology which takes
seriously the historical genesis of the biblical material must
be inductive in character. Theology from this perspective is
the human attempt to articulate the meaning and purpose of
life, and is distinguished from other such attempts (e.g.
literary or philosophical) by its reliance on specifically

religious traditions for the data on which it reflects. The biblical books do not provide normative conclusions or definitive revelations. They provide samples of the religious tradition. They differ from modern systematic theology mainly in their mode of discourse: where theology usually involves philosophical reflection, the biblical books rely on narrative and poetic symbolism. But they too, like modern theological ventures, must be seen as human constructions which attempt to articulate the meaning and purpose of life. Their relevance to the modern age lies not so much in their conclusions, which were closely bound to the historical circumstances which evoked them, as in their method. They illustrate the ways in which the religious tradition can be used to illuminate the changing crises of history. This point is especially obvious in the later biblical books such as Daniel and Maccabees where there is considerable use and adaptation of the earlier biblical tradition. The fact that these books do not simply develop religious conceptions but seek to integrate them with the social and political realities of their day makes them all the more interesting for our purpose. Any theory of revelation or inspiration must fully accommodate the historical and social human factors in the genesis of these books.

The theological understanding of these books raises also the question of the significance of the scriptural canon. In fact, Daniel and 1 and 2 Maccabees illustrate well some of the difficulties involved in taking the canon as a prescriptive factor in theology, as has been proposed by a number of biblical scholars in the nineteen seventies. (See Daniel J. Harrington, *Interpreting the Old Testament*, Postscript, "Canonical Criticism"; No. 1 of this series.) 1 and 2 Maccabees are not found at all in the Hebrew bible and are consequently excluded from the Protestant canon. This is also true of the so-called "Additions to Daniel": the "Prayer of Azariah", the "Song of the Three Young Men," "Susanna" and "Bel and the Dragon." These works are included in the Greek bible (which also includes some works which are not canonical in either Catholicism or Protestantism) and in the Latin Vulgate and were declared canonical by the Council of Trent. In Protestant tradition these books are regarded as Apocrypha (literally "hidden" books), not of equal status with the scriptures but still useful and good to read. The significant point in this divergence of opinion is that the canon is not a clearcut entity but has a soft edge. The canonicity of particular books could be disputed in antiquity and ultimately decisions were made by synagogal and church authorities. The canon, in short, is a selection of authoritative works from the corpus of traditional literature, made or ratified by the competent religious authorities. Canonical works have the status of standard reference works in the religious community. They are not necessarily different in kind from other works of the tradition which survived outside the canon.

These considerations are of some importance for the discussion of Daniel and 1 & 2 Maccabees. As we shall see, Daniel is more closely related to the non-canonical Jewish apocalyptic literature of the Hellenistic period than to any of its biblical precedents. In all three works it is important to realize that inclusion in the canon does not determine the genre, or type of writing. We are not obliged, because a work is canonical, to assume that it is factually accurate and morally edifying. Rather we must look to the literary conventions which govern the work and consider its function in its historical setting. We will pursue these questions more specifically in our discussion of the individual books.

THE BOOK OF DANIEL

The Book of Daniel:
Introduction

TWO MAIN introductory questions arise in connection with the Book of Daniel. The first concerns the date. The second concerns the unity of the book.

The date

The dating of Daniel has aroused more than usual theological passion, as it involves the authenticity of Daniel's prophecies. On the surface, the Book of Daniel consists of a collection of stories about a Jew named Daniel and his companions in the Babylonian exile, followed by a first person account of the visions of the same Daniel. Already in antiquity the date and authorship were questioned by the neo-Platonist philosopher Porphyry (late second century CE) who maintained that the book was written in the time of Antiochus Epiphanes. Daniel's prophecies of events down to the time of Antiochus were written after the fact, and were accurate, whereas the predictions beyond that time were unfulfilled. The cogency of Porphyry's admittedly anti-Christian argument is widely recognized to-day. The issue is not whether a divinely inspired prophet *could* have foretold the events which took place under Antiochus Epiphanes four hundred years before they occurred. The question is whether this possibility carries any *probability*: is it the most satisfactory way to explain what we find in Daniel? Modern critical scholarship has held that it is not.

First, there is the point noted by Porphyry, that beyond a certain point in history the predictions are not fulfilled. The events in Daniel 11:40-45, leading up to the death of Antiochus, are the most significant examples.

Second, there is the question of genre. We now possess a substantial corpus of extra-canonical writings which closely resemble the prophecies of Daniel. These are the apocalyptic writings, and we shall return to them in the Appendix at the end of the commentary on Daniel. Typically they are ascribed to great individuals of antiquity—Enoch, Moses, Ezra, Baruch. The case of Enoch is perhaps the most blatant. Enoch allegedly lived before the flood. Yet a series of writings in his name becomes current, beginning in the third century BCE. These writings show familiarity with the learning and ideas of the Hellenistic age. Their ascription to Enoch was presumably believed in antiquity, at least by a segment of the population, but no modern scholar, conservative or liberal, would attempt to defend their authenticity. They are patently products of the Hellenistic age and the ascription to Enoch is a fiction. This phenomenon is known as pseudepigraphy or pseudonymity, and it was very widespread in antiquity. The logic underlying it is now difficult to grasp. It is likely that the authors thought that their material was appropriate to Enoch, the kind of material that could properly be ascribed to him. Whether they felt some sense of unity with him over and above this is difficult to say. In view of the popularity of pseudepigraphic works we must assume that the populace at large accepted the attribution. At the same time, it is difficult to imagine that the authors were not conscious of the fictional element in their work. The name of an ancient, venerated figure like Enoch or Moses inevitably lent authority to a book. There was little concern for copyright in antiquity. The writers of the Jewish "pseudepigrapha" presumably used the device in good faith to convince the people of matters which they considered important.

When we view the questions of the date and authorship of Daniel against the background of the pseudepigraphic literature, the burden of proof shifts. We can no longer assume that Daniel is the historical author until there is proof to the contrary. Since Daniel resembles the books of Enoch, Ezra, etc. in so many respects, our initial assumption must be that Daniel is, like them, pseudepigraphic. Nothing in the Book of Daniel requires us to abandon that assumption. The visions of Daniel, like those of Enoch, can be quite satisfactorily explained as constructs of the Hellenistic age, which are ascribed to an ancient figure to add to their authority.

The authenticity of the visions is not the only point at issue in the question of dating. There is also the reliability of the information provided in the stories about Daniel in the first half of the book. Numerous problems arise if we attempt to take these chapters as accurate historical accounts. We need mention only the most celebrated instances here. In Daniel, chapter 5, Belshazzar is said to be the son of Nebuchadnezzar. In fact he was the son of Nabonidus. He is also said to be king, which is not technically correct, although he was regent in Babylon for a time. In Daniel 6, Belshazzar is said to have been succeeded by "Darius the Mede." In fact the king who overthrew the Babylonian kingdom was Cyrus the Persian. There was a later Persian monarch named Darius, but history knows of no "Darius the Mede." There have been numerous strained attempts to salvage the historicity of this individual by identifying him with, for example, Gobryas, the general of Cyrus. No such attempt has provided any evidence for the accuracy of the title "Darius the Mede." However well-intentioned such attempts to defend the historicity of Daniel may be, they only distract from the real problems of interpreting the book. One does not get to appreciate a novel by trying to establish that the events actually took place. No one would say that the parables of Jesus necessarily recount historical occurrences or that their value would be any greater if they did. Many of the great books of the world are fictions. Rather than strain credibility in the attempt to save the historicity of Daniel, we should admit that many traditional problems fade away when we recognize that the stories in chapters one to six and those of Bel and the Dragon and Susanna are fictions. They are, except for Susanna, historical fictions, in the sense that they refer to and presuppose an historical situation. That situation, however, need not necessarily be the initial years of the exile of the Jews in Babylon. It could be any time in the Diaspora or scattering of the Jews in the lands of their foreign masters, down to the Hellenistic age.

The unity of the book

Even a casual reader can see that the entire book of Daniel does not come from a single hand. We have already noted the passages which are not found in the Hebrew bible—the Prayer of Azariah, the Song of the Three Young Men, Bel and the Dragon, and Susanna. Even within the text which is found in the Hebrew bible there are signs of disunity. First, the book is written in two languages: Hebrew in 1:1-2:4a and chapters 8 to 12; Aramaic in 2:4b - 7:28. Second, there are two distinct genres in the book: the tales in chaps. 1-6 and the apocalyptic visions in chaps. 7-12. The fact that the division of languages does not coincide with the division of genres has caused endless controversy among biblical scholars.

There is no simple solution to the problem of the two languages. Some commentators have held that the Hebrew chapters were translated from Aramaic. It is true that the Hebrew in chapters 8 to 12 is difficult and broken, but any attempt to remove the problems by translating on the basis of a supposed Aramaic original is purely hypothetical. The earliest fragments of Daniel from the Dead Sea Scrolls already show the transitions between Hebrew and Aramaic as we now know them. We must assume that whoever put the book together was bilingual. Bilingualism would certainly not have been unusual in Jerusalem in the second century BCE. There is wide agreement that the Aramaic tales in chapters 2-6 were already current before the time of Antiochus Epiphanes. The recourse to Hebrew in chapters 8-12 may perhaps be explained by patriotic fervor in a time of crisis. Chap. 7 obviously refers to the same events as 8-12.

My own suggestion for the overlap between Hebrew and Aramaic is that it was a device on the part of the author/ editor to tie the two halves of the book together. The Hebrew of chap. 1 and the Aramaic of chap. 7 provide links between the Aramaic tales and the Hebrew visions. (Chap. 1 may have been translated from Aramaic to provide a Hebrew enclosure for the book as a whole). A similar interlocking of the two halves of the book can be seen in the ordering of the chapters. Chapters 2 to 7 have a concentric arrangement: 2 shares with 7 the motif of the 4 kingdoms; 3 and 6 are tales of miraculous deliverance; 4 and 5 are critiques of Babylonian kings. At the same time the dating of the chapters reinforces the division between the tales and the visions. The tales begin with Nebuchadnezzar king of Babylon, proceed to Belshazzar in chap. 5, Darius the Mede in chap. 6 and end with a reference to Cyrus the Persian in 6:28. This sequence reflects the sequence of kingdoms presumed throughout the book—Babylon, Media, Persia. Chaps. 7 and 8, however, revert to the reign of Belshazzar, followed by chap. 9 in the time of Darius and we finally reach the age of Cyrus in chap. 10. This reversal of the chronological order in chaps. 7 and 8 shows that these chapters were not simply composed as part of a sequence with 2-6. At the same time the author has taken care to tie the traditional tales into the book as a whole, where they serve as an introduction to the visions.

The conclusion that the tales are older material incorporated by the author of Maccabean times follows from several considerations. As we shall see in the commentary, chaps. 7-12 refer clearly and unambiguously to the persecution by Antiochus Epiphanes. By contrast, there is no unambiguous reference to these events in chaps. 1-6. The events in the opening chapters are set in Babylon. Those in chaps. 7-12 are either set in or vitally concern Palestine. The difference in form between the tales and the visions underscores the transition in subject matter. There are also substantial differences in attitude between the two halves of the book. No matter how arrogant the gentile kings appear in chaps. 1-6 they are never beyond hope of reform. By contrast, there is no hope whatever for the gentile kings of chaps. 7-12. The faithful Jews of the tales are rescued alive from the fiery furnace and the lions' den. In chaps. 11 and 12 they are killed and their deliverance is beyond death in the resurrection.

Why then did the author of Maccabean times incorporate those stories about Daniel in his book? The answer to this question is related to his decision to ascribe his visions to Daniel. Daniel was not such a well-known figure as Enoch or Moses. The tales were necessary to establish his identity. Yet the figure of Daniel was important enough for some Jewish groups to generate not only the stories now found in the Book of Daniel but also other Danielic writings which have now been found among the Dead Sea Scrolls of Qumran. The author of the visions of Daniel presumably came from the circles which had collected and transmitted the tales about Daniel. The figure of Daniel had become the ideal representation of the wise Jew who properly understood and dealt with the rule of the gentile kings. Such a figure was a suitable mouthpiece for the visions which assessed and passed judgment on the Hellenistic kingdoms. In chap. 1 Daniel and his companions are chosen because they are skilled in all wisdom, and the Hebrew term is *maskilim*. The same term is used in chaps. 11 and 12 for the faithful Jews who properly resisted Antiochus Epiphanes. The wisdom and fidelity of Daniel in the tales serve as models for the persecuted Jews of the visions.

There are other points at which the tales were relevant to the time of persecution. Most obvious, perhaps, is the fact that Daniel and his companions are shown to be willing to lay down their lives for their faith. The critique of the gentile kings in chaps. 4 and 5 would also be apt enough at the time of Antiochus Epiphanes. Yet these applications of the tales to the persecution of Maccabean times is secondary in nature. What we really see in the Book of Daniel is the transformation of theology in the light of changing political circumstances.

Already in the tales we find varying attitudes towards the gentile kings. Darius is portrayed far more positively than Nebuchadnezzar. Throughout chapters 1 to 6, however, there is a sense that gentile rule is fundamentally compatible with the sovereignty of the God of the Jews. The two can co-exist. Problems are resolved, miraculously if necessary. Such an optimistic view of gentile rule was typical of much of the Jewish Diaspora. The prophet Jeremiah (29:4-7) had already urged the exiles to "seek the welfare of the city where I have sent you into exile, and pray to the Lord on its behalf, for in its welfare you will find your welfare." Daniel 1-6 follows this advice, on the whole. It is highly probable that the tales in chaps. 1-6 were written in exile in the Diaspora, at some point in the Hellenistic age, probably in the third century BCE. The visions, however, were obviously written in Jerusalem in the heat of the persecution and its aftermath. In these circumstances the optimistic attitude towards the gentiles was no longer possible. Instead we find a theology of polarization, where the political problems can only be resolved by divine intervention and the destruction of the gentile rulers.

The genres of Daniel

We have already had occasion to note at several points the importance of the literary genres, or types of writing involved. The apocalyptic genre of chaps. 7-12 will be discussed at some length in the Excursus (pp. 130-145 below). The genre of the tales requires some comment too.

There was a widespread literature in antiquity about wise men and their fortunes at court. The biblical stories of Joseph and Esther are well-known examples. Another is the story of Ahikar, a tale which was popular with Jews and gentiles alike and can be found in R.H. Charles' *Apocrypha and Pseudepigrapha of the Old Testament* (Oxford: Clarendon, 1913; reprint 1963) 2: 715-784. There are several such tales from outside Judaism, especially from Egypt. We will find in the commentary that even within Daniel we must distinguish different types of tales. The pattern and motifs of Daniel 2 are quite different from those of Daniel 3. The main point for the present is to recognize that in all these stories we are dealing with stereotypical conventions. Each story rings its own changes on those conventions, but there is a typical outline to the stories which guides the reader's expectations. So in Daniel 2, 4 and 5 there is a common outline which is also found in the Joseph story in Genesis 41. The king is confronted with dreams or signs which he cannot understand. The gentile wise men cannot understand them either. Daniel succeeds where the wise men failed, and is then exalted to high position. The outline in Daniel 3 and 6 has parallels in the stories of Joseph, Esther and Ahikar. Initially the heroes are in a state of prosperity. Then they are endangered by a plot or accusation and are condemned to death or prison. They are, however, released (there is scope for considerable variation between the different stories on this point). Finally, their wisdom or merit is recognized and they are exalted to positions of honor.

When we recognize the typical, rather folkloric, aspect of these stories, we can see that they should not be read as historical accounts. They are stories intended to entertain and edify. They are to be sure serious stories which try to shape the way people live their lives, but the manner in which they achieve their effect is not dependent on credulity about the historicity of the stories. They require an attitude similar to that with which we approach any serious fiction. There must be a suspension of disbelief to allow us to engage in the narrative action, but we must also be aware that their truth is not literal but symbolic.

The Book of Daniel: Commentary

THE TALES

DANIEL CHAP. 1: JEWISH YOUTHS AT THE GENTILE COURT

1 In the third year of the reign of Jehoiakim king of Judah, Nebuchadnezzar king of Babylon came to Jerusalem and besieged it. ²And the Lord gave Jehoiakim king of Judah into his hand, with some of the vessels of the house of God; and he brought them to the land of Shinar, to the house of his god, and placed the vessels in the treasury of his god. ³Then the king commanded Ashpenaz, his chief eunuch, to bring some of the people of Israel, both of the royal family and of the nobility, ⁴youths without blemish, handsome and skillful in all wisdom, endowed with knowledge, understanding learning, and competent to serve in the king's palace, and to teach them the letters and language of the Chaldeans. ⁵The king assigned them a daily portion of the rich food which the king ate, and of the wine which he drank. They were to be educated for three years, and at the end of that time they were to stand before the king. ⁶Among these were Daniel, Hananiah, Mishael, and Azariah of the tribe of Judah. ⁷And the chief of the eunuchs gave them names: Daniel he called Belteshazzar, Hananiah he called Shadrach, Mishael he called Meshach, and Azariah he called Abednego.

⁸But Daniel resolved that he would not defile himself with the king's rich food, or with the wine which he drank; therefore he asked the chief of the eunuchs to allow him not to defile himself. ⁹And God gave Daniel favor and compassion in the sight of the chief of the eunuchs; ¹⁰and the chief of the eunuchs said to Daniel, "I fear lest my lord the king, who appointed your food and your drink, should see that you were in poorer condition than the youths who are of your own age. So you would endanger my head with the king."¹¹Then Daniel said to the steward whom the chief of the eunuchs had appointed over Daniel, Hananiah, Mishael, and Azariah, ¹²"Test your servants for ten days; let us be given vegetables to eat and water to drink. ¹³Then let our appearance and the appearance of the youths who eat the king's rich food be observed by you, and according to what you see deal with your servants." ¹⁴So he hearkened to them in this matter, and tested them for ten days. ¹⁵At the end of ten days it was seen that they were better in appearance and fatter in flesh than all the youths who ate the king's rich food. ¹⁶So the steward took away their rich food and the wine they were to drink, and gave them vegetables.

¹⁷As for these four youths, God gave them learning and skill in all letters and wisdom; and Daniel had understanding in all visions and dreams. ¹⁸At the end of the time, when the king had commanded that they should be brought in, the chief of the eunuchs brought

them in before Nebuchadnezzar. ¹⁹And the king spoke with them, and among them all none was found like Daniel, Hananiah, Mishael, and Azariah; therefore they stood before the king. ²⁰And in every matter of wisdom and understanding concerning which the king inquired of them, he found them ten times better than all the magicians and enchanters that were in all his kingdom. ²¹And Daniel continued until the first year of King Cyrus.

THE OPENING chapter serves to introduce Daniel and his companions, Hananiah, Mishael and Azariah. They are said to have been among the youths carried off to Babylon. It is significant that any attempt to establish the historical veracity of Daniel runs into trouble in the first verse. The third year of Jehoiakim was 606 BCE. Nebuchadnezzar did not even become king of Babylon until the following year and the first official year of his reign was 604. Jehoiakim had died before Nebuchadnezzar captured Jerusalem in 598. The statement in Daniel may have been mistakenly inferred from 2 Chron 36:5-7 which says that Nebuchadnezzar came up against Jehoiakim and bound him with chains. Confusion was made easier by the fact that Jehoiakim's son and successor was named Jehoiachin, and he was deported to Babylon.

The purpose of Daniel 1 is not in any case to establish the historical details of the capture of Jerusalem, but to set the scene for the following chapters. Note is taken of the capture of some of the temple vessels. They will figure prominently in chap. 5. Most important is the introduction of the young men. They are taken from the royalty and the nobility and trained to serve in the king's palace.

We should note at the outset that the Jewish youths have no objection to being trained in "the letters and language of the Chaldeans" or to entering the royal service.

Throughout the history of the Diaspora there were Jews who occasionally rose to positions of importance at the gentile courts. Nehemiah, one of the great figures of post-exilic Judaism was a cup-bearer to the Persian king, Artaxerxes I, and subsequently governor of the province of Judah. In preparation for this service they were to be educated for three years. Subsequently we find them grouped with the Chaldean wise men, whose skills traditionally included the interpretation of dreams and visions. The Chaldean wise men operated in a distinctly religious context. They engaged in interpreting the signs of the gods, and their reliability rested on the basis of the reliability of the Babylonian gods and religious system.

Daniel and his companions accept the training of the Chaldeans and engage in the same activities, but with different religious pre-suppositions. They undertake to compete with the Chaldeans on their own ground. Their success relative to the Chaldeans becomes an index of the power and wisdom of their God, relative to the gods of Babylon.

It is evident then that Daniel and his companions stop well short of complete assimilation, while they do not isolate themselves from their environment either. Much of the drama of the following chapters concerns the balance of maintaining a strict Israelite faith while operating successfully in the Babylonian world. The thrust of Daniel 1-6 is not only to affirm that this is possible, but to claim that success is dependent on fidelity to the God of the Jews.

Food and drink

The main narrative episode in chap. 1 is directly concerned with the problem of maintaining a distinct identity in the new environment. Daniel and his companions refuse the rich food offered by the king and request a diet of vegetables and water. After ten days they are found to be healthier than those who ate the king's food. The point at issue is not, of course, the dangers of cholesterol or the merits of vegetarianism. It obviously has to do with the observance of *kosher* laws. These laws acquire a special significance in the setting of the exile. They are a visible sign of the distinctiveness of the Jews over against other peoples. It is well known that the distinctive Jewish observances such as circumcision and sabbath rest acquired special importance during the exile. These were matters on which people had to make a decision, as to whether they wanted to be different from others or not. Consequently the distinctive commandments became symbols for the entire Jewish way of life.

We will see the importance of the distinctive commandments again in the Books of Maccabees, where people lay down their lives rather than eat pork. Ancients and moderns alike have questioned whether these customs were worth so high a price, and whether a more accommodating attitude would not have been better. The issue, however, touches some fundamental human instincts. Not only were the pious Jews convinced that these customs were God-given laws, which must be kept at any price, but they also realized that what was at issue was their right to preserve their own customs and decide their own way of life. However irrational some of the customs may now appear to us, we must realize that what was at issue was a matter of principle. Distinctive dietary customs assured the Jews of the exile that they were, after all, a people set apart, that they were special, and that their Jewish way of life was different and therefore important. No society has ever survived without some symbolic practices of this sort. When early Christianity rejected many of the major Jewish symbols, such as circumcision, it quickly found the need to develop new symbols in their place. It was important for early Christianity to be different from Judaism, but the difference was not between the observance of the letter and the freedom of the spirit. The spirit needs symbols too. The continued formalism of Christian symbols is well illustrated in the Didache, or Teaching of the Twelve Apostles, from the early second century CE: "Let not your fasts be with the hypocrites, for they fast on Mondays and Thursdays, but do you fast on Wednesdays and Fridays" (*Didache* 8.1). What is important here is not what is done— Jews and Christians alike fasted—but that there be some symbolic point of difference to distinguish Christians from others. The Jewish dietary observances in Daniel, like the Christian fasts in the Didache, are different for the sake of being different. Such customs may not impress us as the high-points of Judeo-Christian ethics, but they are important. They build the sense of a special, distinct community which is then strong enough to preserve and carry on the more profound ethical teachings. By their food and drink Daniel and his companions signalled their adherence to the full Jewish law. The importance of their stand on this issue is proportional to the importance of preserving the Jewish law as a framework for life.

DANIEL CHAP. 2: NEBUCHADNEZZAR'S DREAM

2 In the second year of the reign of Nebuchadnezzar, Nebuchadnezzar had dreams; and his spirit was troubled, and his sleep left him. ²Then the king commanded that the magicians, the enchanters, the sorcerers, and the Chaldeans be summoned, to tell the king his dreams. So they came in and stood before the king. ³And the king said to them, "I had a dream, and my spirit is troubled to know the dream." ⁴Then the Chaldeans said to the king, "O king, live for ever! Tell your servants the dream, and we will show the interpretation." ⁵The king answered the Chaldeans, "The word from me is sure: if you do not make known to me the dream and its inter-

pretation, you shall be torn limb from limb, and your houses shall be laid in ruins. ⁶But if you show the dream and its interpretation, you shall receive from me gifts and rewards and great honor. Therefore show me the dream and its interpretation." ⁷They answered a second time, "Let the king tell his servants the dream, and we will show its interpretation." ⁸The king answered, "I know with certainty that you are trying to gain time, because you see that the word from me is sure ⁹that if you do not make the dream known to me, there is but one sentence for you. You have agreed to speak lying and corrupt words before me till the times change. Therefore tell me the dream, and I shall know that you can show me its interpretation." ¹⁰The Chaldeans answered the king, "There is not a man on earth who can meet the king's demand; for no great and powerful king has asked such a thing of any magician or enchanter or Chaldean. ¹¹The thing that the king asks is difficult, and none can show it to the king except the gods, whose dwelling is not with flesh."

¹²Because of this the king was angry and very furious, and commanded that all the wise men of Babylon be destroyed. ¹³So the decree went forth that the wise men were to be slain, and they sought Daniel and his companions, to slay them. ¹⁴Then Daniel replied with prudence and discretion to Arioch, the captain of the king's guard, who had gone out to slay the wise men of Babylon; ¹⁵he said to Arioch, the king's captain, "Why is the decree of the king so severe?" Then Arioch made the matter known to Daniel. ¹⁶And Daniel went in and besought the king to appoint him a time, that he might show to the king the interpretation.

¹⁷Then Daniel went to his house and made the matter known to Hananiah, Mishael, and Azariah, his companions, ¹⁸and told them to seek mercy of the God of heaven

concerning this mystery, so that Daniel and his companions might not perish with the rest of the wise men of Babylon. [19]Then the mystery was revealed to Daniel in a vision of the night. Then Daniel blessed the God of heaven. [20] Daniel said:

"Blessed be the name of God forever and ever,
to whom belong wisdom and might.
[21]He changes times and seasons;
he removes kings and sets up kings;
he gives wisdom to the wise
and knowledge to those who have understanding;
[22]he reveals deep and mysterious things;
he knows what is in the darkness
and the light dwells with him.
[23]To thee, O God of my fathers,
I give thanks and praise,
for thou hast given me wisdom and strength,
and hast now made known to me what we asked of
        thee,
for thou hast made known to us the king's matter."

[24]Therefore Daniel went in to Arioch, whom the king had appointed to destroy the wise men of Babylon; he went and said thus to him, "Do not destroy the wise men of Babylon; bring me in before the king, and I will show the king the interpretation."

[25]Then Arioch brought in Daniel before the king in haste, and said thus to him: "I have found among the exiles from Judah a man who can make known to the king the interpretation." [26]The king said to Daniel, whose name was Belteshazzar, "Are you able to make known to me the dream that I have seen and its interpretation?" [27]Daniel answered the king, "No wise men, enchanters, magicians, or astrologers can show to the king the mystery which the king has asked, [28]but there is a God in heaven who reveals mysteries, and he has made

known to King Nebuchadnezzar what will be in the latter days. Your dream and the visions of your head as you lay in bed are these: [29]To you, O king, as you lay in bed came thoughts of what would be hereafter, and he who reveals mysteries made known to you what is to be. [30]But as for me, not because of any wisdom that I have more than all the living has this mystery been revealed to me, but in order that the interpretation may be made known to the king, and that you may know the thoughts of your mind.

[31]"You saw, O king, and behold, a great image. This image, mighty and of exceeding brightness, stood before you, and its appearance was frightening. [32]The head of this image was of fine gold, its breast and arms of silver, its belly and thighs of bronze, [33]its legs of iron, its feet partly of iron and partly of clay. [34]As you looked, a stone was cut out by no human hand, and it smote the image on its feet of iron and clay, and broke them in pieces, [35]then the iron, the clay, the bronze, the silver, and the gold, all together were broken in pieces, and became like the chaff of the summer threshing floors; and the wind carried them away, so that not a trace of them could be found. But the stone that struck the image became a great mountain and filled the whole earth.

[36]"This was the dream; now we will tell the king its interpretation. [37]You, O king, the king of kings, to whom the God of heaven has given the kingdom, the power, and the might, and the glory, [38]and into whose hand he has given, wherever they dwell, the sons of men, the beasts of the field, and the birds of the air, making you rule over them all—you are the head of gold. [39]After you shall arise another kingdom inferior to you, and yet a third kingdom of bronze, which shall rule over all the earth.[40]And there shall be a fourth kingdom, strong as iron, because iron breaks to pieces and shatters all things; and like iron

which crushes, it shall break and crush all these. ⁴¹And as you saw the feet and toes partly of potter's clay and partly of iron, it shall be a divided kingdom; but some of the firmness of iron shall be in it, just as you saw iron mixed with the miry clay. ⁴²And as the toes of the feet were partly iron and partly clay, so the kingdom shall be partly strong and partly brittle. ⁴³As you saw the iron mixed with miry clay, so they will mix with one another in marriage, but they will not hold together, just as iron does not mix with clay. ⁴⁴And in the days of those kings the God of heaven will set up a kingdom which shall never be destroyed, nor shall its sovereignty be left to another people. It shall break in pieces all these kingdoms and bring them to an end, and it shall stand forever; ⁴⁵just as you saw that a stone was cut from a mountain by no human hand, and that it broke in pieces the iron, the bronze, the clay, the silver, and the gold. A great God has made known to the king what shall be hereafter. The dream is certain, and its interpretation sure."

⁴⁶Then King Nebuchadnezzar fell upon his face, and did homage to Daniel, and commanded that an offering and incense be offered up to him. ⁴⁷The king said to Daniel, "Truly, your God is God of gods and Lord of kings, and a revealer of mysteries, for you have been able to reveal this mystery." ⁴⁸Then the king gave Daniel high honors and many great gifts, and made him ruler over the whole province of Babylon, and chief prefect over all the wise men of Babylon. ⁴⁹Daniel made request of the king, and he appointed Shadrach, Meshach, and Abednego over the affairs of the province of Babylon; but Daniel remained at the king's court.

The second chapter, like the first, begins with a chronological problem. It is set in the second year of the reign of Nebuchadnezzar. Yet it supposedly comes after the three year period of training which had been ordered by the same king. The second year of Nebuchadnezzar, 603 BCE, was still earlier than the historical capture of Jerusalem, so while the date of chap. 2 is incompatible with the information of chap. 1, neither is historically defensible.

In fact, the story in Daniel 2 has scant regard for historical verisimilitude. It tells its story with the broad strokes of the folk tale. When the king has his mysterious dream he not only asks the "magicians, enchanters, sorcerers and Chaldeans" to interpret it, but also insists that they tell him the dream itself. In the story, this demand is justified by the concern that the wise men would speak "lying and corrupt words." Yet the king could hardly be so skeptical of his own religious specialists. If he were anxious to know the meaning of the dream he would hardly choose this occasion to experiment with the powers of the diviners. In fact, we will find below that the king pays little attention to the interpretation. The entire focus of the chapter is on the test to see who can find out and interpret a dream which he has not been told. The real function of this test in the story is to underline the author's thesis that true wisdom must be revealed by God. The wise men cannot satisfy the king's command by any human techniques. Accordingly, the test focuses on their gods' ability to reveal mysteries, and ultimately on the superior power of the God of Daniel. This point is explicitly made in 2:11: "The thing that the king asks is difficult, and none can show it to the king except the gods, whose dwelling is not with flesh."

If the king's demand is unreasonable and implausible, so is his reaction. He commands that all the wise men of Babylon be destroyed, including, apparently, even those like Daniel who had not been informed of the matter at all. The hyperbole here is typical of the folk tale. It is significant that here Daniel appears as a colleague of the Babylonian wise men, and he acts to save them as well as himself. His method is simply prayer. It would not be extraordinary for a Babylonian wise man to pray for enlightenment either. The point is that Daniel's God is able to respond to the prayer. Daniel is quick to make this point to the king in 2:27-28. No wise men could show this mystery to the king, but only the God in heaven who reveals mysteries.

The four kingdoms

The actual dream concerns the famous statue of four metals. The sequence of gold, silver, bronze and iron is reminiscent of the Greek poet Hesiod, who used these metals to describe the declining generations of humanity. It is also paralleled in a Persian prophecy, the Bahman Yasht, where Zarathustra sees a tree with four branches. In the Persian work the third metal is steel, but the fourth is mixed iron, recalling Daniel's iron mixed with clay. Further, the Persian document, like Daniel, identifies the metals with the reigns of kings. Nebuchadnezzar's vision draws upon symbolism which was widely known in antiquity.

Daniel interprets the vision as a political oracle. Nebuchadnezzar is the head of gold, plausibly enough in the context of the story, but rather startlingly if we bear in mind that he was the destroyer of Jerusalem. He is followed by kingdoms which are not worse but weaker, of lesser significance. In view of the sequence of kingdoms in the Book of Daniel, these must be identified with the Medes and the Persians. The Persians are given no credit here for ending the Babylonian exile of the Jews and permitting the re-construction of the temple. The fourth kingdom, the feet of iron and clay, is inevitably the Greek empire established by Alexander the Great. This kingdom was divided between Alexander's generals. In the East, the relevant powers were the Ptolemies in Egypt and the Seleucids in Syria. The explanation of the iron mixed with clay as mixture by marriage refers to marriages between the Seleucids and the Ptolemies. There were two such marriages, dated about 250 BCE and 193 BCE. The prophecy in Daniel must at least be later than the first of these marriages.

The sequence of four kingdoms was not original with Daniel. A Roman historian, Aemilius Sura, claimed that there had been four world kingdoms—Assyria, Media, Persia and Greece (Macedonia) but that the sovereignty had now passed to Rome (the passage dates from the early second century BCE). The fourth Sibylline Oracle, a Jewish work, also has a sequence of four kingdoms, Assyria, Media, Persia and Macedonia. The oddity of these lists is that the Medes had never ruled over Syria, Palestine or any western area of the Near East. Evidently, then, the list originated somewhere east of Babylon, perhaps in Persia. It did not arise from the history of the Jews. The Book of Daniel substitutes Babylon for Assyria, since it was Babylon which had destroyed Jerusalem and Daniel was supposed to have lived in the Babylonian exile. Yet the Medes were retained and the unhistorical Darius the Mede was introduced to provide for a Median kingdom. This shows that Daniel was drawing on relatively fixed traditions. It may be that the entire vision of the statue of four metals and its interpretation were taken over from an older source.

The sequence of the four kingdoms lent itself easily to propaganda against the fourth, Hellenistic kingdom. The message was that all previous kingdoms had passed. The mighty empire of the Greeks would pass too. The sequence is used in a very explicitly anti-Hellenistic way in Daniel chap. 7. Significantly, only the fourth, Greek kingdom is represented as oppressive in Daniel 2.

In itself the statue with the four metals contains a potential theology of history. The four metals suggest a gradual process of decline, as if human history were winding down. This was a view of history shared by many Near Eastern peoples in the Hellenistic age, after they had been overrun by the Greeks. The Babylonians of that age might well have looked back on Nebuchadnezzar as a "head of gold," a powerful king whose reign now appeared as a golden age.

The theology of history in the vision does not, however, stop with the decline of the world kingdoms. At the end of the vision, a stone cut by no human hands shatters the image into such small pieces that they are blown away like chaff.This stone then becomes a great mountain, meaning that the God of heaven will set up a kingdom which will never be destroyed and whose sovereignty will never pass to another people. To any Jewish reader, this kingdom must be presumed to be Jewish and the mountain must represent Mt. Zion. Yet, in the context of the story, the Jewish character of the kingdom is not made explicit to Nebuchadnezzar, and he is presumably free to understand that kingdom in any way he wants. Oddly enough he shows no curiosity for further details. Instead he prostrates himself before Daniel and makes him ruler of the whole province of Babylon. Here again the author shows scant regard for plausibility or verisimilitude, but he supplies a satisfying, conventional ending for the story.

The significance of the dream

In its present context in Daniel chap. 2, the main significance of Nebuchadnezzar's dream is that it provides an occasion for demonstrating the superiority of Daniel and his God over the wisdom of the Chaldeans. Even this demonstration, however, already has political implications. Jews in the Diaspora need feel in no way inferior to their Babylonian masters. The superior wisdom of the God of the Jews carries an assurance that he is ultimately in control of history. The gentile kingdoms must serve his purpose.

The latter point, the divine control over history, is the point amplified in Nebuchadnezzar's dream and its interpretation. The orderly sequence of four kingdoms suggests that this is, after all, a managed universe, and that history runs according to a divine plan. Moreover, the conclusion promises that eventually all the world kingdoms will come down with a crash. The apparently simultaneous destruction of the four kingdoms ignores the chronology of historical sequence. Rather, the statue is treated precisely as an image—and given the traditional Jewish antipathy towards images, we might say an idol. The image represents the pretensions of human kingdoms to power and sovereignty. The destruction of the statue symbolizes the destruction of the idolatrous self-esteem of these kingdoms, from the head of gold to the feet of iron, which aspire to power but are mixed with clay.

The message of this chapter is summed up succinctly in the short hymnic passage in 2:20-23. God has wisdom and might: he removes kings and sets up kings, and he gives wisdom to the wise. This passage recalls similar hymnic passages in Second Isaiah, where God frustrates the omens of liars but confirms the word of his servant (Isa 44: 24-26; compare 47:12-13).

The political attitude in Daniel 2

What kind of attitude towards the gentile authorities is suggested by Daniel chap. 2? In view of the destructive conclusion we might expect a revolutionary attitude, urging the overthrow of the gentiles and the establishment of a Jewish kingdom. This, however, is not the message of Daniel 2. In fact the king, Nebuchadnezzar, is shown in favorable light throughout. At the end he heaps honors and promotions on Daniel and his friends and they accept them. Far from rebelling, they remain loyal servants of Nebuchadnezzar. It is true that the splendor of the Babylonian kingdom is to a great extent undermined by the dream and its interpretation. Yet in the divine plan, the kingdom, the power, the might and the glory are given to Nebuchadnezzar—in his time. We are reminded of Jeremiah (27:5-7): "It is I who by my great power and my outstretched arm have made the earth, with the men and animals that are on the earth, and I give it to whomever it seems right to me. Now I have given all these lands into the hand of Nebuchadnezzar, the king of Babylon, my servant, and I have given him also the beasts of the field to serve him. All the nations shall serve him and his son and his grandson, until the time of his own land comes; then many nations and great kings shall make him their slave." The point in Jeremiah is not that Nebuchadnezzar's kingdom is in any sense an ideal polity, but simply that it is ordained for the moment. The fact that his day too will come makes his present dominion easier to bear.

What then is the message of Daniel 2 for the Jewish exiles? It is to serve the lawful gentile authorities. The eschatological expectation of the dream serves not to inspire resistance but to let off pressure, by providing an assurance that the present dispensation is only for a time. The emphasis of the chapter is not on the expectation of an eschatological Jewish kingdom. That is only indirectly alluded to, and the nature of the final fifth kingdom is left almost completely blank, so that different people might envisage it in different ways. Rather, the emphasis falls on the superior wisdom of Daniel. That wisdom is at once the guarantee of the sovereignty of Daniel's God and the gift which enables Daniel to win success at the Babylonian court.

The fact that this story is a fiction does not detract

significantly from its power for the Jews who lived under foreign rule, or indeed for any people who live under a dominion which is alien to them. More important than the historical factuality of the story is the credibility of its message. Does God control the course of history and careers of his servants in this way? Needless to say, even this question cannot be answered with any definitive proof. History is always open to multiple interpretations. What we can say is that the story provides a model for thinking about and imagining the relation of religion and temporal power. This model enabled the Jews of the Diaspora to live and act in a positive and fruitful manner. It may have a similar capability for others in similar situations.

DANIEL CHAP. 3: THE FIERY FURNACE

3 King Nebuchadnezzar made an image of gold, whose height was sixty cubits and its breadth six cubits. He set it up on the plain of Dura, in the province of Babylon. ²Then King Nebuchadnezzar sent to assemble the satraps, the prefects, and the governors, the counselors, the treasurers, the justices, the magistrates, and all the officials of the provinces to come to the dedication of the image which King Nebuchadnezzar had set up. ³Then the satraps, the prefects, and the governors, the counselors, the treasurers, the justices, the magistrates, and all the officials of the provinces, were assembled for the dedication of the image that King Nebuchadnezzar had set up; and they stood before the image that Nebuchadnezzar had set up. ⁴And the herald proclaimed aloud, "You are commanded, O peoples, nations, and languages, ⁵that when you hear the sound of the horn, pipe, lyre, trigon, harp, bagpipe, and every kind of music, you are to fall down and worship the golden image that King Nebuchadnezzar has set up; ⁶and whoever does not fall down and worship shall immediately be cast into a burning fiery furnace.'' ⁷Therefore, as soon as all the peoples heard the sound of the horn, pipe, lyre, trigon, harp, bagpipe, and every kind of music, all the peoples, nations, and languages fell down and worshiped the golden image which King Nebuchadnezzar had set up.

⁸Therefore at that time certain Chaldeans came forward and maliciously accused the Jews. ⁹They said to King Nebuchadnezzar, "O king, live for ever! ¹⁰You, O king, have made a decree, that every man who hears the sound of the horn, pipe, lyre, trigon, harp, bagpipe, and every kind of music, shall fall down and worship the golden image; ¹¹and whoever does not fall down and worship shall be cast into a burning fiery furnace. ¹²There are certain Jews whom you have appointed over the affairs of the province of Babylon: Shadrach, Meshach, and Abednego. These men, O king, pay no heed to you; they do not serve your gods or worship the golden image which you have set up."

¹³Then Nebuchadnezzar in furious rage commanded that Shadrach, Meshach, and Abednego be brought. Then they brought these men before the king. ¹⁴Nebuchadnezzar said to them, "Is it true, O Shadrach, Meshach, and Abednego, that you do not serve my gods or worship the golden image which I have set up? ¹⁵Now if you are ready when you hear the sound of the horn, pipe, lyre, trigon, harp, bagpipe, and every kind of music, to fall down and worship the image which I have made, well and good; but if you do not worship, you shall immediately be cast into a burning fiery furnace; and who is the god that will deliver you out of my hands?"

¹⁶Shadrach, Meshach, and Abednego answered the king,

"O Nebuchadnezzar, we have no need to answer you in this matter. [17]If it be so, our God whom we serve is able to deliver us from the burning fiery furnace; and he will deliver us out of your hand, O king.[18]But if not, be it known to you, O king, that we will not serve your gods or worship the golden image which you have set up."

[19]Then Nebuchadnezzar was full of fury, and the expression of his face was changed against Shadrach, Meshach, and Abednego. He ordered the furnace heated seven times more than it was wont to be heated. [20]And he ordered certain mighty men of his army to bind Shadrach, Meshach, and Abednego, and to cast them into the burning fiery furnace. [21]Then these men were bound in their mantles, their tunics, their hats, and their other garments, and they were cast into the burning fiery furnace. [22]Because the king's order was strict and the furnace very hot, the flame of the fire slew those men who took up Shadrach, Meshach, and Abednego. [23]And these three men, Shadrach, Meshach, and Abednego, fell bound into the burning fiery furnace.

[1]*And they walked about in the midst of the flames, singing hymns to God and blessing the Lord.* [2]*Then Azariah stood and offered this prayer; in the midst of the fire he opened his mouth and said:*
[3]*"Blessed art thou, O Lord, God of our*
        fathers, and worthy of praise;
and thy name is glorified for ever.
[4]*For thou art just in all that thou hast done*
        to us,
and all thy works are true and thy ways
        right,
and all thy judgments are truth.
[5]*Thou hast executed true judgments in all*
        that thou hast brought upon us
and upon Jerusalem, the holy city of our
        fathers,

for in truth and justice thou hast brought all this
    upon us because of our sins.
⁶*For we have sinfully and lawlessly departed from*
    thee,
and have sinned in all things and have not
    obeyed thy commandments. . .
¹¹*For thy name's sake do not give us up utterly,*
and do not break thy covenant,
¹²*and do not withdraw thy mercy from us,*
for the sake of Abraham thy beloved and
    for the sake of Isaac thy servant
and Israel thy holy one. . .
¹⁹*Do not put us to shame,*
but deal with us in thy forbearance
and in thy abundant mercy.
²⁰*Deliver us in accordance with thy*
    marvelous works,
and give glory to⁻thy name, O Lord!
Let all who do harm to thy servants be put
    to shame;
²¹*let them be disgraced and deprived of all*
    power and dominion,
and let their strength be broken.
²²*Let them know that thou art the Lord, the*
    only God,
glorious over the whole world."

²³*Now the king's servants who threw them in did not cease feeding the furnace fires with naphtha, pitch, tow and brush.* ²⁴*And the flame streamed out above the furnace forty-nine cubits,* ²⁵*and it broke through and burned those of the Chaldeans whom it caught about the furnace.* ²⁶*But the angel of the Lord came down into the furnace to be with Azariah and his companions, and drove the fiery flame out of the furnace,* ²⁷*and made the midst of the furnace like a moist whistling wind, so that the fire did not touch them at all or hurt or trouble them.*

[28]*Then the three, as with one mouth, praised and glorified and blessed God in the furnace, saying:*

[29]*"Blessed art thou, O Lord, God of our fathers, and to be praised and highly exalted for ever...*

[35]*"Bless the Lord, all works of the Lord, sing praise to him and highly exalt him for ever.*
[36]*Bless the Lord, you heavens, sing praise to him and highly exalt him for ever....*
[44]*Bless the Lord, fire and heat, sing praise to him and highly exalt him for ever.*
[45]*Bless the Lord, winter cold and summer heat, sing praise to him and highly exalt him for ever....*
[60]*Bless the Lord, you sons of men, sing praise to him and highly exalt him for ever.*
[61]*Bless the Lord, O Israel, sing praise to him and highly exalt him for ever....*
[66]*Bless the Lord, Hananiah, Azariah, and Mishael, sing praise to him and highly exalt him for ever; for he has rescued us from Hades and saved us from the hand of death, and delivered us from the midst of the burning fiery furnace; from the midst of the fire he has delivered us.*
[67]*Give thanks to the Lord, for he is good, for his mercy endures for ever.*
[68]*Bless him, all who worship the Lord, the God of gods, sing praise to him and give thanks to him, for his mercy endures for ever."*

[24]Then King Nebuchadnezzar was astonished and rose up in haste. He said to his counselors, "Did we not cast three men bound into the fire?" They answered the king, "True, O king." [25]He answered, "But I see four men loose, walking in the midst of the fire, and they are not hurt; and the appearance of the fourth is like a son of the gods."

²⁶Then Nebuchadnezzar came near to the door of the burning fiery furnace and said, "Shadrach, Meshach, and Abednego, servants of the Most High God, come forth, and come here!" Then Shadrach, Meshach, and Abednego came out from the fire. ²⁷And the satraps, the prefects, the governors, and the king's counselors gathered together and saw that the fire had not had any power over the bodies of those men; the hair of their heads was not singed, their mantles were not harmed, and no smell of fire had come upon them. ²⁸Nebuchadnezzar said, "Blessed be the God of Shadrach, Meshach, and Abednego, who has sent his angel and delivered his servants, who trusted in him, and set at nought the king's command, and yielded up their bodies rather than serve and worship any god except their own God. ²⁹Therefore I make a decree: Any people, nation, or language that speaks anything against the God of Shadrach, Meshach, and Abednego shall be torn limb from limb, and their houses laid in ruins; for there is no other god who is able to deliver in this way." ³⁰Then the king promoted Shadrach, Meshach, and Abednego in the province of Babylon.

The crisis which provides the drama of Daniel 2 does not arise because of any tension between Judaism and the gentiles. Daniel and his companions are endangered because they are colleagues of the Chaldean wise men. The situation in chapter three is rather different. Here the catalyst is the colossal statue (about ninety feet by nine feet) erected by Nebuchadnezzar, and the demand that everyone worship it. The Jews refuse, and are accused by the Chaldeans, and are then cast into the fiery furnace. In effect, we have here a story of religious persecution.

This story is distinguished from others in the book by the fact that Daniel does not figure in it. It would seem that the story was not composed as part of a Daniel cycle, but was included as another story of Jews in exile, perhaps because of its similarity to Daniel 6. In fact, the references to Azariah, Mishael and Hananiah in the other chapters are probably secondary, inserted by the editors of the tales to provide links with chapter 3, since the youths play no significant part in the action of the other stories. It is unlikely that chapter three is older than the third century BCE, since some of the terms for the musical instruments in verse 5 are Greek in origin. The word *sympōnia,* which is translated "bagpipe" in the RSV, is used as the name of an instrument in connection with Antiochus Epiphanes by the Greek historian Polybius (the older meaning of the word is "harmony"). The administrative terms in vs. 2 are Persian in origin. The historical background of the story is not the Babylonian era to which it is dated, but some centuries later.

The fact that the story involves religious persecution has led some scholars to suppose that it was composed in the time of Antiochus Epiphanes, like the second half of the Book of Daniel. Two points tell against this view. First, in Daniel 3, Nebuchadnezzar is remarkably willing to acknowledge the God of the Jews at the end of the story. No such conversion is envisaged in Daniel 7-12. (2 Maccabees 9 does recount a quite fantastic conversion of Antiochus, but that was written some years after the persecution, and may conceivably be influenced by Daniel 4.) Second, the miraculous rescue of the youths here is in sharp contrast with the fate of the faithful Jews in Daniel 11. If Daniel 3 were composed in the time of Antiochus Epiphanes, we would have to suppose that it was written somewhat earlier than Daniel 7-12, before the persecution reached its height, or was written from a somewhat different viewpoint from the visions.

We should probably not try to tie Daniel 3 too closely to any historical event. The story is essentially a fantasy. Its stereotypical aspects can be seen by comparison with similar stories in Esther, Daniel 6, the story of Bel and the Dragon, and the Third Book of Maccabees, all of which envisage some extraordinary danger and remarkable, unexpected deliverance. There are, of course, historical elements which provide the circumstantial coloring of the tale, such as the administrative terms in verse 2. The construction of colossal statues was not without precedent. In Babylon we hear of a "great golden statue of Zeus" reported by the Greek historian Herodotus (presumably it was the statue of a Babylonian god) and of three golden images on top of the temple of Bel, one of which was forty feet high, according to another historian, Diodorus Siculus. There are scattered references to people being burned alive in antiquity. Jeremiah 29:22 refers to "Zedekiah and Ahab, whom the king of Babylon roasted in the fire." A Jewish historian, Eupolemus, in the second century BCE says that King "Jonachim" (presumably Jehoiakim) attempted to burn Jeremiah alive when the prophet found Jews sacrificing to an image of Bel. The latter story is no less legendary than Daniel 3, but at least we can see that the idea of execution by burning was not peculiar to Daniel. The plot of the story, however, is a fantastic construction which has scant concern for historical verisimilitude.

The attempt of Nebuchadnezzar to compel "all the peoples, nations and languages" to worship the image has no historical basis. (The image is presumably the image of a god, as may be seen from 3:12: "they do not serve your gods or worship the golden image which you have set up".) Even in the persecution by Antiochus Epiphanes, the demand was for sacrifice to the gods rather than worship of a particular idol. (Situations somewhat closer to that envisaged in Daniel 3 developed later under the Romans.) Yet Daniel 3 gives powerful expression to the vulnerability of the Jews in a pagan land. They did not worship the same gods as everyone else. This point was a constant source of suspicion and animosity towards the Jews throughout the ancient world, and often led to the charge of "atheism." Their antipathy to images was also an oddity, which set them apart. We do not know that the Babylonians, Persians or Greeks ever demanded that the Jews worship a specific idol, but the possibility was always there. Especially for those who rose to prominence at a gentile court, there was always the danger that their lack of reverence for idols would give offense to their masters, or would be used against them by their rivals. This is the possibility which is vividly dramatized in Daniel 3.

The story makes free use of hyperbole and exaggeration to heighten the drama. The size of the statue is enormous. All peoples are obliged to worship it. The sound of the orchestra is audible to every nation. The king is impulsive and extreme in his reactions. Yet the king himself does not seek out the Jews. They are betrayed by their rivals, the Chaldeans, and there is a note of envy in the remark that these Jews have been set over the affairs of the province. We may compare here the story of Esther where Haman resents Mordecai's refusal to bow before him. In Esther the charge against the Jews is that "their laws are different from those of every other people and they do not keep the king's laws" (Esther 3:8). In Daniel too there is a mixture of envy and resentment of the fact that the Jews are different.

In Esther, the problem is resolved through the enterprizing action of Esther and Mordecai. In Daniel, there is no room for a human resolution. The challenge of the king goes straight to the religious foundations of the conflict: "who is the god that will deliver you out of my hands?" The Jews attempt no argument, and do not even reproach the king. They willingly accept the challenge because they are confident that their God can save them. They tell the king that they would not worship his gods in any case, but their determination is evidently based on their certainty of the power of their own God.

The story moves to its climax with liberal use of hyperbole. The furnace is heated seven times more than usual, and the flame even burns up the executioners. The Greek addition has the flames rise forty-nine cubits above the furnace and burn up those who were standing around. It also explains that the angel of the Lord comes down to cool the heart of the furnace. The Aramaic text is somewhat less explicit. The king sees a fourth figure in the furnace "like a son of the gods." He is immediately convinced of the power of their God. He praises him, and promotes the Jews in the affairs of the kingdom. The uncompromising fidelity of the Jews to their religion leads once more to success in temporal affairs.

The significance of the story

The hyperbolic, exaggerated manner in which the story is told builds an atmosphere of awe and wonder and underlines the fantastic character of the tale. When the Jews were actually called on to yield up their bodies rather than serve other gods in the time of Antiochus Epiphanes, many found no angel of the Lord to rescue them. When we think of the furnace as the ovens of Auschwitz, the story is no longer marvelous but poignant. In the later chapters of Daniel, the conviction that the faithful will be rescued is transposed to life after death, where, of course, it can be neither disproved nor verified. The story of the fiery furnace was retained, but it was inevitably read in a new light.

The story of the three youths could be a dangerous illusion if it led people to believe that their faith gave them immunity to the flames of the furnace. When it is read in the context of the whole Book of Daniel, however, its metaphorical character becomes evident. Most obviously, it could serve as a vivid symbolic representation of the hope of resurrection, although the original tale evidently envisaged deliverance in this life. Yet the very wonder which pervades the story should discourage us from trying to specify the manner of deliverance with precision. The central affirmation of the story is that "our God whom we serve is able to deliver us from the burning fiery furnace." In the Aramaic text, the manner of deliverance, involving the mysterious one "like a son of the gods" is deliberately enigmatic and mysterious. What is important is that the threat posed by the king and his furnace is not ultimate. The Book of Esther made essentially the same point with less supernatural drama when it had Mordecai tell Esther that even if she failed to act "relief and deliverance will rise for the Jews from another quarter" (Esther 4:14). There is always room for hope, even in the most desperate situation. The power of a king is never absolute. The uncertainty of the future, and our lack of control over the powers that ultimately direct the world, means that we can always hope for some form of deliverance "from another quarter."

The power of Daniel 3 lies in its symbolism. The fiery furnace stands as one of the great images of religious literature. The testing of fine metals in the furnace is a fitting comparison here. Deliverance from the furnace provides a metaphor for deliverance from any desperate situation. We might compare Ezekiel's vision of the valley of dry bones, for an image of comparable power.

For Jews in the Diaspora, a story like Daniel 3 would have a therapeutic effect. On the one hand the story arouses their worst fears—an explicit attempt by the gentile rulers to enforce idolatry under pain of death. On the other hand these fears are allayed by the story of fantastic deliverance. It assures the Jews that there are powers in this world greater than Nebuchadnezzar and that these powers are benevolent, especially to them. In this way the fear of persecution, which was increasingly present in Jewish life in the Diaspora in the Hellenistic period, was exorcized and overcome. Jews could proceed in confidence to pursue their careers in the world of the gentiles. The metaphorical force of the story is scarcely less to-day. It invites us to view the world with the kind of trust necessary to face the fiery furnaces we may confront in life.

The prayer of Azariah

The Catholic edition of Daniel includes two lengthy passages, the prayer of Azariah and the song of the three young men, which are not found in the Aramaic but only in the Greek and Latin. The prayer of Azariah is obviously a foreign body here. It is a typical communal confession, similar to the prayer in Daniel 9. Such prayers are very common in the later books of the Old Testament and in the non-canonical literature of the period. It begins with a confession of God's justice and the sinfulness of Israel, which has failed to observe the covenant. It then invokes the memory of the patriarchs and appeals to the mercy of God. This prayer seems singularly inappropriate in Daniel 3. It is a prayer for all Israel, not just for the three young men. The predicament of the youths is in no way due to sin but to their fidelity to the law. Presumably the prayer was added by a scribe who felt that the situation called for a prayer for deliverance. Yet the insertion only highlights the difference between the theology of Daniel and the theology of the prayer itself.

The prayer is informed by the theology characteristic of the Deuteronomic writings. Distress is a result of sin. Deliverance will follow on repentance. In Daniel, by contrast, distress typically results from fidelity. What is needed is perseverance and endurance rather than repentance. The heroes of Daniel are remarkably confident of their own position. The stories, and also the visions, are designed to bolster that confidence in the face of an alien or even hostile world. They do not lend themselves to the kind of self-criticism expressed in this prayer. We shall return to the contrast between the Deuteronomic theology and Daniel when we discuss the prayer in Daniel 9.

The song of the three young men
The song of the three young men is more appropriate in its context. Its message is simply that God controls all the elements, including fire, and that they praise him by doing that for which they were created. The hymn is reminiscent of Ps. 136 which gives thanks to the Lord for the works of creation. It presents a vision of a world where everything is under control and serves its purpose. This faith in the ultimate providential control of the world underlies the entire Book of Daniel. As always, it is not a matter which can be demonstrated with proof, but it is a perspective on the world which provides a sense of security and an atmosphere of trust.

The hymn of the three young men provides a nice illustration of the metaphorical significance of the story of the fiery furnace. God is praised for snatching us from the netherworld and from the flame. The furnace, like the netherworld, symbolizes the threat of death which in some form always hangs over human life. In giving thanks for deliverance from the furnace, the hymn is giving thanks for the gift of life itself.

DANIEL CHAP. 4: THE MADNESS OF NEBUCHADNEZZAR

4 King Nebuchadnezzar to all peoples, nations, and languages, that dwell in all the earth: Peace be multiplied to you! ²It has seemed good to me to show the signs and

wonders that the Most High God has wrought toward me.
³How great are his signs,
how mighty his wonders!
His kingdom is an everlasting kingdom,
and his dominion is from generation to generation.

⁴I, Nebuchadnezzar, was at ease in my house and prospering in my palace. ⁵I had a dream which made me afraid; as I lay in bed the fancies and the visions of my head alarmed me. ⁶Therefore I made a decree that all the wise men of Babylon should be brought before me, that they might make known to me the interpretation of the dream. ⁷Then the magicians, the enchanters, the Chaldeans, and the astrologers came in; and I told them the dream, but they could not make known to me its interpretation. ⁸At last Daniel came in before me—he who was named Belteshazzar after the name of my god, and in whom is the spirit of the holy gods—and I told him the dream, saying, ⁹"O Belteshazzar, chief of the magicians, because I know that the spirit of the holy gods is in you and that no mystery is difficult for you, here is the dream which I saw; tell me its interpretation. ¹⁰The visions of my head as I lay in bed were these: I saw, and behold, a tree in the midst of the earth; and its height was great. ¹¹The tree grew and became strong, and its top reached to heaven, and it was visible to the end of the whole earth. ¹²Its leaves were fair and its fruit abundant, and in it was food for all. The beasts of the field found shade under it, and the birds of the air dwelt in its branches, and all flesh was fed from it.

¹³ "I saw in the visions of my head as I lay in bed, and behold, a watcher, a holy one, came down from heaven. ¹⁴He cried aloud and said thus, 'Hew down the tree and cut off its branches, strip off its leaves and scatter its fruit; let the beasts flee from under it and the birds from its branches. ¹⁵But leave the stump of its roots in the earth,

bound with a band of iron and bronze, amid the tender grass of the field. Let him be wet with the dew of heaven; let his lot be with the beasts in the grass of the earth; [16]let his mind be changed from a man's, and let a beast's mind be given to him; and let seven times pass over him. [17]The sentence is by the decree of the watchers, the decision by the word of the holy ones, to the end that the living may know that the Most High rules the kingdom of men, and gives it to whom he will, and sets over it the lowliest of men.' [18]This dream I, King Nebuchadnezzar, saw. And you, O Belteshazzar, declare the interpretation, because all the wise men of my kingdom are not able to make known to me the interpretation, but you are able, for the spirit of the holy gods is in you."

[19]Then Daniel, whose name was Belteshazzar, was dismayed for a moment, and his thoughts alarmed him. The king said, "Belteshazzar, let not the dream or the interpretation alarm you." Belteshazzar answered, "My lord, may the dream be for those who hate you and its interpretation for your enemies! [20]The tree you saw, which grew and became strong, so that its top reached to heaven, and it was visible to the end of the whole earth; [21]whose leaves were fair and its fruit abundant, and in which was food for all; under which beasts of the field found shade, and in whose branches the birds of the air dwelt — [22]it is you, O king, who have grown and become strong. Your greatness has grown and reaches to heaven, and your dominion to the ends of the earth. [23]And whereas the king saw a watcher, a holy one, coming down from heaven and saying, 'Hew down the tree and destroy it, but leave the stump of its roots in the earth, bound with a band of iron and bronze, in the tender grass of the field; and let him be wet with the dew of heaven; and let his lot be with the beasts of the field, till seven times pass over him'; [24]this is the interpretation, O king: It is a decree of the Most High, which has come upon my lord the king, [25]that you shall be driven

from among men, and your dwelling shall be with the beasts of the field; you shall be made to eat grass like an ox, and you shall be wet with the dew of heaven, and seven times shall pass over you, till you know that the Most High rules the kingdom of men, and gives it to whom he will. ²⁶And as it was commanded to leave the stump of the roots of the tree, your kingdom shall be sure for you from the time that you know that Heaven rules. ²⁷Therefore, O king, let my counsel be acceptable to you; break off your sins by practicing righteousness, and your iniquities by showing mercy to the oppressed, that there may perhaps be a lengthening of your tranquillity."

²⁸All this came upon King Nebuchadnezzar. ²⁹At the end of twelve months he was walking on the roof of the royal palace of Babylon, ³⁰and the king said, "Is not this great Babylon, which I have built by my mighty power as a royal residence and for the glory of my majesty?" ³¹While the words were still in the king's mouth, there fell a voice from heaven, "O King Nebuchadnezzar, to you it is spoken: The kingdom has departed from you, ³²and you shall be driven from among men, and your dwelling shall be with the beasts of the field; and you shall be made to eat grass like an ox; and seven times shall pass over you, until you have learned that the Most High rules the kingdom of men and gives it to whom he will." ³³Immediately the word was fulfilled upon Nebuchadnezzar. He was driven from among men, and ate grass like an ox, and his body was wet with the dew of the heaven till his hair grew as long as eagles' feathers, and his nails were like birds' claws.

³⁴At the end of the days I, Nebuchadnezzar, lifted my eyes to heaven, and my reason returned
to me, and I blessed the Most High, and praised and honored him who lives for ever;
for his dominion is an everlasting dominion,
and his kingdom endures from generation to generation;

[35]all the inhabitants of the earth are accounted as nothing;
and he does according to his will in the host of heaven
and among the inhabitants of the earth;
and none can stay his hand
or say to him, "What doest thou?"

[36]At the same time my reason returned to me; and for the glory of my kingdom, my majesty and splendor returned to me. My counselors and my lords sought me, and I was established in my kingdom, and still more greatness was added to me. [37]Now I, Nebuchadnezzar, praise and extol and honor the King of heaven; for all his works are right and his ways are just; and those who walk in pride he is able to abase.

Daniel 4 is presented as a proclamation of Nebuchadnezzar "to all peoples, nations and languages," recounting a dream, which was fulfilled in a period of madness, which in turn led to his recognition of the Most High God. The first three verses of the chapter are numbered with chapter 3 in the Aramaic text and in some translations (so 4:1 in the Aramaic corresponds to 4:4 in the RSV).

It is well established now that this story is a variant of a tradition which originally referred to Nabonidus, who was the last king of Babylon before it fell to the Persians. We know from Babylonian sources that Nabonidus spent ten years away from Babylon, basing himself in the remote city of Tema in Arabia. During that time he neglected the temple rituals in Babylon, including the most important festival of the New Year. He was hated by the Babylonian clergy who viewed him as impious. The sojourn in Tema is recounted in an inscription from Harran, in which Nabonidus speaks in the first person. This "confession" or another like it, may explain why the king in Daniel 4 also speaks in the first person.

Recently a document called the Prayer of Nabonidus has been found among the Dead Sea Scrolls of Qumran. This document is presented as a first person proclamation by Nabonidus. It says that he was afflicted with an inflammation for seven years, and was put away from men. When he confessed his sins and faults, God allowed one of the Jewish exiles in Babylon to explain his situation. This document is obviously related to Daniel 4, although neither depends directly on the other. Evidently Daniel 4 is adapting a traditional story. That story had an historical point of departure in the absence of Nabonidus from Babylon, but the development of the story was independent of historical data. The Book of Daniel transfers the story from Nabonidus to the more famous, or notorious, Nebuchadnezzar.

The narrative begins with Nebuchadnezzar's dream. The Chaldeans fail to interpret it, so he calls on Daniel. The contrast between Daniel and the Chaldeans, which was the main focus of Daniel 2, is noted briefly here. Once again, Daniel is the loyal servant of the king. There is no conflict between Jews and gentiles in this story.

The dream itself concerns a great tree. The great tree recalls the cedar of Lebanon in Ezekiel 31, to which the king of Egypt is compared. Here it represents Nebuchadnezzar himself. The beasts and the birds are sheltered by it. Jeremiah (27:6) said that God had given Nebuchadnezzar the beasts of the field to serve him.

The vision continues with the decree of the watchers or holy ones. (This usage of "holy ones" for angels is of some significance for Daniel 7, below.) The tree is cut down and only a stump is left. At this point the allegory breaks down, as some person is sentenced to live like a beast for seven years. Daniel reluctantly explains that the person in question is the king. The moral of the vision is quite straightforward. Because the king has raised himself too high, he must be brought low. Daniel's advice is a rather general admonition to practise righteousness and avoid iniquity, specifying only that he show mercy to the oppressed. The chapter concludes by telling how Nebuchadnezzar was reduced to a bestial state and, after the appointed time, came to recognize the sovereignty of God.

The objection to gentile kings

While there is no conflict between Judaism, as such, and Nebuchadnezzar, Daniel is, however reluctantly, cast in the role of critic of the king, almost as Nathan was to David. The chapter articulates the basic Jewish objection to the gentile kings—they usurp the place of God. There are numerous striking passages in the Old Testament which express this criticism. Isaiah 14 compares the king of Babylon to Lucifer, the Day-Star, Son of Dawn, who tried to rise above the stars of God, and was therefore brought down into the Pit. Ezekiel 28 assails the king of Tyre for his pride, and for saying "I am a god." But he is a man and no god, and will be brought down to the Pit. The hymn in Philippians Chap. 2 reverses this pattern with reference to Christ. Because he emptied himself and did not seek to be equal to God, therefore God exalted him. No biblical theme recurs more insistently, from the opening chapters of Genesis onward, than that man is not God, and cannot become like God. The theme is not peculiar to the bible either. It is essentially the same as the central motif in Greek tragedy. Tragedy occurs when a character succumbs to *hybris,* the pride which aspires to rise above the common lot of humanity. The fall inevitably follows.

Daniel 4 expresses this widespread human insight, that pride goes before a fall, with vivid imagery, even if the images of the tree and the beast do not go very well together. Yet the picture of the mighty Nebuchadnezzar, who had ruled over the beasts of the field, eating grass like an ox, is a memorable one. It reinforces the message of the story, which is summarized in the hymnic passage in 4:34-35: "all the inhabitants of the earth are accounted as nothing . . . and none can stay his (God's) hand." The imagery is powerful for anyone who suffers under the power of a Nebuchadnezzar, ancient or modern.

The perspective on political power

The story lends a definite perspective to political matters. Nebuchadnezzar could rightly claim to have built Babylon up to greatness. The story dramatizes the fragility of the power of even so great a king. When the Book of Daniel was written, the power of Babylon was long since broken. The tree had indeed been felled and only a stump remained. The perspective of this story, then, is rather similar to that of the four kingdoms prophecy in chapter 2.

Despite the extreme humiliation of the king, he is restored at the end. Daniel 4 does not preach the destruction of gentile power, but its reformation. The story is designed as a moral lesson to gentile rulers: humble yourselves, or this may happen to you too. Of course the gentile rulers were unlikely to heed, or even to read, such a warning, but the story must have provided a satisfying sense of moral superiority for the Jews. It helped them to see their rulers in perspective. The fictional repentance of Nebuchadnezzar expressed their hope for a satisfactory resolution of the problem of gentile dominion, not by the destruction of the gentiles, but by their conversion.

DANIEL CHAP. 5: THE WRITING ON THE WALL

> **5** King Belshazzar made a great feast for a thousand of his lords, and drank wine in front of the thousand.

²Belshazzar, when he tasted the wine, commanded that the vessels of gold and of silver which Nebuchadnezzar his father had taken out of the temple in Jerusalem be brought, that the king and his lords, his wives, and his concubines might drink from them. ³Then they brought in the golden and silver vessels which had been taken out of the temple, the house of God in Jerusalem; and the king and his lords, his wives, and his concubines drank from them. ⁴They drank wine, and praised the gods of gold and silver, bronze, iron, wood, and stone.

⁵Immediately the fingers of a man's hand appeared and wrote on the plaster of the wall of the king's palace, opposite the lampstand; and the king saw the hand as it wrote. ⁶Then the king's color changed, and his thoughts alarmed him; his limbs gave way, and his knees knocked together. ⁷The king cried aloud to bring in the enchanters, the Chaldeans, and the astrologers. The king said to the wise men of Babylon, "Whoever reads this writing, and shows me its interpretation, shall be clothed with purple, and have a chain of gold about his neck, and shall be the third ruler in the kingdom." ⁸Then all the king's wise men came in, but they could not read the writing or make known to the king the interpretation. ⁹Then King Belshazzar was greatly alarmed, and his color changed; and his lords were perplexed.

¹⁰The queen, because of the words of the king and his lords, came into the banqueting hall; and the queen said, "O king, live for ever! Let not your thoughts alarm you or your color change. ¹¹There is in your kingdom a man in whom is the spirit of the holy gods. In the days of your father light and understanding and wisdom, like the wisdom of the gods, were found in him, and King Nebuchadnezzar, your father, made him chief of the magicians, enchanters, Chaldeans, and astrolo-

gers, ¹²because an excellent spirit, knowledge, and understanding to interpret dreams, explain riddles, and solve problems were found in this Daniel, whom the king named Belteshazzar. Now let Daniel be called, and he will show the interpretation."

¹³Then Daniel was brought in before the king. The king said to Daniel, "You are that Daniel, one of the exiles of Judah, whom the king my father brought from Judah. ¹⁴I have heard of you that the spirit of the holy gods is in you, and that light and understanding and excellent wisdom are found in you. ¹⁵Now the wise men, the enchanters, have been brought in before me to read this writing and make known to me its interpretation; but they could not show the interpretation of the matter. ¹⁶But I have heard that you can give interpretations and solve problems. Now if you can read the writing and make known to me its interpretation, you shall be clothed with purple, and have a chain of gold about your neck, and shall be the third ruler in the kingdom."

¹⁷Then Daniel answered before the king, "Let your gifts be for yourself, and give your rewards to another; nevertheless I will read the writing to the king and make known to him the interpretation. ¹⁸O king, the Most High God gave Nebuchadnezzar your father kingship and greatness and glory and majesty; ¹⁹and because of the greatness that he gave him, all peoples, nations, and languages trembled and feared before him; whom he would he slew, and whom he would he kept alive; whom he would he raised up, and whom he would he put down. ²⁰But when his heart was lifted up and his spirit was hardened so that he dealt proudly, he was deposed from his kingly throne, and his glory was taken from him; ²¹he was driven from among men, and his mind was made like that of a beast, and his dwelling was with the wild asses; he was fed grass like an ox, and his body

was wet with the dew of heaven, until he knew that the Most High God rules the kingdom of men, and sets over it whom he will. ²²And you his son, Belshazzar, have not humbled your heart, though you knew all this, ²³but you have lifted up yourself against the Lord of heaven; and the vessels of his house have been brought in before you, and you and your lords, your wives, and your concubines have drunk wine from them; and you have praised the gods of silver and gold, of bronze, iron, wood, and stone, which do not see or hear or know, but the God in whose hand is your breath, and whose are all your ways, you have not honored.

²⁴"Then from his presence the hand was sent, and this writing was inscribed. ²⁵And this is the writing that was inscribed: MENE, MENE, TEKEL, and PARSIN. ²⁶This is the interpretation of the matter: MENE, God has numbered the days of your kingdom and brought it to an end; ²⁷TEKEL, you have been weighed in the balances and found wanting; ²⁸PERES, your kingdom is divided and given to the Medes and Persians."

²⁹Then Belshazzar commanded, and Daniel was clothed with purple, a chain of gold was put about his neck, and proclamation was made concerning him, that he should be the third ruler in the kingdom.

³⁰That very night Belshazzar the Chaldean king was slain. ³¹And Darius the Mede received the kingdom, being about sixty-two years old.

There was an historical Belshazzar, and he was in fact the one who governed Babylon when it fell to the Persians. He was not, however, king of Babylon, but regent in the absence of Nabonidus, and he was son of Nabonidus, not of Nebuchadnezzar. There was a legend, reported by the Greek historians Herodotus and Xenophon that Babylon was captured during a nocturnal festival. So, like the other stories in

Daniel, the story of Belshazzar's feast has a certain amount of historical coloring. The fictional character of the story is underlined in the unhistorical reference to Darius the Mede at the end.

Again, the story is a vivid one. Belshazzar is shown as a figure of decadent luxury, drinking wine "in front of thousands" with his wives and his concubines. His greatest offence in the eyes of a Jewish author is that he brings out the vessels which had been taken from the Jerusalem temple, and uses them as goblets while praising the gods of gold and silver. The temple vessels figure prominently in the books of Maccabees, and undoubtedly this story received added point in Maccabean times. Yet the vessels had also been taken by the Babylonians, and the story in Daniel 5 could have been composed anytime thereafter as a dramatization of the disregard of the gentile kings who ruled the earth for the things which Jews held most sacred.

Few images in the bible are more hauntingly evocative than the fingers writing on the wall. The scene has become proverbial for imminent destruction which is destined and cannot be evaded. It conveys not only the riddle to be deciphered but also the sense of a mysterious hand guiding the course of events.

As in Daniel 2 and 4, the Chaldean wise men fail to provide an interpretation. The test of wisdom frames the story here. The rewards promised to Daniel are part of the conventions of the tale, although the honor of becoming third ruler in the kingdom becomes rather dubious in view of the imminent destruction. Daniel accepts the honors, although he disavows any interest in them at first. Even here Daniel is a loyal subject, although he is more sharply critical of Belshazzar than he ever was of Nebuchadnezzar. If he disavows interest in the honors, it is surely because of the perspective provided by the writing on the wall.

The message of the chapter is stated quite clearly by

Daniel before he proceeds to the interpretation. The lesson of the previous chapter is recounted. Belshazzar appears as a counterpart to Nebuchadnezzar. The former monarch was humbled, and then restored. Belshazzar was not deterred by this example but showed his arrogance in the treatment of the temple vessels.

The actual writing on the wall, Mene, Mene, Tekel and Parsin, is deliberately enigmatic, and it continues to inspire scholarly speculation. There is wide consensus that the words are nouns and refer to weights or monetary units— the mina, shekel and half-minas. What significance these weights may have had is still unclear. The shekel is the least valuable of the three, the proportions being 60, 1, 13. Most commentators agree that the weights refer to kings or kingdoms, but disagree as to the exact references. There is also disagreement as to whether the duplication of mina is original. In any case, Daniel ignores the exact meaning of the terms and offers a pun on each: mene suggests the numbering of the days, tekel the weighing of the king and peres (altering slightly the original word) is taken as an allusion to the Persians.

The chapter concludes with abrupt finality. Daniel is honored in accordance with the king's promise, and the king is killed that night.

The judgment on the king

Daniel 5 complements Daniel 4 by providing a story in which the arrogant king does not repent, and is killed. It reinforces the message of the previous chapter that the mighty can be brought low. However fictional the story, the fall of Babylon was indeed historical. The story, which has the city fall on the very night of the feast when Belshazzar profaned the temple vessels, makes its point by the ironic juxtaposition of events. We are reminded of the gospel warning: "Fool! This night your soul is required of you" (Luke 12:20). The uncertainty of the hour of death is the great leveller of high and low, king and subject.

Even though Belshazzar is given no time to repent, Daniel 5 does not envisage the overthrow of gentile power as such. The kingdom passes to Darius the Mede. The judgment on the king takes place within the context of continuing gentile rule. The message is that there are good gentile kings and bad ones. The good ones are those who humble themselves, treat the sacred things with respect and acknowledge the God of heaven. It is not clear that Daniel expected the repudiation of all pagan gods and the sole worship of the God of Israel. Some gentile kings, such as Cyrus of Persia, could speak of the chief god of any people as the God of heaven. (So, for example, he told the Babylonians that Marduk, god of Babylon, had given the city over to him.) This kind of respectful treatment is what the Jews probably hoped for and sometimes got. The story of Belshazzar was a fable intended to chasten the arrogant. Needless to say, the story was unlikely to have any effect on the actual rulers, but it was reassuring for the Jewish subjects. It provided a fantasy of what would happen if any monarch did not treat their sacred things with respect.

The story is pervaded by a sense of wonder and mystery. Behind the scene of history is the hand that writes the words of doom on the wall. The divine control of history may not always be obvious, but on occasion the hand and the writing become visible. While such a hidden force controls events no human can afford to be as arrogant as Belshazzar.

Even more obviously than the previous chapters this story transcends its political context and becomes a moral tale of universal relevance, a tale of the hiddenness of destiny and the fall of the proud.

DANIEL CHAP. 6: THE LIONS' DEN

> **6** It pleased Darius to set over the kingdom a hundred and twenty satraps, to be throughout the whole kingdom;

²and over them three presidents, of whom Daniel was one, to whom these satraps should give account, so that the king might suffer no loss. ³Then this Daniel became distinguished above all the other presidents and satraps, because an excellent spirit was in him; and the king planned to set him over the whole kingdom. ⁴Then the presidents and the satraps sought to find a ground for complaint against Daniel with regard to the kingdom; but they could find no ground for complaint or any fault, because he was faithful, and no error or fault was found in him. ⁵Then these men said, "We shall not find any ground for complaint against this Daniel unless we find it in connection with the law of his God."

⁶Then these presidents and satraps came by agreement to the king and said to him, "O King Darius, live for ever! ⁷All the presidents of the kingdom, the prefects and the satraps, the counselors and the governors are agreed that the king should establish an ordinance and enforce an interdict, that whoever makes petition to any god or man for thirty days, except to you, O king, shall be cast into the den of lions. ⁸Now, O king, establish the interdict and sign the document so that it cannot be changed according to the law of the Medes and the Persians, which cannot be revoked." ⁹Therefore King Darius signed the document and interdict.

¹⁰When Daniel knew that the document had been signed, he went to his house where he had windows in his upper chamber open toward Jerusalem; and he got down on his knees three times a day and prayed and gave thanks before his God, as he had done previously. ¹¹Then these men came by agreement and found Daniel making petition and supplication before his God. ¹²Then they came near and said before the king, concerning the interdict, "O king! Did you not sign an interdict, that any man who makes petition to any god or man within thirty days ex-

cept to you, O king, shall be cast into the den of lions?''
The king answered, ''The thing stands fast, according to
the law of the Medes and Persians, which cannot be
revoked.''[13] Then they answered before the king, ''That
Daniel, who is one of the exiles from Judah, pays no heed
to you, O king, or the interdict you have signed, but
makes his petition three times a day.''

[14]Then the king, when he heard these words, was much
distressed, and set his mind to deliver Daniel; and he
labored till the sun went down to rescue him. [15]Then these
men came by agreement to the king, and said to the king,
''Know, O king, that it is a law of the Medes and Persians
that no interdict or ordinance which the king establishes
can be changed.''

[16]Then the king commanded, and Daniel was brought
and cast into the den of lions. The king said to Daniel,
''May your God, whom you serve continually, deliver
you!'' [17]And a stone was brought and laid upon the
mouth of the den, and the king sealed it with his own signet and with the signet of his lords, that nothing might be
changed concerning Daniel. [18]Then the king went to his
palace, and spent the night fasting; no diversions were
brought to him, and sleep fled from him.

[19]Then, at break of day, the king arose and went in
haste to the den of lions. [20]When he came near to the den
where Daniel was, he cried out in a tone of anguish and
said to Daniel, ''O Daniel, servant of the living God, has
your God, whom you serve continually, been able to deliver you from the lions?'' [21]Then Daniel said to the king,
''O king, live for ever! [22]My God sent his angel and shut
the lions' mouths, and they have not hurt me, because I
was found blameless before him; and also before you, O
king, I have done no wrong.'' [23]Then the king was exceedingly glad, and commanded that Daniel be taken up
out of the den. So Daniel was taken up out of the den, and

no kind of hurt was found upon him, because he had trusted in his God. ²⁴And the king commanded, and those men who had accused Daniel were brought and cast into the den of lions—they, their children, and their wives; and before they reached the bottom of the den the lions overpowered them and broke all their bones in pieces.

²⁵Then King Darius wrote to all the peoples, nations, and languages that dwell in all the earth: "Peace be multiplied to you. ²⁶I make a decree, that in all my royal dominion men tremble and fear before the God of Daniel,

for he is the living God,
enduring for ever;
his kingdom shall never be destroyed,
and his dominion shall be to the end.
²⁷He delivers and rescues,
he works signs and wonders
in heaven and on earth,
he who has saved Daniel
from the power of the lions."

²⁸So this Daniel propsered during the reign of Darius and the reign of Cyrus the Persian.

In Daniel 6 we find yet another vivid picture which has impressed itself on the popular imagination even when the outline of the story has been lost. Daniel in the lions' den has become a figure for the innocent defenceless person surrounded by dangers, but surviving by the force of righteousness. The metaphorical potential of this image transcends the historical context of the story.

This story, like the others, has some historical coloring. Darius I of Persia did in fact set up satrapies throughout the empire, but here Darius is supposed to be a Mede who ruled before Cyrus the Great of Persia. The story itself has little concern for historical plausibility. The main historical ingredient in the story is the rivalry between Jewish and gentile courtiers and the resentment caused by the success of the Jew. In this respect Daniel 6 is especially close to Esther. Unlike Esther, however, Daniel 6 singles out "the law of his God" as the ground on which the gentiles can contrive to bring a complaint against the Jew. As we have seen above, much of the resentment against the Jews in the ancient world was due to the fact that they had different laws and religious observances from others. It was, in fact, the law of their God which made them a group apart. Daniel 6 does not suggest that keeping the Jewish law was in any way incompatible with loyal service to Darius. On the contrary, Daniel is a faultless servant of the king, and the king, moreover, appreciates this. Only troublemakers try to create a tension between Jewish law and the service of the crown. Yet the story shows an awareness of the potential danger to the Jews because of their distinct religion. Like Daniel 3, this story has initially a nightmarish quality. It fantasizes the kind of trap that could lie in store for the Jew who rose to prominence in the gentile world, and aroused the resentment of his rivals. The therapeutic value of the story lies in showing how the danger is overcome.

The trap set for Daniel is to have the king enact a law forbidding anyone to make a petition of any god or man for thirty days, except to himself. The idea is farfetched, and quite implausible, but it suffices to get the plot in motion. In all these stories, the kings are highly simplified stereotypes, who react with extremes of emotion and are usually susceptible to anything their advisers may suggest. The stereotypical character of the story is heightened by "the law of the Medes and the Persians, which cannot be revoked." We hear of the immutability of the laws of the Medes and Persians also in Esther and in the Greek historian Diodorus Siculus. Here it serves to set up a situation which cannot be resolved by human means but becomes a test of the power of God.

It should be noted that despite the rashness of the king in passing this law, he is throughout a sympathetic figure. He is distressed at the unforeseen consequence of his edict and wishes to deliver Daniel. He even prays that Daniel's god will deliver him. The issue here is not any conflict with gentile power as such. The conflict is with the malicious and resentful courtiers.

As in Daniel 3, the resolution is achieved through miraculous deliverance: "My God sent his angel and shut the lions' mouths." Not all Jews were so fortunate. This is not the stuff of historical reality, but of fantasy. Its value lies in the confidence and trust it inspires. As the Psalmist had written: "Even though I walk through the valley of the shadow of death, I fear no evil; for thou art with me" (Ps 23:4). As we shall see, the fantasy of miraculous deliverance was no longer sufficient in the face of actual persecution. In less urgent times it gave the Jews of the exile a sense of security, especially since in Daniel 6 it reassured them of the benevolence not only of God but of the king.

The note of vengeance

The response of the king to Daniel's deliverance introduces a note which we have scarcely heard before in the Book of Daniel: the king commands that Daniel's accusers, with their children and their wives, be thrown to the lions, and their bones are broken before they reach the bottom of the pit. This is not only poetic justice. It is vengeance, which extends even to the presumably innocent wives and children. There is ample biblical precedent for such sentiments. We may think of the jubilant conclusion of the Book of Esther, when the Jews were permitted to slay seventy five thousand of those who hated them (Esther 9:16) or of the fervent prayer of the Psalmist: "daughter of Babylon, you devastator! . . . Happy shall he be who takes your little ones and dashes them against the rock!" (Ps. 137: 8-9). Such sentiments may seem distasteful in the light of the gospel message of loving our enemies. Yet Christians should remember that no book in the bible shows a stronger spirit of vengeance than the Christian Apocalypse of John, and that if Paul advised the Romans to give food and drink to their enemies, it was so as to heap burning coals upon their heads (Rom 12:20). Few people can endure the harassment and malice of others without some desire for vengeance. It is better to be frank and acknowledge this than to pretend we have no such feelings, when they may very well be influencing our actions subconsciously. It may also be better to vent such feelings in a fantasy or story than in violent action.

The element of vengeance in Daniel 6 is very minor. The emphasis at the end of the story is on the praise of God in the mouth of the Persian king. The hymnic passage re-affirms a familiar biblical theme: God can save from the jaws of death. While human kingdoms rise and fall, his kingdom is forever. God here represents the power that guides the universe, beyond the limits of humanity. This power is made manifest in the unexpected events, the fall of the tyrant or the rescue of the condemned man, the events which ordinarily people would not have foreseen. The kingdom which continues while dynasties rise and fall is the kingdom of life itself.

The Tales in Retrospect

When we look back on the tales in Daniel 1-6, we may be impressed with their general optimism. The stories reflect the determination of the Jews to live and prosper under gentile rule, while maintaining uncompromising fidelity to their law. In fact, a major thesis of these stories is that success in the gentile world is directly dependent on fidelity to the Law.

The stories, which are evident fantasies, suggest a theological basis for Diaspora life. Whereas the prayer of Azariah, like the older Deuteronomistic theology, saw the exile as a punishment for sin, Daniel sees the rule of the gentiles as part of a long-term divine plan. The four kingdoms have their appointed times. Their sovereignty is not absolute. Good gentile kings will in some way acknowledge the God of heaven. The arrogant will be struck down. Ultimately all four kingdoms will pass. What is crucial is that this entire development is subject to the power of God. Each kingdom is transient and can be disposed of by God as he wishes.

The wise Jew, typified by Daniel, has a superior position in so far as he understands all this. If for the present, temporal power is in the hands of his enemies, he need feel no danger. His God, who supervises history, will deliver him, from fiery furnace or lions' den. Furthermore, even if an occasional ruler is arrogant, they usually appreciate the wisdom and loyalty of the Jew and honor him accordingly.

This view of the world was evidently compatible enough with the realities of life for some period of the history of the Diaspora. It was severely strained by the events under Antiochus Epiphanes. We may compare the way in which the optimistic liberal theology of the early part of this century was shattered by the two World Wars, and especially by the Jewish Holocaust under Hitler. While there is occasional malice, resentment and arrogance in the gentile world viewed by the tales, it is evil on a small scale. Ultimately God is in his heaven and all's well with the world. In the visions from the time of Antiochus Epiphanes, God is still in his heaven, but all is not well with the world. The fantasies of deliverance from fiery furnace and lions' den were no more adequate for that crisis than they were for Auschwitz. A different genre of religious literature was called for, even more fantastic in its imagery, but one which gave greater recognition to the enormity of evil and the difficulty of human hope.

THE VISIONS

DANIEL CHAP. 7: THE BEASTS FROM THE SEA AND "ONE LIKE A SON OF MAN"

7 In the first year of Belshazzar king of Babylon, Daniel had a dream and visions of his head as he lay in his bed. Then he wrote down the dream, and told the sum of the matter. ²Daniel said, "I saw in my vision by night, and behold, the four winds of heaven were stirring up the great sea. ³And four great beasts came up out of the sea, different from one another. ⁴The first was like a lion and had eagles' wings. Then as I looked its wings were plucked off, and it was lifted up from the ground and made to stand upon two feet like a man; and the mind of a man was given to it. ⁵And behold, another beast, a second one, like a bear. It was raised up on one side; it had three ribs in its mouth between its teeth; and it was told, 'Arise, devour much flesh.' ⁶After this I looked, and lo, another, like a leopard, with four wings of a bird on its back; and the beast had four heads; and dominion was given to it. ⁷After this I saw in the night visions, and behold, a fourth beast, terrible and dreadful and exceedingly strong; and it had great iron teeth; it devoured and broke in pieces, and stamped the residue with its feet. It was different from all the beasts that were before it; and it had ten horns. ⁸I considered the horns, and behold, there came up among them another horn, a little one, before which three of the first horns were plucked up by the roots; and behold, in this horn were eyes like the eyes of a man, and a mouth speaking great things. ⁹As I looked,

> thrones were placed
> and one that was ancient of days took his seat;
> his raiment was white as snow,
> and the hair of his head like pure wool;
> his throne was fiery flames,
> its wheels were burning fire.

¹⁰A stream of fire issued

> and came forth from before him;
> a thousand thousands served him,
> and ten thousand times ten thousand stood before him;
> the court sat in judgment,
> and the books were opened.

¹¹I looked then because of the sound of the great words which the horn was speaking. And as I looked, the beast was slain, and its body destroyed and given over to be burned with fire. ¹²As for the rest of the beasts, their dominion was taken away, but their lives were prolonged for a season and a time. ¹³I saw in the night vision,

> and behold, with the clouds of heaven
> there came one like a son of man
> and he came to the Ancient of Days and was
>   presented before him.

¹⁴And to him was given dominion

> and glory and kingdom,
> that all peoples, nations, and languages
> should serve him;
> his dominion is an everlasting dominion,
> which shall not pass away,
> and his kingdom one
> that shall not be destroyed.

¹⁵"As for me, Daniel, my spirit within me was anxious and the visions of my head alarmed me. ¹⁶I approached one of those who stood there and asked him the truth concerning all this. So he told me, and made known to me the

interpretation of the things. [17]"These four great beasts are four kings who shall arise out of the earth. [18]But the saints of the Most High shall receive the kingdom, and possess the kingdom for ever, for ever and ever.'

[19]"Then I desired to know the truth concerning the fourth beast, which was different from all the rest, exceedingly terrible, with its teeth of iron and claws of bronze; and which devoured and broke in pieces, and stamped the residue with its feet; [20]and concerning the ten horns that were on its head, and the other horn which came up and before which three of them fell, the horn which had eyes and a mouth that spoke great things, and which seemed greater than its fellows. [21]As I looked, this horn made war with the saints, and prevailed over them, [22]until the Ancient of Days came, and judgment was given for the saints of the Most High, and the time came when the saints received the kingdom.

[23]"Thus he said: 'As for the fourth beast,
　　there shall be a fourth kingdom on earth,
　　which shall be different from all the kingdoms,
　　and it shall devour the whole earth, and trample it
　　　　down, and break it to pieces.
[24]As for the ten horns,
　　out of this kingdom
　　ten kings shall arise,
　　and another shall arise after them;
　　he shall be different from the former ones,
　　and shall put down three kings.
[25]He shall speak words against the Most High,
　　and shall wear out the saints of the Most High,
　　and shall think to change the times and the law;
　　and they shall be given into his hand for a time, two
　　　　times, and half a time.
[26]But the court shall sit in judgment, and his dominion
　　　　shall be taken away,
　　to be consumed and destroyed to the end.

> ²⁷And the kingdom and the dominion and the greatness
> of the kingdoms under the whole heaven
> shall be given to the people of the saints of the Most
> High;
> their kingdom shall be an everlasting kingdom,
> and all dominions shall serve and obey them.'
> ²⁸"Here is the end of the matter. As for me, Daniel, my
> thoughts greatly alarmed me, and my color changed; but
> I kept the matter in my mind."

Daniel 7 is without doubt the most powerful chapter in the book, and one of the most powerful in the entire bible. It draws on traditional symbolism which had roots further back than the emergence of Israel as a nation. It provided the New Testament with some of its most memorable imagery.

The scene is set in the first year of Belshazzar, thus breaking the sequential ordering of the chapters which had been followed up to this point. Unlike the earlier chapters, Daniel is now the one who has the dream, and it is interpreted for him by an angel. Interpretation is no longer within the capacity of human beings. The revelation is emphatically out of this world.

The beasts from the sea

The vision involves, first, a great sea stirred up by the four winds of heaven. Then four great beasts come up out of the sea, hybrid and awesome. Of these, the fourth receives most attention. It has ten horns, and an eleventh, a little horn, which appears as an extraneous growth. The scene then moves to the divine throne. Judgment is passed and the fourth beast is slain. Then appears "one like a son of man" on the clouds of heaven, and he receives "dominion and glory and kingdom."

The initial interpretation of this vision is given to Daniel by "one of those who stood there," an angel. The first part of the vision is summarized in a sentence: "These four great beasts are four kings who shall arise on the earth.'' It should be obvious to any reader that this statement is not an adequate substitute for the vision. A great beast "terrible and dreadful and exceedingly strong" with iron teeth, devouring and tearing in pieces, is not a neutral description of a kingdom. The interpretation only tells us, in the briefest way possible, what the vision is about. It makes no attempt to capture the emotional impact of the vision or to convey what has been said about the four kingdoms.

In fact, the imagery of the vision is loaded, over and above what can be grasped at first sight by the reader unfamiliar with the tradition. We may begin with the great sea. It is apparent from many passages in the Old Testament that the sea could signify more than an inanimate body of water. We read that when God created the world:
"By his power he stilled the sea;
By his understanding he smote Rahab.
By his wind the heavens were made fair;
His hand pierced the fleeing serpent.'' (Job 26:12-13)
Again in Ps. 89:9-11 we find a hymn to God as creator:
"Thou didst rule the raging of the sea;
when its waves rise, thou stillest them.
Thou didst crush Rahab like a carcass,
thou didst scatter thy enemies with thy mighty arm''
and in Ps. 74:13-17:
"Thou didst divide the sea by thy might;
thou didst break the heads of the dragons on the waters.
Thou didst crush the heads of Leviathan . . .
Thou hast fixed all the bounds of the earth.''
Even from these few examples we can see that the sea is not a neutral entity. These passages see the work of creation not as a production of matter out of nothing, but as the imposition of order where there was chaos before. This in fact is what creation means in virtually all ancient mythology. Even Genesis doesn't begin with nothing, but with waste and

void, *tōhū wā-bōhū*, chaos and disorder. In the passages we have cited the chaos is symbolized by the sea, fleeting monsters and dragons in the sea, two of which are named as Rahab and Leviathan. Now the reader will look in vain, in Genesis or in any of the prose narratives of the bible, for an account of a battle between God and Rahab or Leviathan. What we have here are snatches of an older mythology, which may have played a significant part in the religion of ancient Israel but found little place in the bible.

Much light has been thrown on this mythology by the discovery of Canaanite myths from about 1500 BCE at Ugarit in northern Syria, in 1929. In the Ugaritic myths we find the god of fertility, Baal, engaged in a series of combats with forces which represent chaos in some form. One of the opponents of Baal was named Mot, or Death. The symbolism here hardly needs comment. More importantly for Daniel, another opponent of Baal was Yamm or Sea, and we hear of a struggle in which Baal overcomes Sea with two clubs. Other passages in the Ugaritic myths refer to a battle in which Baal "smote Lotan, the ancient dragon, destroyed the crooked serpent, Shilyat with the seven heads." Yet another passage has the Canaanite goddess Anat smite Sea, destroy "El's river Rabbim," muzzle the dragon and smite the crooked serpent of seven heads. Lotan is the prototype of the mysterious Leviathan of the biblical texts. Rabbim (many or mighty) often appears as an adjective for the waters of the sea. In Daniel, a form of the same adjective is used. The great sea is *yammā' rabbā.* The seven-headed monster re-appears in Revelation 12, 13 and 17.

It is apparent, then, that when Daniel sees four monstrous beasts coming up out of the sea, the imagery of his vision has rich and traditional associations. It evokes a sense that the monsters which had been subdued at creation were again let loose on the world. The evocation of the primordial myth is in no way contradicted by the statement that the beasts are four kings. Throughout the Old Testament the imagery drawn from the myths was used to refer to historical and political events. Rahab is used as a code-name for Egypt (Isa 30:7, Ps. 87:4). In Isa 17:12-14 we read that the nations roar like the roaring of many waters, but God will rebuke them and they will flee away. The sea-imagery was readily applicable to the Exodus. One of the finest illustrations of the use of this imagery is in Isa 51:9-10. The prophet is celebrating the release of the Jews from the Babylonian exile. He asks God

"Was it not thou that didst cut Rahab in pieces,
  that didst pierce the dragon?
Was it not thou that didst dry up the sea,
  the waters of the great deep;
that didst make the depths of the sea a way
  for the redeemed to pass over?
And the ransomed of the Lord shall return . . ."

Here three events are compared: the mythical battle with the dragon and Rahab, the splitting of the sea at the Exodus, and the liberation of the Jews from the exile. The battle with the monster becomes a metaphor for the two other great crises of Israel's history.

We can now better appreciate the significance of Daniel's vision. It did indeed refer to four kings or kingdoms. The motif of the four kingdoms is evidently taken over from Daniel 2, and indirectly from the political propaganda of the Hellenistic world. In Daniel 7, however, the four kingdoms are viewed rather differently. They arise from the turbulent sea. They are the forces of chaos, released on the world. The descriptions of the individual beasts are drawn in part from biblical imagery. (Hosea 13 lists a lion, a bear and a leopard.) They must also be related to the monsters in the sea in the Canaanite myths and Old Testament passages. In Daniel 2, the four kingdoms were granted their alloted time by God. Here they are forces of anarchy and rebellion. The world ruled by the gentiles is no longer acceptable. Daniel's vision, colored no doubt by the experience of persecution under Antiochus Epiphanes, is a vision of a world in tumult, analogous to what the poet W.B. Yeats saw in our own century:

"Things fall apart, the center cannot hold.
Mere anarchy is loosed upon the world."

The sea and its monsters were not isolated motifs. They were part of a traditional story. In the Ugaritic myths, Sea and the various monsters were defeated by Baal. In the Old Testament passages the sea was subdued by Yahweh and the monsters were slain. The battle between Yahweh and the monsters, originally located in the creation, had been projected forward to the end-time in the Book of Isaiah:

"In that day the Lord with his hard and great strong sword will punish Leviathan the fleeing serpent, Leviathan the twisting serpent, and he will slay the dragon that is in the sea" (Isa 27:1).

While the appearance of the beasts strikes terror into Daniel and the reader alike, we know that in the end they will be subdued.

The heavenly judgment

The scene moves abruptly from the blasphemies of the little horn to the heavenly judgment scene. The Ancient of Days is evidently God. Daniel doesn't hesitate to claim that he saw God, and offer a description of him. This way of describing God also has an old tradition behind it, reaching back ultimately to the Canaanite god El. The description of the throne owes something to the famous vision of Ezekiel. We find a similar description in the apocalyptic Book of Enoch. The effect of the introduction of God, the fire all around him and the myriad of angels, is one of splendor and awe. This scene, too, may inspire terror, but it offsets the terror of the beasts.

The judgment scene unfolds. The books of judgment are a common apocalyptic motif which we will meet again in Daniel 12. Records are kept in heaven. All will be accounted for. The fourth beast, which had sprouted the little horn, is slain and its body thrown in the fire. This is no time for mercy towards one's enemies. The judgment pays little heed to the chronological order of the kingdoms. All are judged at once. The first three survive the fourth. The concern of the author is not with chronological sequence but with relative value judgments. As we know from chapter 2, the fourth kingdom is the Greek, and it is with this kingdom that the author is primarily concerned, although the other kingdoms too are beasts, and are condemned.

The judgment of the beasts is followed by the advent of "one like a son of man" who comes "with the clouds of heaven." The entourage of clouds is significant. In the Ugaritic myths, Baal, the conqueror of sea, is the rider of the clouds. In the Old Testament it is Yahweh who rides on the clouds. Since Yahweh is already present as the Ancient of Days, the "one like a son of man" cannot be the divinity himself. Yet the entourage of clouds marks him as a supernatural, heavenly figure.

In the angel's interpretation in vss. 17-18, the "one like a son of man" is not explicitly identified. Instead we are told that "the saints of the Most High" will receive the kingdom which was given to the "one like a son of man" in the vision. This does not necessarily mean that he is a collective figure, identical with them, but it does mean that he represents them in some way.

The identity of the "saints" or holy ones has itself been a matter of much controversy. The Aramaic word is the adjective "holy" used substantively, as a noun. In the great majority of cases where this word is used as a noun in Hebrew or Aramaic it refers to angels. We have already met this usage in Daniel 4. We will meet it again in Daniel 8. At the same time, the holy ones obviously bear some relation to the persecuted Jews. Since the four beasts represent four kingdoms, we should expect that the "one like a son of man" and the "saints" also represent a human people. The passage in Dan 7: 19-27 makes clear that the vision relates to the persecution of the Jews by Antiochus Epiphanes, and 7:27 says that the kingdom is given to the people of the holy ones.

There is no doubt that both the "one like a son of man" and the "saints of the Most High" represent the persecuted Jews. The question is, what is the manner of representation, and the nature of the symbolism? We have seen that the four beasts are not neutral ciphers which can be replaced adequately by a statement about four kings. The beasts, and the sea, express the force of chaos underlying the four kingdoms. Correspondingly, the "one like a son of man" on the clouds of heaven represents not only the persecuted Jews but a heavenly power which supports them. The very fact that the term "holy ones" is commonly used for angels, suggests that the persecuted Jews are in some way associated with angels. In short, the conflict is not viewed in Daniel 7 as a purely human struggle between Antiochus and the Jews. Behind both are supernatural forces and it is on the supernatural level that the decisive battle is fought.

The conceptual world of the visions of Daniel is made much clearer in chapter 10. There Daniel is told that there is an ongoing battle between Michael, the "prince" or patron angel of Israel, aided by Gabriel, and the "princes" or angels of Persia and Greece. In chapter 12, Michael arises in victory. We will discuss this conception of the heavenly battle below. For the present we must note the light it sheds on the "holy ones" of Daniel 7. Michael in chapter 10 is the patron and representative of the Jewish people. When he triumphs, they triumph. Similarly in chapter 7, if the kingdom is given to the "holy ones" it is equally given to the people of the holy ones, the faithful Jews. In the light of chapter 10, the "one like a son of man" may well be identified with Michael, representative and leader at once of the heavenly host and of the Jewish people. That the one like a son of man is an angelic being is supported by the fact that the interpreting angel in Daniel 8 also has the appearance of a man and angelic "men" appear again in chapters 10 and 12. The "son of man" in the Similitudes of Enoch, a Jewish work heavily dependent on Daniel, is said to be like one of the holy angels (1 Enoch 46:1). In Rev 14:14 "one like a son of man" appears seated on a cloud, who is evidently an angel (not Christ, in this instance). Daniel 7 does not make an explicit identification, but leaves the figure deliberately enigmatic. The important point is that he is a heavenly figure and represents the supernatural power supporting the persecuted Jews.

The little horn

In 7:19 Daniel focuses the vision on the fourth beast, which was different from all the rest. The violence of this beast is emphasized. It has ten horns, representing ten kings. (This imagery is picked up again in Revelation 13.) In addition there is a little horn which is the most offensive of all. The little horn is clearly identifiable with Antiochus Epiphanes. Yet it is not adequately interpreted by the simple identification. We may note, to begin, that the angelic statement in vs. 17, that the four beasts were four kings, was slightly misleading. The fourth beast is not an individual king, but the Greek empire, a quasi-demonic force of which the individual kings (horns) are only manifestations (just as the beast itself is an embodiment of the deeper forces of chaos symbolized by the sea). The little horn appears as an unnatural additional outgrowth, and the evil of the entire beast comes to a focus here. The mouth that spoke great things is the blasphemous mouth of the king who claimed to be a god made manifest. (Epiphanes means manifest. Some of his contemporaries held that he was *epimanes,* mad.) We are told that this horn made war on the saints and prevailed over them. The reference is obviously to the persecution of the Jews by Antiochus. This passage does not, however, show that the saints must be simply equated with the Jews, any more than the horn can be simply identified with the king. Rather, the idea is that corresponding to the conflict on earth there is a conflict in heaven, as is clearly expressed in chapter ten. When Antiochus is prevailing over the Jews on earth, the power of the beast is prevailing over the angelic counterparts of the Jews. We will find the temporary defeat of the angelic host even more strikingly expressed in chapters 8 and 11. The triumph of Antiochus is temporary. Although he can change the times (the calendar, which was very important for the temple service) and the law, his allotted time is a time, two times and half a time—three and a half years. We will find variations on this figure in the later chapters.

The kingdom

The kingdom which is given to the people of the holy ones is left tantalizingly vague. The only point that is clear is that all will serve it. Presumably the Jews will have power and dominion on earth and their angelic counterparts in heaven. Daniel, however, is not interested in providing blueprints for a political administration. It is enough that the beast will be destroyed and that power and dominion, in whatever form, will be given to the persecuted Jews.

The impact of the vision

How does this vision address the crisis of the times of Antiochus Epiphanes, and how does it help the persecuted Jews? First we should note that Antiochus and his times are never explicitly mentioned, even when they are being clearly alluded to. They are never considered directly. The vision-ary Daniel is supposed to be seeing all this in the reign of Belshazzar in the mid-sixth, not in the second, century BCE. The technique of pseudonymity, by which a work is ascribed to a famous ancient sage, has many effects, and we will see more of them in chapters 10 and 12. For the present we may note that the whole setting of the vision is transposed from that of the real author to a more ancient time. The author's setting is to some degree concealed. The events of Antiochus' reign are not considered in their historical specificity, but are taken up into an allegory which expresses the typical and repeatable rather than the unique.

Second, the allegorical language achieves a considerable manipulation of the emotions. The beasts are awesome and terrifying, especially if one is aware of the traditional associations of the imagery. Initially the vision heightens rather than lessens the terror of the situation. It views the gentile kingdoms as beasts, embodiments of primeval chaos, rather than as human institutions. Given this way of looking at the situation, compromise is impossible. As Paul would say, the struggle is not against flesh and blood but against principalities and powers (Eph 6:12).

Yet the terror of the beasts is emphatically and definitively allayed. The heavenly court is even more awesome than the beasts. If the "one like a son of man" remains somewhat enigmatic, this only adds to the aura of mystery. The tradi-tional pattern of the story makes the defeat of the beasts in-evitable. The claim that all this had been foretold long ago by Daniel also adds to the sense that everything is controlled by destiny.

Mircea Eliade, the great historian of religion, has said that one of the purposes of myth is to conquer the terror of his-tory—the loneliness of unique unrepeatable occurrences. Daniel's vision achieves this effect by showing that what is happening is not strictly unique or unprecedented. It is a reenactment of a struggle as old as creation, between the heavenly rider of the clouds and the beasts from the sea.

Finally, and perhaps more fundamentally, by stressing the supernatural backdrop of the conflict, Daniel 7 suggests that success is not in the hands of mortals. In one sense, this relieves anxiety, since full responsibility for the outcome does not rest on human shoulders. At the same time, the outcome is all the more certain because it is in the hands of God.

The truth of the vision

It is at this last point that the question of the truthfulness and value of the vision arises most directly. First, what warrant have we for saying that superhuman powers are at work? Is this not mere obscurantism, which hinders the human resolution of problems? Second, what guarantee have we that the outcome of our struggles is sure and for the best?

On the first question, it is surely obvious that the language of the sea and the beasts is symbolic: it is trying to suggest and evoke something which cannot be expressed in a literal, univocal way. What it suggests is that Antiochus Epiphanes embodied a power of evil which was greater than what he alone could contrive. In part, his actions were a culmination of centuries of world history, of the rise of the world empires and the spread of Hellenism. In part, too, we must say that the individual king may not have foreseen or understood all the ramifications of his actions, and may not have been fully master of his own impulses. The surplus of evil, over and above the king's intentional action, is symbolized in the imagery of the beasts. In our own century many have felt a similar surplus of evil in Hitler and the Nazis. Correspondingly, the angelic host and the "one like a son of man" are no less symbolic. They express the unexpected resources and the unpredictable historical influence of those who withstood the persecution even unto death.

On the second question, the certainty of the outcome, we must say that Daniel was wise in refusing to specify the nature of the future kingdom. The term kingdom is itself a metaphor here, just as it is in the New Testament. It refers, not to a political administration but to transcendence, to the fully satisfying outcome of the religious struggle. Of course, even then we have never any guarantee that such an outcome is assured. When Daniel becomes more specific in chapter 11 he is embarrassingly wrong on the details that can be verified. The value of the certainty promised by Daniel can not, however, be assessed in terms of the accuracy of his predictions. It can only be judged pragmatically in the way it helped people cope in a time of crisis and the kind of action it inspired. There can be little doubt that certainty of relief helped people stand their ground in the face of persecution. We will see later, in chapter 11, what kind of action it inspired.

The relevance of the vision

Daniel 7 was composed to address one very specific historical crisis, the persecution of the Jews by Antiochus Epiphanes. We have seen that part of the vision's technique was to minimize the specific historical references and assimilate that crisis to a primeval mythic pattern. Because of that technique Daniel 7 transcends its historical situation easily. In every generation there are beasts which rise from the sea and those who hope for a "son of man" to bring deliverance where none is humanly available. We find a powerful re-use of Daniel's imagery in the New Testament Book of Revelation, where the beast is the Roman Empire and the savior is Christ. In our own time, the horror of the Nazi attempt to exterminate the Jews is a poignantly appropriate instance where the old Jewish symbolism fits easily. Identifying beasts has its dangers to be sure and the use of this symbolism isn't always justified. Unfortunately, however, there are all too many situations where it is justified, where chaos appears to be loosed on the world and we can only hope for a deliverance which we cannot ourselves provide.

DANIEL CHAP. 8: THE RAM AND THE GOAT

8 In the third year of the reign of King Belshazzar a vision appeared to me, Daniel, after that which appeared to me at the first. ²And I saw in the vision; and when I saw, I was in Susa the capital, which is in the province of Elam; and I saw in the vision, and I was at the river Ulai. ³I raised my eyes and saw, and behold, a ram standing on the bank of the river. It had two horns; and both horns were high, but one was higher than the other, and the higher one came up last. ⁴I saw the ram charging westward and northward and southward; no beast could stand before him, and there was no one who could rescue from his power; he did as he pleased and magnified himself.

⁵As I was considering, behold, a he-goat came from the west across the face of the whole earth, without touching the ground; and the goat had a conspicuous horn between his eyes. ⁶He came to the ram with the two horns, which I had seen standing on the bank of the river, and he ran at him in his mighty wrath. ⁷I saw him come close to the ram, and he was enraged against him and struck the ram and broke his two horns; and the ram had no power to stand before him, but he cast him down to the ground and trampled upon him; and there was no one who could rescue the ram from his power. ⁸Then the he-goat magnified himself exceedingly; but when he was strong, the great horn was broken, and instead of it there came up four conspicuous horns toward the four winds of heaven.

⁹Out of one of them came forth a little horn, which grew exceedingly great toward the south, toward the east, and toward the glorious land. ¹⁰It grew great, even to the

host of heaven; and some of the host of the stars it cast down to the ground, and trampled upon them. [11]It magnified itself, even up to the Prince of the host; and the continual burnt offering was taken away from him, and the place of his sanctuary was overthrown. [12]And the host was given over to it together with the continual burnt offering through transgression; and truth was cast down to the ground, and the horn acted and prospered. [13]Then I heard a holy one speaking; and another holy one said to the one that spoke, "For how long is the vision concerning the continual burnt offering, the transgression that makes desolate, and the giving over of the sanctuary and host to be trampled under foot?" [14]And he said to him, "For two thousand and three hundred evenings and mornings; then the sanctuary shall be restored to its rightful state."

[15]When I, Daniel, had seen the vision, I sought to understand it; and behold, there stood before me one having the appearance of a man. [16]And I heard a man's voice between the banks of the Ulai, and it called "Gabriel, make this man understand the vision." [17]So he came near where I stood; and when he came, I was frightened and fell upon my face. But he said to me, "Understand, O son of man, that the vision is for the time of the end."

[18]As he was speaking to me, I fell into a deep sleep with my face to the ground; but he touched me and set me on my feet. [19]He said, "Behold, I will make known to you what shall be at the latter end of the indignation; for it pertains to the appointed time of the end. [20]As for the ram which you saw with the two horns, these are the kings of Media and Persia. [21]And the he-goat is the king of Greece; and the great horn between his eyes is the first king. [22]As for the horn that was broken, in place of which four others arose, four kingdoms shall arise from his nation, but not with his power. [23]And at the latter end of their rule, when the transgressors have reached their full

measure, a king of bold countenance, one who understands riddles, shall arise. ²⁴His power shall be great, and
he shall cause fearful destruction, and shall succeed in
what he does, and destroy mighty men and the people of
the saints. ²⁵By his cunning he shall make deceit prosper
under his hand, and in his own mind he shall magnify
himself. Without warning he shall destroy many; and he
shall even rise up against the Prince of princes; but, by no
human hand, he shall be broken. ²⁶The vision of the evenings and the mornings which has been told is true; but
seal up the vision, for it pertains to many days hence."

²⁷And I, Daniel, was overcome and lay sick for some
days; then I rose and went about the king's business; but I
was appalled by the vision and did not understand it.

The vision in Daniel 8 is closely parallel to that in Daniel 7
using different symbolism. We are told explicitly that the
ram represents Media and Persia and that the he-goat represents Greece. The choice of these symbols was determined
by the astral symbolism of the Hellenistic age. The ram is the
constellation Aries which presided over Persia according to
the astrologer Teucer of Babylon. The goat represents Cap-
ricorn which presided over Greece. As in Daniel 7, the symbols represent not only the earthly kingdoms but the superhuman powers behind them. The initial fight between the
ram and the he-goat represents the overthrow of the Persian
empire by Alexander the Great, but it represents it as a
heavenly battle between astral powers.

The main focus of the chapter is on the little horn, an image taken directly from Daniel 7. In Daniel 8, however, the
horn is set in the context of astral symbolism. We are told
that the horn attacked the host of heaven and cast some of
the stars to the ground and trampled them, and even rose up
against the prince of the host (presumably God himself).
The career of Antiochus is again being viewed here in the

light of a mythic pattern. While the myth in question has
roots in the old Ugaritic mythology, it is also vividly expressed in the bible, in Isaiah 14:12-15:

> "How you are fallen from heaven, O Day-Star, Son of
>   Dawn!
> How you are cut down to the ground, you who laid the
>   nations low!
> You said in your heart, 'I will ascend to heaven;
> above the stars of God I will set my throne on high;
> I will sit on the mount of assembly in the far north;
> I will ascend above the heights of the clouds,
> I will make myself like the Most High.'
> But you are brought down to Sheol, to the depths of the
>   Pit."

The passage in Isaiah is referring to the king of Babylon. It
evidently presupposes a story about the Day Star. Some
light has been thrown on that story by a fragmentary
Ugaritic myth which tells how the Day Star attempted to
take over the throne of Baal. Already in Isaiah, the story
had become a powerful metaphor for the rise and fall of a
human king. When the career of Antiochus is told in terms
of this story, we are led to see a superhuman dimension to
it, but we can also anticipate how the story will end.

When the little horn casts some of the host of the stars to
the ground, we have a precise parallel to the statement in
Daniel 7 that he will wear out the saints of the Most High.
In both cases the human activity in question is the persecution of the Jews. In Daniel 8, the historical context is quite
explicitly indicated by the references to the profanation of
the temple and the cessation of the continual burnt offering. Yet the host of the stars clearly indicates that the
battle is also raging on another level. Throughout antiquity
the stars were regarded as divine or quasi-divine beings. In

ancient Israel, they were equated with the host of heaven. In some contexts they were viewed negatively, because pagans worshipped the host of heaven. So for example Deut 4:19 warns against worshipping the heavenly bodies, the host of heaven. In other cases they are viewed positively, as God's heavenly host. In Judges 5:20 the stars are said to fight with Israel against Sisera. In Job 38:7 they are linked with the sons of God, shouting for joy at creation. There is a vast interest in the stars in the first Book of Enoch, a composite Jewish work which is roughly contemporary with Daniel, and there again we find the stars equated with angels. In Daniel 8, the host of heaven is not inanimate either, as can be seen from the attack of the little horn.

There was a widespread conception in antiquity that battles were not only fought between human combatants but also involved supernatural forces. We may think here of the role of the stars in Judges 5, or of the mysterious commander of the army of the Lord who appears to Joshua in Joshua 5:13-15. We will find in the Books of Maccabees that this conception was still alive in the second century BCE. One of the most striking formulations is found in the Dead Sea War Scroll, where the sectarians of Qumran were preparing for the final battle: "Valliant warriors of the angelic host are among our numbered men, and the hero of war is with our congregation; the host of his spirits is with our foot-soldiers and horsemen" (1QM col. 12).

It is against this background that the role of the heavenly host in Daniel 8 must be understood. The struggle is not simply between Antiochus and the Jews. The conflict has another, supernatural, dimension, and it is on the supernatural level that it will be resolved.

The application of the vision

The vision is interpreted for Daniel by an angelic "man." (Much of this episode, including the way in which Daniel is addressed as "son of man," is reminiscent of the Book of Ezekiel.) It is already apparent, from the interchange between the angelic "holy ones" in 8:13-14, that the greatest outrage of the persecution is the profanation of the temple and the disruption of the service.

These angels introduce another note, which was only sounded in passing in Daniel 7. There is an appointed time for the end. In 8:14 this time is specified as 2,300 evenings and mornings. This figure (1,150 days) roughly corresponds to the three and a half years mentioned in chapter 7. We will find different specific figures in chapter 12, and there it will be apparent that Daniel did not provide precise reliable predictions. We can appreciate, however, that for those who were enduring the persecution of Antiochus the specificity of the figure had some psychological value. We will return to this problem in the following chapters.

The conclusion of the interpretation is abrupt: "by no human hand he shall be broken." Daniel 8 tells us even less than Daniel 7 about what may be expected to follow the fall of the king. Two points are made. First, he will be broken. The vision is more concerned with the cessation of the present evil than with the positive vision of what may follow. Second, the fall will be brought about "by no human hand." Here we begin to get a sense of the kind of action advocated by the vision. Evidently there will be little support for the Maccabees here, since no human hand is effective. If the persecution will be brought to an end by some heavenly power, piety may be more important than active rebellion. We shall see Daniel's position more clearly in chapter 11.

At the end, Daniel is told to seal up the vision. Here we have a piece of literary fiction. The author must explain why a revelation supposedly given to Daniel long ago has not hitherto become known. The command also adds to the general impression of mystery.

Daniel's sickness, which is typical of his reaction to the

revelations throughout the second half of the book, underlines again the overpowering character of the vision. This
material is not presented as the kind of reasonable view that
anyone could come up with. It is out of this world, and must
be explained by an angel. One cannot argue with it. One can
only accept or reject.

The impact of this vision is closely similar to that of chapter 7. At the heart of it is the transfer of the focus of attention
from the human to the supernatural plane. While the gravity
of the crisis is heightened, there is also the assurance that the
time is appointed and deliverance is certain.

The continued relevance of the chapter lies again in its
metaphorical power. The little horn, like the Day-Star in Isa
14, provides a vivid characterization of arrogant power in
any age.

DANIEL CHAP. 9: THE SEVENTY WEEKS OF YEARS

9 In the first year of Darius the son of Ahasuerus, by birth
a Mede, who became king over the realm of the Chaldeans — [2]in the first year of his reign, I, Daniel, perceived
in the books the number of years which, according to the
word of the Lord to Jeremiah the prophet, must pass
before the end of the desolations of Jerusalem, namely,
seventy years.

[3]Then I turned my face to the Lord God, seeking him by
prayer and supplications with fasting and sackcloth and
ashes. [4]I prayed to the Lord my God and made confession, saying, "O Lord, the great and terrible God, who
keeps covenant and steadfast love with those who love
him and keep his commandments, [5]we have sinned and
done wrong and acted wickedly and rebelled, turning
aside from thy commandments and ordinances; [6]we have
not listened to thy servants the prophets, who spoke in thy

name to our kings, our princes, and our fathers, and to all the people of the land.... [17]Now therefore, O our God, hearken to the prayer of thy servant and to his supplications, and for thy own sake, O Lord, cause thy face to shine upon thy sanctuary, which is desolate. [18]O my God, incline thy ear and hear; open thy eyes and behold our desolations, and the city which is called by thy name; for we do not present our supplications before thee on the ground of our righteousness, but on the ground of thy great mercy. [19]O Lord, hear; O Lord, forgive; O Lord, give heed and act; delay not, for thy own sake, O my God, because thy city and thy people are called by thy name."

[20]While I was speaking and praying, confessing my sin and the sin of my people Israel, and presenting my supplication before the Lord my God for the holy hill of my God; [21]while I was speaking in prayer, the man Gabriel, whom I had seen in the vision at the first, came to me in swift flight at the time of the evening sacrifice. [22]He came and he said to me, "O Daniel, I have now come out to give you wisdom and understanding. [23]At the beginning of your supplications a word went forth, and I have come to tell it to you, for you are greatly beloved; therefore consider the word and understand the vision.

[24]"Seventy weeks of years are decreed concerning your people and your holy city, to finish the transgression, to put an end to sin, and to atone for iniquity, to bring in everlasting righteousness, to seal both vision and prophet, and to anoint a most holy place. [25]Know therefore and understand that from the going forth of the word to restore and build Jerusalem to the coming of the anointed one, a prince, there shall be seven weeks. Then for sixty-two weeks it shall be built again with squares and moat, but in a troubled time. [26]And after the sixty-two weeks, an anointed one shall be cut off, and shall have nothing; and

the people of the prince who is to come shall destroy the
city and the sanctuary. Its end shall come with a flood,
and to the end there shall be war; desolations are decreed.
[27]And he shall make a strong covenant with many for one
week; and for half of the week he shall cause sacrifice and
offering to cease; and upon the wing of abominations
shall come one who makes desolate, until the decreed end
is poured out on the desolator."

Daniel 9 differs from the other revelations in the second
half of the book, in so far as it is explicitly an interpretation of an older biblical text. As such it provides an interesting example of the re-use of scripture, in situations
other than that of the original author.

The scriptural passages in question are Jeremiah
25:11-12; 29:10, which say that "these nations shall serve
the king of Babylon seventy years. Then after seventy years
are completed, I will punish the king of Babylon."
Historically, the prophecy was not accurate. Less than
seventy years elapsed before the fall of Babylon and the
restoration of the Jews from the exile. Furthermore, many
Jews of the Maccabean era doubted whether the restoration of the Persian era was an adequate fulfillment of the
prophecy. We may note at the outset, that Daniel does not
presume that the straightforward figure of 70 years should
be taken literally. All of scripture is regarded as
mysterious, just as the allegorical visions are, and must be
explained by an angel.

The prayer of Daniel

Between the initial reference to the seventy years and the
angel's interpretation, we find a lengthy prayer on the lips
of Daniel. This prayer is similar to the prayer of Azariah in
chapter 3. It belongs to a set type of covenantal prayer,
common in the post-exilic period. Scholars are divided as
to whether this prayer is an original part of the Book of

Daniel. The quality of the Hebrew is noticeably different from the surrounding passages, and there is strong probability that the prayer is a traditional piece which has been inserted here.

As in the prayer of Azariah, there is a discrepancy between the theology of the prayer and the theology of the Book of Daniel. The prayer is Deuteronomic in spirit. It begins with a confession of sin and of the righteousness of God. All the calamities which have befallen the Jews are in fulfilment of the law of Moses, because they have broken the covenant. Then the prayer points out that the people has become a byword and the sanctuary is desolate, and beseeches God to act because of his mercy, and because the people is called by his name. The assumption throughout is that distress is due to sin and one ought to pray to God to change the course of events.

This Deuteronomic theology was one common Jewish way of explaining such disasters as the Babylonian exile. It is therefore entirely natural that Azariah might seek to explain the whole framework of the Diaspora in this way, or that Daniel might so address the desolation of Jerusalem, whether in the Babylonian era or in the time of Antiochus Epiphanes. Yet we find that the angel had set out to give Daniel wisdom and understanding even at the beginning of the prayer, before the prayer could be heard. What the angel discloses is that the course of history is set. God does not change it in response to prayer. The desolation of Jerusalem may be due to sin, but it is also part of a master plan. There is a set time for its deliverance. What is required of Jews such as Daniel is not repentance, for they are greatly beloved, but understanding of what is happening, which will enable them to have the necessary patience and endurance.

The angel's interpretation

The angel interprets the seventy years of Jeremiah as

seventy weeks of years. This procedure is instructive for
our understanding of Daniel's own predictions. Evidently,
if a number does not appear to be exact, it is not rejected,
but reinterpreted.

The number given by Jeremiah, which itself was a
rounded figure of seven decades, is now multiplied seven
fold to give 490 years. This is 100 years more than the
figure given by Ezekiel (4:5) which was cited in the so-
called Damascus Document from Qumran at a time close
to the composition of Daniel. Daniel's figure is not correct
by modern calculations and there is no evidence that it was
based on a different, ancient, system of calculation.
Rather it would seem to be inspired by the idea of the
jubilee year, which is described in Leviticus 25. Just as the
week is terminated by a sabbath day, so a week of years
was terminated by a sabbatical year and seven weeks of
years, 49 years, by a jubilee year. The jubilee year was holy
and was a time to proclaim "liberty throughout the land"
(Lev 25:10). Among the more notable provisions was the
release of Jews who had become enslaved to other Jews.
Daniel's reinterpretation of Jeremiah might then be described as "sabbatical eschatology" since it looks forward
to a final definitive jubilee when the troubles of Jerusalem
would come to an end.

Daniel's schema is closely paralleled in the so-called "Apocalypse of Weeks," which was written about the same time as
Daniel and is now incorporated in 1 Enoch 93 and 91. There all
history is divided into ten "weeks," but a decisive turning point
comes in the seventh week when "an apostate generation will
arise and many will be its deeds, but all its deeds will be apostasy, and at its end the chosen righteous from the eternal plant
of righteousness will be chosen, to whom will be given seven-
fold teaching concerning the whole creation." (1 Enoch 93:9-
10). Elsewhere in 1 Enoch the figure of 70 generations is used
for the imprisonment of the demonic "Watchers" (1 Enoch
10:12) and 70 "shepherds" are said to rule over Israel after the

destruction of the temple by the Babylonians (1 Enoch 89:59). It is apparent then that Daniel's 70 weeks of years is not so much a calculation of actual time as a conventional schema for a set period.

The distribution of the seventy weeks is also of interest. The first seven weeks constitute the period "from the going forth of the word to restore and build Jerusalem to the coming of an anointed one, a prince." The "going forth of the word" refers back to 9:23 ("At the beginning of your supplications a word went forth") so the point of departure is Daniel's prayer in the reign of the (unhistorical) Darius the Mede. The coming of an anointed one should be understood, by analogy with 9:26, to refer to Joshua the first high priest after the exile. (Zerubbabel, the governor, is a possible alternative). Then sixty two weeks pass virtually without comment. The interest is focused on the last week. This begins when the anointed one is cut off—i.e. with the murder of the legitimate high priest Onias III (see below at 2 Mac 4:34). The main outrage of this period is, again, the disruption of the temple cult, and there is an allusion to "the abomination that makes desolate"—the pagan altar erected on top of the altar of sacrifice in the temple. But the allotted time for the profanation of the temple is only half a week—three and a half years. The end is near.

Once more Daniel is concerned with the cessation of present evil, not with a new order to follow it. Even the evil which is to cease is described in very general terms in vs. 24—"to finish the transgression, put an end to sin, and to atone for iniquity." The only specific evil is the profanation of the temple. Thereafter "everlasting righteousness" will be ushered in. The temple will no longer be profaned, but we are not even told clearly whether the new order will be earthly or on some other plane. The message of the chapter is simply that an end is decreed for the desolator.

The prophecy of the seventy weeks of years shows in more

developed form an idea which was already present in the four kingdoms. The duration of history is measured out in advance. One of the advantages in ascribing the work to Daniel is that he can "foretell" a lengthy process of history which has already elapsed. We will see this device more clearly in chapter 11. The Jews of the author's actual time can locate themselves in this larger framework and see that they are near the end. Relief is in sight. The "end" in question is not an absolute end. It is the end of gentile domination and of the distress of Jerusalem.

The truth of the prophecy

The impact of this chapter derives mainly from the sense that all is determined in advance. The present can be endured because the end is certain. It is apparent to us that this certainty is not really derived from the prophecy of Jeremiah. Jeremiah only provides the jumping-off board. His prediction is used as a metaphor for a set period of time, and even then it has to be adjusted to maintain credibility. The real source of the certainty is the need of the people in a time of persecution. They need the assurance that their distress will not be indefinite in duration.

At this point, the question of truth arises. The prophecy of the seventy weeks of years cannot be reconciled with historical fact. Its point of departure is the reign of the unhistorical Darius the Mede. The time from the profanation of the temple by the Syrians to its purification by the Maccabees was exactly three years, not three and a half (see 1 Mac 4:54; 2 Mac 10:3-5, commentary), and the more exact numbers of days given in chapters 8 and 12 contradict each other. The point at issue is not the magnitude of the error, but the way in which Daniel's language should be understood. The truth of Daniel is not to be found in exact prediction. It is rather pragmatic in nature. Its value lies in the support it gave to the persecuted Jews in doing what they believed was right. Beyond this, the insistence that there was a decreed end could also lay claim to the truth expressed in the schema of the four kingdoms. All things pass. The end of Antiochus, and of the persecution, was inevitable sooner or later. The concrete prophecies of seventy weeks of years, and three and a half years, made it easier for the persecuted Jews to realize that their sufferings would not last indefinitely.

DANIEL CHAP. 10: THE BATTLE IN HEAVEN

10 In the third year of Cyrus king of Persia a word was revealed to Daniel, who was named Belteshazzar. And the word was true, and it was a great conflict. And he understood the word and had understanding of the vision.

²In those days I, Daniel, was mourning for three weeks. ³I ate no delicacies, no meat or wine entered my mouth, nor did I anoint myself at all, for the full three weeks. ⁴On the twenty-fourth day of the first month, as I was standing on the bank of the great river, that is, the Tigris, ⁵I lifted up my eyes and looked, and behold, a man clothed in linen, whose loins were girded with gold of Uphaz. ⁶His body was like beryl, his face like the appearance of lightning, his eyes like flaming torches, his arms and legs like the gleam of burnished bronze, and the sound of his words like the noise of a multitude. ⁷And I, Daniel, alone saw the vision, for the men who were with me did not see the vision, but a great trembling fell upon them, and they fled to hide themselves. ⁸So I was left alone and saw this great vision, and no strength was left in me; my radiant appearance was fearfully changed, and I retained no strength. ⁹Then I heard the sound of his words; and when I heard the sound of his words, I fell on my face in a deep sleep with my face to the ground.

[10]And behold, a hand touched me and set me trembling on my hands and knees. [11]And he said to me, "O Daniel, man greatly beloved, give heed to the words that I speak to you, and stand upright, for now I have been sent to you." While he was speaking this word to me, I stood up trembling. [12]Then he said to me, "Fear not, Daniel, for from the first day that you set your mind to understand and humbled yourself before your God, your words have been heard, and I have come because of your words. [13]The prince of the kingdom of Persia withstood me twenty-one days; but Michael, one of the chief princes, came to help me, so I left him there with the prince of the kingdom of Persia [14]and came to make you understand what is to befall your people in the latter days. For the vision is for days yet to come."

[15]When he had spoken to me according to these words, I turned my face toward the ground and was dumb. [16]And behold, one in the likeness of the sons of men touched my lips; then I opened my mouth and spoke. I said to him who stood before me, "O my lord, by reason of the vision pains have come upon me, and I retain no strength. [17]How can my lord's servant talk with my lord? For now no strength remains in me, and no breath is left in me."

[18]Again one having the appearance of a man touched me and strengthened me. [19]And he said, "O man greatly beloved, fear not, peace be with you; be strong and of good courage." And when he spoke to me, I was strengthened and said, "Let my lord speak, for you have strengthened me." [20]Then he said, "Do you know why I have come to you? But now I will return to fight against the prince of Persia; and when I am through with him, lo, the prince of Greece will come. [21]But I will tell you what is inscribed in the book of truth: there is none who contends by my side against these except Michael, your prince. 11 And as for me, in the first year

of Darius the Mede, I stood up to confirm and strengthen
him.

Chapters 10-12 belong together and constitute one long
revelatory unit. They are broken up here only to facilitate
commentary.

In Daniel 10, it is not entirely clear whether Daniel is
supposed to have seen a great conflict in a vision, or
whether his vision consists only of the angel, who then
gives him the revelation orally. In any case, there is some
vision, and Daniel prepares for it by fasting. The connection between fasting and ecstatic experience is well-known.
It may be that the author of the visions of Daniel actually
had a visionary experience, even though he writes under
the pseudonym of Daniel. At least we must say that he was
familiar with some of the techniques of visionaries and the
physical and emotional side-effects of the visionary state.
Much of Daniel 10 is concerned to show how Daniel found
the revelation overpowering. Although much of the revelation concerns the events of Hellenistic history, it is not
presented as a history lesson, but as an otherworldly revelation of the hidden significance of these events.

The angelic "man" who appears to Daniel is reminiscent
of a similar "man" in Ezekiel 8. By analogy with 9:21 we
may assume that he is identified as Gabriel. Significantly
for our understanding of Daniel 7, the angel is said to be
"in the likeness of the sons of men" in 10:16.

The revelation given by the angel is concerned with a
"great conflict" (or, alternatively "a great host"). This
conflict has two dimensions. The human dimension is
developed at length in chapter 11, in a thinly disguised account of Hellenistic history. Chapter 10, however, shows
us the heavenly backdrop of these events. The angel,
Gabriel, is involved in a struggle with the "prince" of Persia, and after him the "prince" of Greece will come.
Gabriel is assisted by one of the chief "princes," Michael,

who is also called "your prince" i.e. is the prince of Israel.
It is apparent here that "princes" are in fact the patron
angels of the nations. The battle ends in 12:1 when Michael
"arises" in victory.

The conception of a battle between angelic princes is an
adaptation of a common mythological conception of the
ancient world. Over every people there is a god. If two
peoples do battle, the more significant battle is really being
waged between their gods. Two biblical passages can serve
to illustrate this conception. In Deut. 32:8 we read:

> "When the Most High gave to the nations their in-
> heritance,
>   when he separated the sons of men,
>   he fixed the bounds of the peoples
>   according to the number of the sons of God."

(So RSV, following the Greek reading and supported now
by evidence from the Dead Sea Scrolls. The received
Hebrew text reads "sons of Israel" to avoid the suggestion
of polytheism.)

According to this passage, every nation has a god (one
of the sons of God) over it. Israel's God is Yahweh. In early Israel the existence of other gods was not denied, only
that they had efficacy or power.

The second passage is in Isa 36:18-20, in an address to
the people of Jerusalem by the commander of the Assyrian
army who was calling on them to surrender:

> "Beware lest Hezekiah mislead you by saying, 'The
> Lord will deliver us.' Has any of the gods of the nations
> delivered his land out of the hand of the king of
> Assyria? Where are the gods of Hamath and Arpad?
> Where are the gods of Sepharvaim? Have they delivered
> Samaria out of my hand? Who among all the gods of
> these countries have delivered their countries out of my
> hand, that the Lord should deliver Jerusalem out of my
> hand?"

The king of Assyria also attributed his own success to a god. What we see from this passage is that behind every nation stands a god, who does battle on behalf of his people. The "princes" of Daniel 10 are clearly an adaptation of this conception.

In assessing the significance of this conception it is important to bear in mind that there is a prince of Greece as well as a prince of Israel and that this conception was widely shared in the ancient world. The princes are not actual existing persons, human or heavenly. They are symbolic representations of their peoples. This is not to deny that people in antiquity thought of these princes as really existing, and even regarded them as more powerful and important than humans of flesh and blood. From a modern critical perspective, however, we must realize that the prince of Greece cannot be imagined apart from Greece itself. He is projected, on the basis of the human political data. He is then imagined to have more power than his human counterparts, and to be capable of acting over against them on occasion. Nevertheless, he is tied to them. He is a personification of some depth dimension pertaining to the people of Greece.

While we may no longer believe in such patron angels, the conception is not without its validity. Like the beasts and the "son of man" figure in Daniel 7, the heavenly princes symbolize a surplus of power and meaning, over and above what is rationally controlled, whether it is for good or evil. The prince of Greece symbolizes the whole impact of Hellenistic civilization, far beyond what was consciously controlled by Antiochus Epiphanes. Michael, prince of Israel, represents a resource for the persecuted Jews, beyond what they could expect of themselves. Michael is a projected, imagined figure, but he could be psychologically effective.

By placing the battle in the hands of the angelic princes, Daniel prepares the way for his conception of the appropriate action in the situation. The outcome of the struggle does not depend on human action. All is foretold, and is inscribed in the book of truth (10:21). The course of history is set. The human task is to get on the right side.

DANIEL CHAP. 11: THE HELLENISTIC WARS

[2]"And now I will show you the truth. Behold, three more kings shall arise in Persia; and a fourth shall be far richer than all of them; and when he has become strong through his riches, he shall stir up all against the kingdom of Greece. [3]Then a mighty king shall arise, who shall rule with great dominion and do according to his will. [4]And when he has arisen, his kingdom shall be broken and divided toward the four winds of heaven, but not to his posterity, nor according to the dominion with which he ruled; for his kingdom shall be plucked up and go to others besides these.

[5]"Then the king of the south shall be strong, but one of his princes shall be stronger than he and his dominion shall be a great dominion. [6]After some years they shall make an alliance, and the daughter of the king of the south shall come to the king of the north to make peace; but she shall not retain the strength of her arm, and he and his offspring shall not endure; but she shall be given up, and her attendants, her child, and he who got possession of her....

[21]In his place shall arise a contemptible person to whom royal majesty has not been given; he shall come in without warning and obtain the kingdom by flatteries.

[22]Armies shall be utterly swept away before him and broken, and the prince of the covenant also.

[23]And from the time that an alliance is made with him he shall act deceitfully; and he shall become strong with a small people. [24]Without warning he shall come into the richest parts of the province; and he shall do what neither his fathers nor his fathers' fathers have done,

scattering among them plunder, spoil, and goods. He shall devise plans against strongholds, but only for a time. ²⁵And he shall stir up his power and his courage against the king of the south with a great army; and the king of the south shall wage war with an exceedingly great and mighty army; but he shall not stand, for plots shall be devised against him.²⁶Even those who eat his rich food shall be his undoing; his army shall be swept away, and many shall fall down slain. ²⁷And as for the two kings, their minds shall be bent on mischief; they shall speak lies at the same table, but to no avail; for the end is yet to be at the time appointed. ²⁸And he shall return to his land with great substance, but his heart shall be set against the holy covenant. And he shall work his will, and return to his own land.

²⁹"At the time appointed he shall return and come into the south; but it shall not be this time as it was before. ³⁰For ships of Kittim shall come against him, and he shall be afraid and withdraw, and shall turn back and be enraged and take action against the holy covenant. He shall turn back and give heed to those who forsake the holy covenant. ³¹Forces from him shall appear and profane the temple and fortress, and shall take away the continual burnt offering. And they shall set up the abomination that makes desolate. ³²He shall seduce with flattery those who violate the covenant; but the people who know their God shall stand firm and take action.

³³And those among the people who are wise shall make many understand, though they shall fall by sword and flame, by captivity and plunder, for some days. ³⁴When they fall, they shall receive a little help. And many shall join themselves to them with flattery; ³⁵and some of those who are wise shall fall, to refine and to cleanse them and to make them white, until the time of the end, for it is yet for the time appointed.

³⁶"And the king shall do according to his will; he shall

exalt himself and magnify himself above every god, and shall speak astonishing things against the God of gods. He shall prosper till the indignation is accomplished; for what is determined shall be done. [37]He shall give no heed to the gods of his fathers, or to the one beloved by women; he shall not give heed to any other god, for he shall magnify himself above all. [38]He shall honor the god of fortresses instead of these; a god whom his fathers did not know he shall honor with gold and silver, with precious stones and costly gifts. [39]He shall deal with the strongest fortresses by the help of a foreign god; those who acknowledge him he shall magnify with honor. He shall make them rulers over many and shall divide the land for a price.

[40]"At the time of the end the king of the south shall attack him; but the king of the north shall rush upon him like a whirlwind, with chariots and horsemen, and with many ships; and he shall come into countries and shall overflow and pass through. [41]He shall come into the glorious land. And tens of thousands shall fall, but these shall be delivered out of his hand: Edom and Moab and the main part of the Ammonites. [42]He shall stretch out his hand against the countries, and the land of Egypt shall not escape. [43]He shall become ruler of the treasures of gold and of silver, and all the precious things of Egypt; and the Libyans and the Ethiopians shall follow in his train. [44]But tidings from the east and the north shall alarm him, and he shall go forth with great fury to exterminate and utterly destroy many. [45]And he shall pitch his palatial tents between the sea and the glorious holy mountain; yet he shall come to his end, with none to help him."

Daniel 11 provides a thinly veiled account of the history of the Near East from the last kings of Persia to Antiochus Epiphanes. No names are directly named although the characters are easily recognized. The main reason for the lack of specific names is that the chapter is affecting an oracular style. Since all these things are being foretold centuries in advance, they must not be stated too explicitly. Further, the lack of names adds a sense of mystery to the account and permits the reader the pleasure of decoding the mystery.

One of the more obvious purposes of pseudonymity becomes apparent in Daniel 11. Since Daniel supposedly lived before all these events, he can provide a very accurate "prediction" after the fact. The reader can verify that all these things happened in sequence, down to the career of Antiochus Epiphanes. The assumption is built up that the rest will happen too, and will happen soon. This device is undoubtedly a pious fraud, but we can appreciate how it would give hope and assurance to the persecuted Jews. The prophecy must be judged by the kind of action it supported rather than by its authenticity. We may note, incidentally, that because of the accurate prophecy after the fact, we can tell at what point the book of Daniel was written, since beyond a certain point the "predictions" are no longer fulfilled (from 11:40 on).

The detail in which the history is recounted is designed primarily to build up the reliability of the real prediction at the end, and provide an impression of certainty. There is only a very limited attempt to describe a pattern in history, and this appears in the rise and fall of Antiochus III (the Great) and Antiochus IV (Epiphanes). We need not decode the entire history here. The great king in 11:3 is Alexander. Thereafter, the kings of the north are the Seleucids of Syria (so named after Seleucus I; the kings of this line were named either Seleucus or Antiochus). The kings of the south are the Ptolemies of Egypt. The marriages between the dynasties are noted in 11:6 and 11:17.

The career of Antiochus Epiphanes

The main interest of the chapter lies in the career of Antiochus Epiphanes, who is introduced in 11:21 as "a contemptible person." The "prince of the covenant" in 11:22 is the Jewish high-priest and the reference is to the displacement of Onias III by Jason the Hellenizer. Daniel accurately chronicles Antiochus' two expeditions against Egypt in 169 and 168 BCE, the first successful, the second ending with the humiliation at the hands of the Kittim, the Romans. (The word Kittim was derived from Citium in Cyprus, and was originally applied to any people who came from the West.) Dan 11:30-32 describes the outbreak of the persecution, and the profanation of the temple. While we are told already in 11:28 that his heart is set against the holy covenant, we are also told in 11:30 that "he shall turn back and give heed to those who forsake the holy covenant." In short, the initiative came from within the Jewish community in some part. The Hellenizing faction in Jerusalem, which supported the adoption of a Greek way of life, are those who are seduced by flattery. The abomination that makes desolate in 11:31 is the pagan altar erected on the altar of sacrifice in the temple.

The conduct advocated by Daniel

The clearest formulation of the attitude and conduct advocated by the Book of Daniel is found in 11:32-34. The people who know their God, or the wise, the *maskilim,* are the heroes of the book and we must assume that the author counted himself among them. Their wisdom presumably consists in their understanding the supernatural framework of events, as revealed in the Book of Daniel itself. Their task is to teach, to make the "many", the masses, understand. At no point is there any suggestion that they should resort to force of arms. Since the outcome of the struggle is already decided, and is in the hands of God and his angels, violence is not required. Instead, the wise fall, by sword and flame, and this is to purify them and make them white. They are, in effect, martyrs. The result of their martyrdom will be apparent in chap. 12. For the present they have the assurance that the appointed time is coming.

In 11:34 it is said that when the wise fall they will receive "a little help." This expression has usually been taken as a slighting reference to the Maccabees. This is possible, but by no means certain. It is not apparent that the "wise" of Daniel would have regarded the blood-stained Maccabees as a help at all. It may be that the expression means that few will really join their cause, although a number will join with flattery or insincerely.

The characterization of the king

Daniel 11:36-39 returns to the account of the king. As in Daniel 8, he is said to exalt himself above every god. "Every god" here may include the pagan gods, but it could also refer to the heavenly host. Antiochus' policy of Hellenization is represented as an outrage not only against the Jews but also against his own ancestral religion. Apollo, the traditional patron of the Seleucids, was replaced by Zeus Olympius. The epithet "god of fortresses" should probably be taken as a sarcastic comment on the role of the fortress Acra, which Antiochus erected in Jerusalem (see 1 Mac 1:33-34). The breach with tradition is thought to be blasphemous even by pagan standards.

The events predicted in 11:40-45 are not historical but are an eschatological scenario which may be based in part on Ezekiel 38-39. Antiochus, like Gog, is a king from the north, who will invade the land of Israel and fall there. This is not how Antiochus met his death, so we know that this prophecy was composed before he actually died late in 164 BCE, or at least before news of his death reached Jerusalem. Once again, the significance of the passage does not lie in its prediction but in its characterization of Antiochus as an eschatological figure, like Gog, of mythical proportions, and in its assurance that even such a figure must come to an end.

DANIEL CHAP. 12:1-3: THE RESURRECTION

12 "At that time shall arise Michael, the great prince who has charge of your people. And there shall be a time of trouble, such as never has been since there was a nation till that time; but at that time your people shall be delivered, every one whose name shall be found written in the book. ²And many of those who sleep in the dust of the earth shall awake, some to everlasting life, and some to shame and everlasting contempt. ³And those who are wise shall shine like the brightness of the firmament; and those who turn many to righteousness, like the stars for ever and ever.

The climax of the long revelation of chapters 10 and 11, and indeed of the entire Book of Daniel, comes in chapter 12. The demise of Antiochus will coincide with the triumph of Michael in the heavenly battle. Since he is the "prince" who has charge over the Jewish people, his triumph is their triumph. At that time they will be delivered. Not all Jews are numbered among the elect, however, but only those whose names are found written in the book. The most significant aspect of the deliverance is the resurrection of the dead. We are told that many who sleep in the dust of the earth (which possibly means Sheol or Hades, the abode of the dead) will awake, some to everlasting life, some to shame and contempt. Daniel does not envisage a universal resurrection. Only those rise who merit eternal reward or punishment. We are left to assume that the mass of humanity is, as Kipling put it, neither good enough to merit heaven nor bad enough to merit hell. Among the good, the wise teachers, the *maskilim* are singled out for special honor. They will be like the stars for ever and ever. We have seen in earlier chapters that the stars were often identified with the angelic host. Shining like the stars is not only a vivid metaphor for brilliant glory. Its significance can be seen from a passage in 1 Enoch 104, which promises the righteous that they "will shine as the lights of heaven, and the portals of heaven will be opened to you" and that they will become "companions to the hosts of heaven." The same conception is found in the Similitudes of Enoch, a work which drew heavily on Daniel, where we read that "the dwelling-places of the righteous are with the holy angels" (39:5). Again in the New Testament Jesus tells the Sadducees that when men rise from the dead they are like the angels in heaven (Mark 12:25 and parallels).

The introduction of the idea of the resurrection of the dead throws a new light on the preceding chapters. We can now appreciate why the *maskilim* or wise teachers were willing to lay down their lives in peaceful resistance. Just as the forces involved in the struggle between Antiochus and the Jews were not only those that met the eye, the stakes in that struggle were not of the temporal order either. For the wise, the goal of life was to be properly purified and in tune with the angelic world, with a view to enjoying an eternal fellowship with the angels. As we shall see, the goal of the Maccabees was rather different, and of a more immediate kind.

We have noted in the previous chapters that Daniel is extremely reticent about the state of things which is to follow the "end" or the victory over Antiochus. In chapter 7, that state was expressed as a kingdom, characterized by power and glory. In chapter 12, the main feature is the resurrection. Neither chapter attempts a complete description. It is not clear from Daniel 12 whether all history on earth will come to an end, as is apparently envisaged in some New Testament passages. Nothing is said about the people who are still alive at the end. It may be that life goes on, presumably now under a Jewish kingdom. The wise who shine like stars are not necessarily only the martyrs. They may also include their colleagues who were not martyred. As Paul put it, "we shall not all sleep but we shall all be changed" (1Cor

15:51). Daniel does not undertake to provide a full systematic doctrine of the last things. He speaks only of what is of most importance to him, and that is evidently the destiny of the wise teachers or *maskilim*. Daniel may also have expected a Jewish kingdom on earth, but that is not the focus of his interest. As the entire second half of the book offers heavenly wisdom, communicated by angels, so also the high point of the conclusion is the hope of life in fellowship with the angels beyond death.

The belief in resurrection

Daniel 12 is the earliest biblical passage which expresses unambiguously the hope of reward after death. The standard conception in ancient Israel was that the shade of the person survived in Sheol or Hades, but this was only a shadowy existence, which could not be described as life. There are a few passages in the Old Testament which hint at life after death, most notably Isaiah 26:19 ("thy dead shall live, their bodies shall rise"). Taken in context, however, these passages refer, not to the resurrection of individuals, but to the restoration of the Israelite people from a state like death, such as the Babylonian exile. This metaphorical use of the idea of resurrection is most vividly expressed in Ezekiel's famous vision of the valley of the dry bones, where we are told explicitly that "these bones are the whole house of Israel" (Ezekiel 37:11).

The belief in the resurrection of individuals and the judgment after death was introduced into Judaism in the apocalyptic writings, notably 1 Enoch, some parts of which are older than Daniel and date to the third century BCE. We should note that the earliest witnesses do not think in terms of the restoration of the body on earth, but of the elevation of the spirit from Sheol to the presence of God. (The spirit was still conceived in a quasi-physical form.) While Daniel 12 is not fully explicit on the matter, the emphasis on the star-like transformation of the wise also suggests exaltation to heaven.

Daniel 12 is not, then, the earliest Jewish expression of belief in resurrection, since earlier attestation is found in 1 Enoch. Yet Daniel provides a good illustration of the function of that belief and of the way in which it arose. Obviously there is no question of verification or of objective evidence. The resurrection is an integral part of the apocalyptic revelation. It is offered on the authority of the angel and can only be accepted or rejected. We have seen already that the truth of such a claim cannot be assessed on grounds of objective factuality, but only pragmatically, in terms of the conduct it inspired. The belief in resurrection in Daniel is the basis for the stance of the martyrs. It is the hope that enables them to lay down their lives rather than comply with the demands of the tyrant. We will have ample opportunity to reflect on the logic of this position in the stories of the martyrs in 2 Maccabees.

The significance and value of the belief

The historical significance of the apocalyptic belief in resurrection is enormous. It provided the framework for much of the New Testament. It laid the groundwork which made the Christian proclamation of the resurrection of Jesus credible. St. Paul saw this clearly when he wrote to the Corinthians: "if there is no resurrection of the dead, then Christ has not been raised." (1 Cor. 15:16). An empty tomb could be explained in various ways (as can be seen from the Jewish charge in Matt 27:13, that the disciples stole the body). Visions of the risen Christ could be dismissed as hallucinations by people who did not believe, in principle, that resurrection was possible. The apocalyptic belief in resurrection was one important background against which the resurrection of Jesus could be understood. The resurrection of Jesus was perceived by the early Christians as an integral part of the general resurrection, and of a full apocalyptic scenario. Christ was the first fruits of those who had fallen asleep. The apocalyptic vision of Daniel was not, then, an historical peculiarity but shared the view of the world which became the basis for the rise of Christianity, and so had an immense influence on western history.

Despite the historical impact of the apocalyptic belief in resurrection, the question must inevitably arise whether it is a mere illusion. We have seen that the resurrection in Daniel 12 is part of a lengthy apocalyptic revelation, and that much of the preceding "prediction" must be acknowledged to have been written after the fact. Is the credibility of the resurrection thereby undermined?

Here again we must insist that this is not a matter in which verification or empirical proof is possible. The certainty provided by the angel in antiquity is not available to the modern student who reads the book critically. The symbolic character of the belief should be obvious from the variety of ways in which life after death is conceived, and from the discrepancy between Daniel's eclectic resurrection and later views of universal afterlife. We are not dealing here with hard facts. The resurrection is a hope, which can never be disproved, but which can only be envisaged through the resources of the human imagination.

The value of the belief in resurrection in Daniel must be measured in terms of the action it inspired. Martyrs are always admirable for their courage, and there is an inherent human dignity in the refusal to submit to a tyrant. The hope of the resurrection symbolizes the sense of transcendent value which claims that some things are more important than physical reality, and are even worth the price of life. It provided a way of looking at the world which releases people from the power of any blackmail, by diminishing the threat of the ultimate weapon of blackmail, death. If this is illusion, it can be an inspiring illusion, and in the Maccabean crisis it inspired some of the most striking gestures in biblical history. It is true that others, including the Hebrew prophets, dealt with the threat of death in other ways, without recourse to belief in resurrection.Our task for the present is not to compare and evaluate the different biblical theologies, but to appreciate the motivating power of the vision of a judgment beyond death, as it is articulated in Daniel.

DANIEL CHAP. 12: 4-13: THE CONCLUSION

4But you, Daniel, shut up the words, and seal the book, until the time of the end. Many shall run to and fro, and knowledge shall increase."

5Then I Daniel looked, and behold, two others stood, one on this bank of the stream and one on that bank of the stream. 6And I said to the man clothed in linen, who was above the waters of the stream, "How long shall it be till the end of these wonders?" 7The man clothed in linen, who was above the waters of the stream, raised his right hand and his left hand toward heaven; and I heard him swear by him who lives for ever that it would be for a time, two times, and half a time; and that when the shattering of the power of the holy people comes to an end all these things would be accomplished. 8I heard, but I did not understand. Then I said, "O my lord, what shall be the issue of these things?" 9He said, "Go your way, Daniel, for the words are shut up and sealed until the time of the end. 10Many shall purify themselves, and make themselves white, and be refined; but the wicked shall do wickedly; and none of the wicked shall understand; but those who are wise shall understand. 11And from the time that the continual burnt offering is taken away, and the abomination that makes desolate is set up, there shall be a thousand two hundred and ninety days. 12Blessed is he who waits and comes to the thousand three hundred and thirty-five days. [13]But go your way till the end; and you shall rest, and shall stand in your allotted place at the end of the days."

Daniel is told to seal the book, as he had been told to seal the vision in chap. 8. This is a literary fiction, designed in part to explain why the book has not been in circulation since the alleged time of Daniel. It is assumed that, at the actual time of the Maccabean crisis, the seal is broken.

Apocalyptic writings are often regarded as esoteric, or secret, because of passages such as this. It is certainly true that in Daniel the revelation is regarded as a mystery which is not normally accessible to humanity. It is not clear however whether the apocalyptic writers deliberately restricted the circulation of their books. This is more likely in the case of sectarian documents such as the Qumran scrolls than in the case of Daniel, which was written to address a national crisis. The wise in Daniel 11 are said to "make many understand." While their message may be a mystery in its origin, they have a missionary goal within the Jewish people. The apocalyptic message of Daniel is not the speculation of a closed circle, but is directed to the transformation of the people.

What Daniel seeks to convey is a kind of wisdom. "None of the wicked shall understand, but those who are wise will understand" (12:10). The "understanding" of Daniel is, of course, a rather exceptional way of looking at the world, as a theatre of supernatural forces, where the time of the end is guaranteed. As we have seen above, the wisdom of this world view can only be assessed in terms of the action it inspired. It should be noted, however, that wisdom does not provide one simple, objectively verifiable view of reality. The understanding of reality is inseparably bound up with value judgments and the style of life which is regarded as desirable. Even within the same religious tradition of

Judaism there was room for considerable diversity as we shall see when we turn to Maccabees.

The Hebrew/Aramaic Book of Daniel concludes with a specific prediction of the time until the end, or rather, with three specific predictions: three and a half years, a thousand two hundred and ninety days and a thousand three hundred and thirty-five days. The actual time that elapsed from the desecration of the temple to its reconstruction was less than any of these (see 1 Mac 4:54). The fact that these contradictory figures were allowed to stand side by side is remarkable. It did not prevent the Jewish historian Josephus, writing at the end of the first century CE from claiming that Daniel surpassed the other prophets by not only foretelling what would happen but by also specifying when it would happen. Evidently Josephus did not take the numbers in Daniel literally. From Daniel's own treatment of the seventy years of Jeremiah, we may question whether he took them literally either. The specific numbers lent an impression of specificity, which had psychological importance for his readers, but the juxtaposition of contradictory numbers was an admission that we know not the day nor the hour. The truth of Daniel lies in the inevitability that all things human will come to an end.

The Visions in Retrospect

The visions of Daniel 7-12 present a view of the world which is sharply different from that of the tales in chapters 1-6. To be sure, there is continuity. Throughout the Book of Daniel it is assumed that the God of Israel controls the destinies of all peoples. His dominion is not publicly evident. It is seen through special revelations by the wise, such as Daniel, and through exceptional acts of deliverance. This is the common ground which underlies the entire book. In the light of the crisis under Antiochus, however, this theology took on significantly new aspects. First, the gentile kingdoms were no longer seen as potential servants of God. Instead, they were in revolt, like the little horn which raised itself against the stars, or they were eruptions of chaos like the beasts from the sea. They can not be reformed, only destroyed. Second, the reward in store for the wise and righteous is no longer success at the pagan court, or even earthly success at all. The ultimate reward is to shine like the stars in the after life.

The visions, unlike the tales, provide an ideology of resistance. While the tales maintained an uncompromising fidelity to the Jewish tradition, they did so while striving to affirm loyalty to the kingdom of the day. In the visions, the authority of the gentiles is emphatically rejected. We might expect here some correspondence between Daniel and modern liberation theology, and there surely is an analogy in the sharp rejection of oppressive powers. Yet a few qualifications should be made. The wise of Daniel appear to be strictly non-violent. Their contribution to the resistance movement lies in piety, and in the understanding which they foster. This in turn is related to their goal. Unlike the Maccabees they are not primarily working for a national Jewish state or for a social and economic vision. Their aspirations are primarily negative—the overthrow of the oppressive power. Their ultimate reward is not such that it can be achieved through the transformation of the political order. Moreover, while they do "stand firm and take action" the achievement of their goals is strictly in the hands of God and the heavenly host.

The revolution in the Book of Daniel is a revolution in the imagination. It changes our way of looking at the political and social order. Such a change of consciousness can of course be fundamental to political revolution. In itself, however, its primary effect is to enable people to cope with the existing order, rather than to change it. The power of the Syrians in Jerusalem was in fact broken by the violence of the Maccabees, more directly than by the visions of the wise. Yet the visions too played their part in the resistance, and they also preserved the integrity of a strand of the Jewish tradition which was not represented by the Maccabees.

We shall return, as we discuss the Books of Maccabees, to the relative merits of the perspectives of Daniel and the Maccabees. For the present, we would emphasize that the differences within Daniel itself point up the historical relativity of any theological perspective on politics and history. As we have seen repeatedly, both the tales and the visions of Daniel are fantasy literature, and are measured primarily by their adequacy for the needs of the people. Those needs differed, from the rather benign rule of the Persians and the Ptolemies to the persecution of Antiochus Epiphanes. We shall see in the Books of Maccabees that even in a single historical context one single perspective cannot be pronounced normative. These biblical books provide a range of models for viewing and responding to the crises of history. We must decide for ourselves which, if any, of these models provides the best guidance for our own time.

THE ADDITIONS TO THE BOOK OF DANIEL

In addition to the prayer of Azariah and the Song of the Three Young Men in Daniel 3, the Greek and Latin translations of Daniel include two stories not found in the Hebrew bible, Susanna and Bel and the Dragon. These are included in Catholic editions of the bible as chapters 13 and 14. In some of the ancient versions the story of Susanna appears as the opening chapter of the book, presumably because it refers to Daniel as "a young lad" in vs. 45.

SUSANNA

13 There was a man living in Babylon whose name was Joakim. ²And he took a wife named Susanna, the daughter of Hilkiah, a very beautiful woman and one who feared the Lord. ³Her parents were righteous, and had taught their daughter according to the law of Moses. ⁴Joakim was very rich, and had a spacious garden adjoining his house; and the Jews used to come to him because he was the most honored of them all.

⁵In that year two elders from the people were appointed as judges. Concerning them the Lord had said: "Iniquity came forth from Babylon, from elders who were judges, who were supposed to govern the people." ⁶These men were frequently at Joakim's house, and all who had suits at law came to them.

⁷When the people departed at noon, Susanna would go into her husband's garden to walk. ⁸The two elders used to see her every day, going in and walking about, and they began to desire her. ⁹And they perverted their minds and turned their eyes from looking to Heaven or remembering righteous judgments. ¹⁰Both were overwhelmed with passion for her, but they did not tell each other of their distress, ¹¹for they were ashamed to disclose their lustful desire to possess her. ¹²And they watched eagerly, day after day, to see her.

¹³They said to each other, "Let us go home, for it is mealtime." ¹⁴And when they went out, they parted from each other. But turning back, they met again; and when each pressed the other for the reason, they confessed their lust. And then together they arranged for a time when they could find her alone.

¹⁵Once, while they were watching for an opportune day, she went in as before with only two maids, and wished to bathe in the garden, for it was very hot. ¹⁶And no one was there except the two elders, who had hid themselves and were watching her. ¹⁷She said to her maids, "Bring me oil and ointments, and shut the garden doors so that I may bathe." ¹⁸They did as they had been commanded; and they did not see the elders, because they were hidden.

¹⁹When the maids had gone out, the two elders rose and ran to her, and said: ²⁰"Look, the garden doors are shut, no one sees us, and we are in love with you; so give your consent, and lie with us. ²¹If you refuse, we will testify against you that a young man was with you, and this was why you sent your maids away."

²²Susanna sighed deeply, and said, "I am hemmed in on every side. For if I do this thing, it is death for me; and if I do not, I shall not escape your hands. ²³I choose not to do it and to fall into your hands, rather than to sin in the sight of the Lord."

²⁴Then Susanna cried out with a loud voice, and the two elders shouted against her. ²⁵And one of them ran out and opened the garden doors. ²⁶When the household servants heard the shouting in the garden, they rushed in at the side door to see what had happened to her. ²⁷And when the elders told their tale, the servants were greatly ashamed, for nothing like this had ever been said about Susanna. . . .

⁴¹The assembly believed them, because they were elders of the people and judges; and they condemned her to death.

⁴²Then Susanna cried out with a loud voice, and said, "O eternal God, who dost discern what is secret, who art aware of all things before they come to be, ⁴³thou knowest that these men have borne false witness against me. And now I am to die! Yet I have done none of the things that they have wickedly invented against me!"

⁴⁴The Lord heard her cry. ⁴⁵And as she was being led away to be put to death, God aroused the holy spirit of a young lad named Daniel; ⁴⁶and he cried with a loud voice, "I am innocent of the blood of this woman."

⁴⁷All the people turned to him, and said, "What is this that you have said?" ⁴⁸Taking his stand in the midst of them, he said, "Are you such fools, you sons of Israel? Have you condemned a daughter of Israel without examination and without learning the facts? ⁴⁹Return to the place of judgment. For these men have borne false witness against her."

⁵⁰Then all the people returned in haste. And the elders said to him, "Come, sit among us and inform us, for God has given you that right." ⁵¹And Daniel said to them, "Separate them far from each other, and I will examine them."

⁵²When they were separated from each other, he summoned one of them and said to him, "You old relic of

wicked days, your sins have now come home, which you have committed in the past, ⁵³pronouncing unjust judgments, condemning the innocent and letting the guilty go free, though the Lord said, 'Do not put to death an innocent and righteous person.'⁵⁴Now then, if you really saw her, tell me this: Under what tree did you see them being intimate with each other?" He answered, "Under a mastic tree." ⁵⁵And Daniel said, "Very well! You have lied against your own head, for the angel of God has received the sentence from God and will immediately cut you in two."

⁵⁶Then he put him aside, and commanded them to bring the other. And he said to him, "You offspring of Canaan and not of Judah, beauty has deceived you and lust has perverted your heart. ⁵⁷This is how you both have been dealing with the daughters of Israel, and they were intimate with you through fear; but a daughter of Judah would not endure your wickedness. ⁵⁸Now then, tell me: Under what tree did you catch them being intimate with each other?" He answered, "Under an evergreen oak." ⁵⁹And Daniel said to him, "Very well! You also have lied against your own head, for the angel of God is waiting with his sword to saw you in two, that he may destroy you both."

⁶⁰Then all the assembly shouted loudly and blessed God, who saves those who hope in him. ⁶¹And they rose against the two elders, for out of their own mouths Daniel had convicted them of bearing false witness; ⁶²and they did to them as they had wickedly planned to do to their neighbor; acting in accordance with the law of Moses, they put them to death. Thus innocent blood was saved that day.

⁶³And Hilkiah and his wife praised God for their daughter Susanna, and so did Joakim her husband and all

her kindred, because nothing shameful was found in her. ⁶⁴And from that day onward Daniel had a great reputation among the people.

The story of Susanna is a moral tale, unrelated to the substance of the Book of Daniel. The connection with Daniel lies in the latter's name, which means "my judge is God" (or possibly "judge of God" or even "God has judged"). The story illustrates two themes: the virtue of the Jewish woman Susanna ("a lily") and the wise judgment of Daniel. The latter theme is the basis for the Shakespearian phrase "a Daniel come to judgment."

The story is a very simple one. The two elders are entirely wicked. They are corrupt judges and liars, in addition to their lust. Susanna, by contrast, is entirely virtuous. The theme of attempted seduction is of course a stock one in folklore and literature. (In the biblical tradition, the Joseph story provides an example which was often re-told in the New Testament era.) Here the plot is uncomplicated by any hesitation on the part of Susanna or indeed by anything that would make the proposed seduction attractive. At the outset, the choice is set up between sin, and an accusation leading to death. In this respect there is an analogy with the stories in Daniel 3 and 6. In this case, however, the deliverance requires no miracle or revelation, but only the intelligent intervention of Daniel.

Despite its simplicity, the story is noteworthy in a few respects. First, it is set entirely within the bounds of Judaism. The wicked old men and the virtuous Susanna are alike Jews. Moreover, the elders are judges and held in high esteem by the people. Evidently, high esteem within a religious community is not a dependable guide to character. When the community has to choose between the word of the elders and the word of a woman, the choice is simple. Before Daniel arrives no one attempts to defend Susanna, and she is apparently given no opportunity to speak before she is condemned. We are remined of the story of Judah and Tamar in Genesis 38, where Judah quite blithely condemns his daughter-in-law to death for fornication until he realizes that he himself was her partner. The biblical tradition reflects a male-dominated society and religion, where the woman's viewpoint was seldom heard. Yet there are at least rare flashes of recognition that the dominant prejudices of society were only prejudices and that the woman could be justified over the man.

The wisdom of Daniel

The wisdom displayed by Daniel seems very simple. It involves no more than an elementary cross-examination of the witnesses. The real wisdom of Daniel lies in the recognition that this step was necessary, that the judges were not reliable witnesses and that Susanna was "a daughter of Israel." His wisdom lies in the ability to cut through prejudice. The theme that God is no respecter of persons is a favorite one in the biblical tradition. The lesson of Susanna is, similarly, that neither membership of the chosen people nor rank within it count for anything or ensure virtuous conduct. The heroes of the story are characters who have little initial status—the woman Susanna, and Daniel, who is a mere lad. Virtue and wisdom can be found in such unranked people as well as, or perhaps better than in the revered authorities.

BEL AND THE DRAGON

14 When King Astyages was laid with his fathers, Cyrus the Persian received his kingdom. ²And Daniel was a companion of the king, and was the most honored of his friends.

³Now the Babylonians had an idol called Bel, and every

day they spent on it twelve bushels of fine flour and forty sheep and fifty gallons of wine. ⁴The king revered it and went every day to worship it. But Daniel worshiped his own God.

⁵And the king said to him, "Why do you not worship Bel?" He answered, "Because I do not revere man-made idols, but the living God, who created heaven and earth and has dominion over all flesh."

⁶The king said to him, "Do you not think that Bel is a living God? Do you not see how much he eats and drinks every day?" ⁷Then Daniel laughed, and said, "Do not be deceived, O king; for this is but clay inside and brass outside, and it never ate or drank anything."

⁸Then the king was angry, and he called his priests and said to them, "If you do not tell me who is eating these provisions, you shall die. ⁹But if you prove that Bel is eating them, Daniel shall die, because he blasphemed against Bel." And Daniel said to the king, "Let it be done as you have said."

¹⁰Now there were seventy priests of Bel, besides their wives and children. And the king went with Daniel into the temple of Bel. ¹¹And the priests of Bel said, "Behold, we are going outside; you yourself, O king, shall set forth the food and mix and place the wine, and shut the door and seal it with your signet. ¹²And when you return in the morning, if you do not find that Bel has eaten it all, we will die; or else Daniel will, who is telling lies about us." ¹³They were unconcerned, for beneath the table they had made a hidden entrance, through which they used to go in regularly and consume the provisions. ¹⁴When they had gone out, the king set forth the food for Bel. Then Daniel ordered his servants to bring ashes and they sifted them throughout the whole temple in the presence of the king alone. Then they went out, shut the door and sealed it with the king's signet, and departed. ¹⁵In the night the

priests came with their wives and children, as they were accustomed to do, and ate and drank everything.

¹⁶Early in the morning the king rose and came, and Daniel with him. ¹⁷And the king said, "Are the seals unbroken, Daniel?" He answered, "They are unbroken, O king." ¹⁸As soon as the doors were opened, the king looked at the table, and shouted in a loud voice, "You are great, O Bel; and with you there is no deceit, none at all."

¹⁹Then Daniel laughed, and restrained the king from going in, and said, "Look at the floor, and notice whose footsteps these are." ²⁰The king said, "I see the footsteps of men and women and children."

²¹Then the king was enraged, and he seized the priests and their wives and children; and they showed him the secret doors through which they were accustomed to enter and devour what was on the table. ²²Therefore the king put them to death, and gave Bel over to Daniel, who destroyed it and its temple.

²³There was also a great dragon, which the Babylonians revered. ²⁴And the king said to Daniel, "You cannot deny that this is a living god; so worship him." ²⁵Daniel said, "I will worship the Lord my God, for he is the living God. ²⁶But if you, O king, will give me permission, I will slay the dragon without sword or club." The king said, "I give you permission."

²⁷Then Daniel took pitch, fat, and hair, and boiled them together and made cakes, which he fed to the dragon. The dragon ate them, and burst open. And Daniel said, "See what you have been worshiping!"

²⁸When the Babylonians heard it, they were very indignant and conspired against the king, saying, "The king has become a Jew; he has destroyed Bel, and slain the dragon, and slaughtered the priests." ²⁹Going to the king, they said, "Hand Daniel over to us, or else we will kill you and your household." ³⁰The king saw that they were

pressing him hard, and under compulsion he handed Daniel over to them.

[31]They threw Daniel into the lions' den, and he was there for six days. [32]There were seven lions in the den, and every day they had been given two human bodies and two sheep; but these were not given to them now, so that they might devour Daniel.

[33]Now the prophet Habakkuk was in Judea. He had boiled pottage and had broken bread into a bowl, and was going into the field to take it to the reapers. [34]But the angel of the Lord said to Habakkuk, "Take the dinner which you have to Babylon, to Daniel, in the lions' den." [35]Habakkuk said, "Sir, I have never seen Babylon, and I know nothing about the den." [36]Then the angel of the Lord took him by the crown of his head, and lifted him by his hair and set him down in Babylon, right over the den, with the rushing sound of the wind itself.

[37]Then Habakkuk shouted, "Daniel! Daniel! Take the dinner which God has sent you." [38]And Daniel said, "Thou hast remembered me, O God, and has not forsaken those who love thee." [39]So Daniel arose and ate. And the angel of God immediately returned Habakkuk to his own place.

[40]On the seventh day the king came to mourn for Daniel. When he came to the den he looked in, and there sat Daniel. [41]And the king shouted with a loud voice, "Thou art great, O Lord God of Daniel, and there is no other besides thee." [42]And he pulled Daniel out, and threw into the den the men who had attempted his destruction, and they were devoured immediately before his eyes.

The stories of Bel and the Dragon are very different from Susanna. Their affinity with Daniel 3 and 6 is highlighted by the motif of the lions' den. Evidently this motif had become attached to Daniel and came to figure in otherwise independent stories.

The primary theme of these stories is polemic against Babylonian idolatry. This theme was well developed in Second Isaiah, especially in Isa 44. The story of Bel (Bel-Marduk, the chief god of Babylon) goes beyond Second Isaiah in suggesting calculated deception on the part of the priests. Needless to say there is no ecumenical spirit here, and no attempt to understand Babylonian religion from within. The intention is simply to mock, and distortion is a standard method of mockery. We should not base our opinion of pagan religions on Jewish or Christian polemics, just as we would not base our opinions of Judaism or Christianity on the ridicule of outsiders.

As in Daniel 6, the king is represented as sympathetic to Daniel. The king in question here is Cyrus the Great of Persia, the king who released the Jews from the Babylonian captivity and was noted for his tolerant attitudes to other peoples. His predecessor here is named Astyages, who was in fact the king of Media defeated by Cyrus. This story thus dispenses with the unhistorical Darius the Mede, but it still implies that the Medes had ruled over Babylon, which was not the case. The Persian king who actually destroyed the statue and temple of Bel was Xerxes I, and his action was not motivated by any opposition to idolatry, but by desire for plunder. It may well be that the Jewish story is an imaginative elaboration of Jer 51:44: "And I will punish Bel in Babylon, and take out of his mouth what he has swallowed."

The snake or dragon in the second story is introduced as a ridiculous "living god." There is no evidence that the Babylonians worshipped live snakes, although snake worship was ancient in Greece and Egypt, and was also known in Babylonia. Animal worship was especially prominent in Egypt and there are frequent polemics against it in the Hellenistic Jewish literature.

The king remains sympathetic to Daniel even when he hands him over. Jews of the Diaspora liked to fantasize that their rulers would take their side against their rivals. The charge that the king had become a Jew was not as farfetched as it might seem, although it is anachronistic in the time of Cyrus, when Judaism was still perceived as an ethnic-political entity rather than as a cult. In the first century CE, Queen Helena of Adiabene in Mesopotamia converted to Judaism, and the king, Izates, would have done so but for the fear that his subjects would not accept a Jewish king. It should be noted that throughout this story Judaism is conceived as a religion, fully compatible with loyalty to the Babylonian state.

The final episode, involving Habakkuk, is the most wildly fantastic part of the story. The prophet Habakkuk was active before the fall of Jerusalem to the Babylonians and could scarcely have been still active in the time of Cyrus. The chronological difficulty becomes irrelevant in any case in view of the extravagantly supernatural way in which Habakkuk is transported to Babylon. This episode, like the preservation of Daniel in the lions' den (now for seven days) builds up to the acclamation of the king, that there is no god like the god of Daniel. The satisfaction of the story is made complete by the prompt destruction of Daniel's enemies.

Bel and the Dragon returns us to the conceptual and imaginative world of the tales in Daniel 1-6, although this chapter is probably later in origin. The story views idolatry as the main obstacle to the success of the Jews in the Diaspora. It provides a fantasy of how that obstacle might be removed, with the good will of a ruler, and how the Jews might be delivered from the inevitable resentment of their enemies. Tales such as these were not likely to make an impact on the gentiles. If any gentiles happened to read them, they could only resent the pretensions of the Jews.

Rather the stories were designed to reassure the Jews that the pagan religions were absurd and that their own God was superior.

Idolatry

Idolatry, in the simple sense of these stories is not a significant issue in the modern world. Our idols are more subtle and diverse. Commercial products and the images of the mass media are surely among them. The story of Bel and the Dragon has some metaphorical potential in this regard. The deception of the priests of Bel is representative of the deceit of those who put forth idols and ideals for their own advantage. We may be reminded here of some brands of religion whose salesmen devour the contributions which they have demanded while insisting that the offerings were offered to God. The snake that burst open suggests that some idols can be undone by their own greed. The living God worshipped by Daniel represents, at least, liberation and independence from the manipulating clutches of idolatry. While the deliverance of Daniel from the lions' den is a fantasy, his willingness to face the lions rather than participate in idolatry is a striking metaphor for the freedom of the individual from the gods that are no gods.

EXCURSUS ON THE APOCALYPTIC GENRE

THE VISIONS of Daniel belong to a genre of literature called apocalypses, which was widespread in Judaism around the turn of the era and had a profound influence on early Christianity.

What is an apocalypse?

The word apocalypse means "revelation" in Greek, but is used more narrowly to describe a specific category of revelatory literature. In modern scholarship, the name was extended to the genre by analogy with the Apocalypse of John, which is in fact the oldest document which is explicitly introduced as an apocalypse in its own text. The label was common in antiquity, in Jewish, Christian and pagan literature, from about 100 CE on. While earlier works, like the visions of Daniel, were not originally labelled as apocalypses, they have been recognized as apocalypses in modern scholarship because they share the defining characteristics of the later examples of the genre.

An apocalypse is a revelation, marked by specific characteristics in both the manner in which it is communicated and in its content. There is always some element of a vision, although in some cases, such as Daniel 10, that element may be minimal. Since the initial revelation is mysterious, it must be explained by a heavenly mediator, usually an angel. The human recipient of the revelation is, typically,

said to be an ancient, venerated figure, such as Daniel or
Enoch. The identity of the actual author is thus concealed
beneath a pseudonym. (A few early Christian apocalypses
are apparently not pseudonymous, but all the Jewish ones
are.)

The content of the revelation has two aspects. One is
temporal. There is always a concern with a future,
eschatological judgment. The history prior to this judgment may be outlined in greater or lesser detail. In many
cases there is a review of history, which is divided into set
periods (e.g. four kingdoms, seventy weeks of years). At
the end there is a period of acute crisis, often involving the
signs of the end. The judgment leads to the reward of the
good and punishment of the wicked in a life beyond death.
The second aspect of the content of an apocalypse is
spatial. There is always a supernatural world above (or
below) the visible one. This world may be manifested in the
actions of angels or demons, as happens in Daniel, or it
may be described in the context of a heavenly journey. In
many apocalypses this heavenly world is where the just
have their final reward. Individual apocalypses may place
their primary emphasis on either the temporal or the
spatial aspect, but both are always present.

What we have outlined above are the common elements
by which an apocalypse may be identified. They constitute
a literary structure (e.g. they always describe how the
revelation is received) and they also constitute a world
view. Every apocalypse carries some assumptions about
the nature of the world. It is a world dominated by supernatural powers, and subject to a definitive eschatological
judgment. For the individual, this world is not the end. As
in any genre, we must allow for considerable diversity
among the actual apocalypses. The common elements
noted above do not make up the full specific message of
any one work. Rather they constitute a framework, a set of

presuppositions within which different problems may be addressed and different messages developed. In this sense, what is common to the apocalyptic genre is a method rather than a specific message. The framework of the genre is applied to the varying problems addressed by the individual works and sets those problems in an apocalyptic perspective. So, for example in Daniel, the persecution of Antiochus Epiphanes is seen against the backdrop of a heavenly battle and coming judgment.

The earliest Jewish apocalypses

The earliest Jewish apocalypses are found in the first Book of Enoch. 1 Enoch is a collection of writings, all ascribed to Enoch. It has survived in full only in Ethiopic translations, but Aramaic fragments have now been found in the Dead Sea Scrolls. (Greek fragments have also survived.) We now know from the Aramaic fragments that some sections of 1 Enoch must have originated in the third century BCE, if not earlier. The sections in question are the Book of the Watchers (1 Enoch 1-36) and the Astronomical Book (1 Enoch 72-82). This information has changed our view of the development of the apocalyptic literature to a great degree. Previously, Daniel was thought to contain the first full-blown apocalypse. While Daniel was significantly different from the Old Testament prophets, there was enough continuity to support the idea that the apocalypses were a late form of prophecy. Daniel's visions were reminiscent of Ezekiel, and the expectation of an eschatological judgment had clear prophetic prototypes. In the earliest sections of 1 Enoch, however, there is much more speculation on cosmological and astronomical lore. The lines of continuity with prophecy are not so clear. The interest in a supernatural heavenly world which dominates the Enoch literature stands in sharp contrast with the this-worldly emphasis which is characteristic of the Old Testament as a whole.

The Book of the Watchers as an illustration

It may be useful at this point to discuss briefly the Enochic Book of the Watchers as a specimen of the genre apocalypse from outside the bible. The work breaks down into three parts. First, there is an introduction in chapters 1-5 which contrasts the regularity of nature with the irregularity of sinners. Second, there is the story of the Watchers in chaps. 6-16 and finally there is the account of Enoch's journeys in 17-36.

The story of the Watchers is an imaginative expansion of the cryptic passage in Genesis 6, where the "sons of God" come down and fornicate with the daughters of men and beget giants. The Watchers, angelic beings, take the place of the sons of God. In 1 Enoch 6-16 there are two strands to the story. One emphasizes the sexual sin of the Watchers, which led to the birth of the giants and consequently to the spread of violence. The other emphasizes that the Watchers revealed mysteries which should have been kept secret. These include the making of weapons, and again violence results. Finally the good angels bring petition to God and the Watchers are condemned. They are bound under the hills of the earth for seventy generations, and then they will be thrown into the fire. The earth is cleansed from all corruption.

In the apocalyptic literature, stories about supernatural beings usually refer, on one level, to some historical events. We can safely presume that this is also true in the Book of the Watchers. The story has obvious allegorical potential. So, scholars have suggested that the Watchers represent the Hellenistic kings, who burst into the Near East from outside, regarded themselves as gods and brought with them many mysteries of technological civilization. Others have suggested that they represent the priests in Jerusalem. Priests were supposed to be like angels because of their proximity to God in the cult. In the years before the Maccabean revolt, the Jerusalem priesthood had gone through a considerable process of Hellenization and some of the priests might well have been regarded by traditionalists as fallen angels.

Either of these identifications of the human referents in the story is plausible enough, but, unlike Daniel, the Book of the Watchers provides no hint of the historical events underlying the text. We may safely say that the story presupposes some kind of crisis. The violence and general disruption of the story was, at least, most readily applicable to a situation where there was some disturbance. 1 Enoch, however, does not describe that disturbance with any specific detail. As it now stands the story of the Watchers could have been applied to any of a wide range of historical incidents. Moreover, because of its lack of explicit references, the story could be applied over and over again long after the original situation passed.

It appears then that the identity of the author and of his situation is concealed behind the story of the Watchers. The author does not mention any crisis of the Hellenistic age. Instead, the action is transferred to the mythical time of Enoch, before the flood. The pseudonymous use of Enoch's name is part of this transposition.

What is achieved by telling the story of the Watchers rather than speaking directly of the author's own time? Several things. First, the mysterious Watchers, and their offspring, whose height was three thousand cubits and who devoured all the toil of men, have a far greater impact on the imagination than ordinary mortals. The author was in effect saying that the troubles of his age were not of human making. Supernatural forces had been released in the world. Second, the story of the Watchers distracts the attention from the specific historical details of a particular crisis. Since these events are supposed to have happened long ago, the new events of the Hellenistic age are not unique. They are only re-enactments of a typical pattern.

Since we know how the ancient story ended, we can anticipate how the events of the present will turn out. In this way the ancient story lends perspective to the present. It also relieves anxiety, by providing reassurance that this pattern of events has been acted out before. Third, since the story is not strictly tied to historical references, it can be used over and over again with reference to new situations. The meaning of the story is not exhausted by any one application.

The otherworldly journey

The story of the Watchers is one means by which the author responded to the crisis of his day. The journeys of Enoch in chaps. 17-36 are another complementary means. Enoch is introduced already in chap. 12, when he is asked to intercede for the Watchers. He takes up their petition for mercy to God, but it is rejected. In the process, however, we see that Enoch is the opposite of the Watchers. They are heavenly beings who have fallen to earth. He is a human being who is taken up to heaven. The revelation they give is worthless. Enoch reveals the true mystery.

Already in chap. 14 Enoch is lifted up to heaven and has a vision of the throne of God. (The description of the divine throne is remarkably similar to that in Daniel 7.) The journeys proper begin in chap. 17. Enoch is guided by the angels to the most remote parts of creation. He sees the cornerstone of the earth and the pillars of heaven, the mouths of all the rivers and the storehouses of the winds. The focus of his tour, however, is on the places of judgment. He sees the prison for the stars and the host of heaven, where they are kept for the day of judgment. He also sees the places where "the spirits of the souls of the dead" are kept, separated into three compartments: the sinners, the righteous and sinners who have been punished during their life. He sees the place of the final judgment, the tree of life and the valley of Gehenna. The last chapters of the work complete a comprehensive tour of the outer limits of creation.

Like the story of the Watchers, Enoch's journeys contain no reference to the historical circumstances of the author. In the context of the book, this entire revelation is addressed by Enoch to the Watchers. The revelation includes the place where the Watchers will be punished, but it is also directly relevant to the destiny of humanity, righteous and wicked. It contains lengthy assurances that the wicked will be punished and the righteous rewarded. This retribution, or system of reward and punishment, is set in a cosmic context. Enoch reveals not only how one historical crisis will be resolved, but how the whole creation is set up and works. The problems of specific human beings at a particular time in history are viewed in perspective against the backdrop of the whole creation.

Here again, the revelation of Enoch shifts the attention away from the historical present. In this case the revelation focuses on places rather than on a story of the past, but the effect is very similar. The revelation shows that there is another world beyond this one. Its reality is assured, because Enoch has seen it. The apparently superfluous details add to the impression of realism. Enoch has not only seen the places of judgment, but everything that there is to be seen. This entire supernatural world is of immediate relevance to human affairs because of the judgment. The places of the judgment are already there. The judgment is inevitable, and it is not in the hands of men. So, if historical circumstances leave little hope for the future in this world, we need not despair. Any historical situation must be viewed within the framework of the supernatural world and the inevitable judgment revealed by Enoch.

The Book of the Watchers describes the supernatural world in much more detail than does Daniel. Yet Daniel presupposes a similar framework. There again the problems of the world are due to the activity of supernatural powers, and the resolution of those problems is also determined on the supernatural level. The ultimate judgment is a judgment beyond death. The crises of world history are set in a transcendent, supernatural framework.

The Book of the Watchers, like Daniel, is a construct to help people cope in times of duress. Endurance is possible, because the outcome is assured. If things go badly in this world, all is not lost. Even death itself loses some of its terror since there is life beyond it.

The imaginative character of this construct is readily obvious in the Book of Enoch. Enoch is an obviously legendary figure. His revelations about the judgment and supernatural world incorporate various traditions and are scarcely consistent within themselves. When we read a number of heavenly journeys—others by Enoch, some by Baruch and Abraham—it is no longer possible to entertain any idea that these are objective, literal accounts of real places. They are fantasies of imaginary places. Yet they should not be dismissed as worthless. They symbolize the conviction that some things in life are transcendent. We are subject to powers and influences beyond that which is consciously willed by other human beings. Most important are the convictions that justice and life itself have values which can not be negated by the apparent triumph of evil in this world from time to time.

The Old Testament precedents

The heavily supernatural emphasis of the early apocalypses stands in sharp contrast to what we find in most of the Old Testament. This is not to say that there is no continuity. The enigmatic passage about "sons of God" in Genesis 6, on which the story of the Watchers is based, should serve as a warning that there was much more mythology in ancient Israel than has survived in the canonical bible. Genesis 6 is clearly an abbreviation of a longer story. It is now impossible to say whether the story abbreviated in Genesis corresponded to what we now find in Enoch to any significant degree.

The closest Old Testament parallels to the apocalyptic literature are found in the late prophetic books, especially those written after the Babylonian exile. Ezekiel already shows the developed use of allegories which is typical of the later apocalypses. The idea that revelation must be mediated or explained by an angel is found in the Book of Zechariah. Perhaps the closest analogue to the apocalypses is found in Isaiah 24-27, a late composition which is often called the Apocalypse of Isaiah. In these chapters we find extensive use of mythological symbolism, presumably to describe the crisis of the author's own day. Especially striking are the promises that God will swallow up Death forever and slay the dragon that is in the sea. Another passage is intriguing in the light of Enoch's references to the imprisonment of the Watchers and the host of heaven:

> "On that day the Lord will punish the host of heaven,
>   in heaven, and the kings of the earth, on the
>   earth.
> They will be gathered together as prisoners in a pit;
>   they will be shut up in a prison, and after many
>   days they will be punished." (Isa 24:21-22).

Isa 24-27 is a collection of oracles, and it never provides a narrative elaboration of these mythological references. It seems obvious that the prophet was drawing on mythological stories, which are not now available to us. It is possible then that the supernatural world of Enoch was not so great an innovation in ancient Israel as it now appears.

Yet it must be said that there is no full-blown apocalypse in the Old Testament prior to Daniel. As far as we can now see, the apocalyptic genre developed in Judaism in the Hellenistic age. The apocalypses drew freely on older biblical traditions but were also influenced to some degree by Persian, Babylonian and other traditions which were current in the Hellenistic age. The emphasis on the supernatural world, and the expectation of life after death were both common in the Hellenistic world. The acceptance of the belief in personal reward and punishment after death is perhaps the element which most radically distinguishes the apocalypses from the late prophetic books, although this belief must be seen as part of the comprehensive world view of the apocalypses.

The extent of the apocalyptic literature

The ideas and symbols which are characteristic of the apocalypses became increasingly widespread in Judaism from the second century BCE on and are found in varying degrees in documents which do not have the literary form of apocalypses. It is often thought that apocalyptic ideas flourished especially in sectarian circles, such as the Essenes of Qumran. While this is true, such ideas were never restricted to sects. The book of Daniel was accepted into the canon. Two of the later apocalypses, from the end of the first century CE, 4 Ezra and 2 Baruch, seem to have originated in Pharisaic circles.

In addition to the Book of the Watchers, a number of other early apocalypses are found in 1 Enoch. The Astronomical Book can now be dated no later than the third century BCE. The Apocalypse of Weeks (1 Enoch 93; 91: 12-19) and the Animal Apocalypse (1 Enoch 83-90) were written around the time of the Maccabean revolt. The Animal Apocalypse was apparently written in support of the Maccabees. The latter two apocalypses are closer to Daniel than is the Book of the Watchers, in the sense that they have less cosmological speculation and more focus on history. Yet the Book of the Watchers is clearly presupposed in the Animal Apocalypse. It is possible that these Enochic apocalypses come from a single movement, possibly sectarian, although even this is not certain. The book of Daniel, while it shares the same presuppositions about the nature of the world, cannot be ascribed to the same movement. We have seen that Daniel shows no enthusiasm for the Maccabean rebellion. The Animal Apocalypse, by contrast, says that a sword was given to the persecuted Jews and this sword plays a significant part in their deliverance.

The Dead Sea Scrolls

Both Daniel and the early parts of 1 Enoch were preserved among the Dead Sea Scrolls at Qumran. The community at Qumran is generally believed to have belonged to the Essene sect and to have flourished from the middle of the second century BCE until it was destroyed by the Romans in 70 CE. (The settlement was interrupted for a short period at the end of the first century BCE). The community had an extensive library, which included biblical books and other literature (such as the early Enoch material) of diverse origin. There were also documents which were distinctively sectarian and were products of the community itself. In so far as we can now tell, no apocalypses were produced at Qumran. Yet many of the sectarian documents were heavily influenced by apocalyptic ideas and shared an apocalyptic view of the world. The Community Rule claimed that humanity was divided between two Spirits, of Light and Darkness. The Sons of Light were guided by an Angel or Prince of Light. The Sons of Darkness were dominated by an Angel of Darkness. God "has established the spirits in equal measure until the final age" when the judgment will be executed. A remarkable document called the War Scroll provides instructions for a final battle between the Sons of Light, under the Angel Michael, and the Sons of Darkness, under Belial. The Sons of Light include both the human community and their angelic counterparts. The scrolls are remarkably reticent on the subject of life after death, but, when we read in the Community Rule that the Sons of Darkness will have everlasting damnation in the fires of the dark regions, we must assume that the Sons of Light have a corresponding reward. The Thanksgiving Hymns suggest that the members of the community have been already saved from death and admitted to the fellowship of the heavenly host: "I thank thee Lord for thou hast redeemed my soul from the Pit. . .that it may enter into community with the congregation of the Sons of Heaven."

The later apocalypses

The Qumran community is our best illustration of a concrete sociological situation where apocalyptic ideas flourished. It is also our best example of a Jewish sect: a community distinctly separated from the rest of Judaism with procedures for admission and expulsion. We cannot assume that all, or any, of the apocalypses were composed in such a sectarian setting.

One section of 1 Enoch, the Similitudes (1 Enoch 37-71) has not been found at Qumran. Its absence may be due to a relatively late date, although it was almost certainly composed before 70 CE. It is unlikely that any of the Enoch literature was composed at Qumran, and we should not be too surprised if the collection of Enochic books was not absolutely complete. The Similitudes are heavily influenced both by the earlier Enochic apocalypses and by Daniel. They are especially important because a figure called "that son of man" plays a central role. He is an angelic being, higher than the other angels. In 1 Enoch 71 he is identified as Enoch, but the passage is an addition to the Similitudes, possibly intended to contradict the Christian use of the title

Son of Man for Jesus. The Similitudes do not provide exact indications of the time and place of their composition. They look beyond this world for a judgment, and so reflect dissatisfaction with the present order of things, but there is no reason to believe that they were written in a time of intense persecution, as Daniel was.

Two other clusters of apocalyptic writings may serve to fill out our sketch of the distribution of the genre. One consists of the great apocalypses from the end of the first century CE, 4 Ezra and 2 Baruch. The other consists of a group of heavenly journeys from Egyptian Judaism, all probably from the first century CE.

4 Ezra and 2 Baruch are believed to have been written in Pharisaic circles, some time after the fall of Jerusalem to the Romans in 70 CE. They are concerned with the problem of the justice of God. 4 Ezra is reminiscent of Job in its moving expression of the problem of suffering. (2 Baruch is generally more optimistic, and may have been written as a response to 4 Ezra.) Whereas the Enoch tradition has assumed that Enoch, though a human being, had been granted intimate knowledge of the heavenly world, Ezra has neither ascended to heaven nor descended to hell. Moreover, he is initially dissatisfied with the angel's promise of a coming judgment, since so few will be saved. Yet in the later chapters his questioning is stilled. In chap. 9 he is directed into a field, where he sits among the flowers and eats the plants. He then has three visions of the end that is to come. The second is presented as an interpretation of Daniel 7. The fourth kingdom is now an eagle which rises out of the sea, and represents Rome. The third vision has a man rising from the sea, and flying with the clouds. This figure is reminiscent of the "one like a son of man" in Daniel. Ezra's problems are overcome by the repeated effect of these visions and in the end he praises God.

4 Ezra represents the dilemma of a Jew after the fall of

Jerusalem, who found no satisfaction in the traditional doctrines of reward and punishment, and is led somewhat reluctantly to accept the apocalyptic perspective. It should be noted that this perspective does not fully determine the author's theology. 2 Baruch pointedly disputes with 4 Ezra on many matters, such as the efficacy of the law and the extent of human responsibility. Yet it does so within the same apocalyptic perspective, with a view to the judgment that is to come.

The second cluster of apocalypses includes 3 Baruch, 2 Enoch and the Testament of Abraham. These works resemble the Book of the Watchers rather than Daniel, in so far as they describe heavenly journeys, and do not provide reviews of history. (Other documents of the Egyptian Diaspora, the Sibylline Oracles, are closer to Daniel in this respect.) 3 Baruch may serve as our illustration.

The apocalypse begins with a brief account of how Baruch was lamenting over the destruction of Jerusalem. An angel appears to him, and tells him: "Do not be so concerned over the salvation of Jerusalem.... Come and I will show you the mysteries of God." The mysteries are revealed in a tour of five heavens. They include cosmological mysteries, but also the punishments of sinners and the rewards of the just. At the end Baruch is no longer lamenting over Jerusalem, but gives glory to God. The apocalypse does not directly address the problem of the destruction of Jerusalem. Rather it distracts the reader by changing the frame of reference. By the end, the original problem is seen in a new perspective.

The common perspective of the apocalypses

This brief overview of the apocalyptic literature may help to clarify what is meant when the adjective apocalyptic is applied to the visions of Daniel. What is involved is not strictly a common theology, but rather common presuppositions and a common technique. The problems addressed by the different apocalypses vary, but in all cases there is *some* underlying problem. The great crises of the profanation of the temple by Antiochus Epiphanes and its destruction by the Romans, are the points of departure for many apocalypses, but not all have so specific a setting. In the case of some parts of 1 Enoch we cannot be sure of the setting at all. In all cases, however, the underlying problem is viewed in the context of a symbolic universe, which is dominated by supernatural powers and is destined for a definitive judgment. The problems of the present are placed in perspective. They will not be resolved by human means alone, and they will not last forever. So the reader is enabled to cope. The specific conduct demanded of the reader differs from one work to another, but the presuppositions about the nature of the world and human destiny are constant. To say that the visions of Daniel are apocalyptic is to affirm that they share the apocalyptic presuppositions about the nature of the world.

The significance of the apocalyptic world-view

The historical significance of the apocalyptic world-view is enormous, mainly because of its influence on Christianity. There is only one full-blown apocalypse in the New Testament, the Apocalypse of John. The apocalyptic world view, however, is pervasive in the New Testament. The resurrection of Christ was viewed as an apocalyptic event, ushering in the last days. While Jesus' own conception of the kingdom of God is a matter of perennial dispute, there is no doubt that the early Christians saw it as an apocalyptic kingdom, to be ushered in when the Son of Man came on the clouds of heaven with his angels.

The apocalyptic literature has often been something of an embarrassment for the Church. Not all apocalypses insisted that the end must be soon, but the canonical Book of

Daniel did, and this expectation was widespread in the New Testament. Paul told the Corinthians, as a "mystery," that they would not all die but they would all be changed (1 Cor 15:51, compare 1 Thess 4:17) and had to restrain the Thessalonians from thinking that the day of the Lord had already come (2 Thess 2). Two thousand years later, we know that this expectation was disappointed. The recurring attempts in every century to calculate the time of the end have similarly failed. We have seen that it is in the nature of an apocalypse that it can be re-applied to different situations. In this sense, those who apply Daniel or Revelation to the events of our own day may be quite justified. We must be mindful, however, that these books are not reliable predictions. They are symbolic expressions which are never fully exhausted by any one situation. They are constructs of the imagination, designed to motivate people and sustain them in the face of problems. If we want to assess their value we must ask how far they meet the needs of people at any specific time, and how far they inspire praiseworthy action. Their truth is not a matter of factual detail. Yet the apocalypses gave powerful expression to the sense that this world is passing away and we have not here a lasting city. No matter how long planet earth may continue, the transitoriness of the world is a fundamental truth in the life of any person, institution or society.

FIRST MACCABEES

First Maccabees:
Introduction

IN SHARP contrast to the highly symbolic language of
Daniel, 1 Maccabees makes the impression of a straightforward historical account. In fact, it is universally recognized
as a major source of historical information, although it is
not without errors. Yet, no historical account is entirely objective. First Maccabees is inspired by a distinct conception
of the nature of the Jewish religion and is thoroughly theological. It is also an ideological document which has rightly
been described as propaganda for the Maccabean, or Hasmonean, house.

The date of composition

1 Maccabees was originally written in Hebrew but sur-
vives in the Greek translation. It was not included in the
canon of the Hebrew bible. The book was written at some
point in the last third of the second century BCE. The narrative extends to the death of Simon and the accession of
John Hyrcanus in 134 BCE. The concluding formulaic
statement in 16:23-24, that the rest of the deeds of John are
written in the chronicles of the high priesthood, is based on

biblical models (e.g. 2 Kings 20:20 on Hezekiah). Some have thought that this statement presupposes the death of John (104 BCE) but this is not necessary. If it did, we should expect that some mention would be made of John's successor, Alexander Jannaeus. In any case, 1 Maccabees was clearly written before Pompey's conquest of Jerusalem in 63 BCE.

The use of sources

While the later events recorded may still have been fresh in the author's mind, the persecution of Antiochus and the subsequent revolt were thirty to fifty years in the past when the book was written. The author's sources may have included both oral tradition and written material. The diversity of sources is shown by the fact that two distinct dating systems are used. Throughout the book, dates are figured from the beginning of the Seleucid monarchy. There were two ways of figuring that era. The official Syrian usage, or Seleucid era, was counted from the first day of October (Dios, the Hebrew Tishri) of 312 BCE. The Babylonian era, which was followed approximately by the Jews, figured the dates from the first of April (Hebrew Nisan, Greek Artemisios) of 311 BCE. Both systems are attested in 1 Maccabees—e.g. the re-dedication of the temple is dated on the Babylonian/Jewish system, while the death of Antiochus of Epiphanes is given according to the Seleucid system. It seems probable then that the author was drawing on various records or archives for his material. Moreover, he cites some 14 official documents and letters in the book. These appear to be substantially authentic, although they are not necessarily cited in full, and a few, such as the correspondence with Sparta in chapters 12 and 14 are controversial. On the whole, however, the author of 1 Maccabees emerges as a responsible historian, even if he does give an ideological and theological slant to his material.

The book falls easily into four sections. The first deals

with the persecution (1:11-2:70, preceded by a brief introduction in 1:1-10). The others deal in turn with the careers of Judas (3:1-9:22), Jonathan (9:23-12:53) and Simon (13:1-16:22).

The theology of the book

Our concern in this commentary is primarily with the theological and ideological aspects of the work, rather than with the rich historical information it provides. At the heart of the book is the presentation of the family of the Maccabees as "the family of those men through whom deliverance was given to Israel" (5:62). Their slogan, on the lips of Mattathias in 2:27, is to be zealous for the law and support the covenant, but their view of their religious obligations is evidently different from that presented in Daniel. The Maccabees are repeatedly viewed in the light of Old Testament models and even take on messianic dimensions. There is a sharp antithesis between Jews and gentiles, but the antithesis applies mainly to the immediate neighbors of the Jews. More distant nations, such as Rome and Sparta are viewed as potential friends. We will also find that the Maccabees could adopt a friendly attitude even towards the Syrian kings when it was advantageous to do so.

The main questions raised by 1 Maccabees are the religious justification of violence and of nationalism. It is evident from the Book of Daniel that not even all the Jews of their day gave wholehearted approval to the Maccabees. Yet they were the ones who effected the liberation of Judaea and revitalized the distinctive identity of the Jews. Then again, their achievement should not be exaggerated. The liberation they brought about was temporary. The later Hasmonean kings were quite oppressive, and incurred the enmity of the Pharisees. When other Jews followed the example of the Maccabees in the first century CE and launched a violent rebellion against Rome, the results were catastrophic. The lessons of history are always ambiguous. The success of the Maccabees does not prove that they are a model to be imitated in other situations.

The story of the Maccabees acquires paradigmatic significance for the modern history of Israel, but also for the various strands of liberation theology in the Christian world. It provides an occasion to reflect on the nature and problems of such movements, although the lessons of the past can never be applied to the present without due consideration of the differences in the situations.

First Maccabees:
Commentary

1 MAC 1:1-10: THE INTRODUCTION

1 After Alexander son of Philip, the Macedonian, who came from the land of Kittim, had defeated Darius, king of the Persians and the Medes, he succeeded him as king. (He had previously become king of Greece.) [2]He fought many battles, conquered strongholds, and put to death the kings of the earth. [3]He advanced to the ends of the earth, and plundered many nations. When the earth became quiet before him, he was exalted, and his heart was lifted up. [4]He gathered a very strong army and ruled over countries, nations, and princes, and they became tributary to him.

[5]After this he fell sick and perceived that he was dying. [6]So he summoned his most honored officers, who had been brought up with him from youth, and divided his kingdom among them while he was still alive. [7]And after Alexander had reigned twelve years, he died.

[8]Then his officers began to rule, each in his own place. [9]They all put on crowns after his death, and so did their

sons after them for many years; and they caused many evils on the earth.

¹⁰From them came forth a sinful root, Antiochus Epiphanes, son of Antiochus the king; he had been a hostage in Rome. He began to reign in the one hundred and thirty-seventh year of the kingdom of the Greeks.

The book begins with a very rapid historical resume. The conquests of Alexander are seen as the ultimate source of the trouble which came to the surface with the advent of Antiochus Epiphanes in 175 BCE. The author's theologizing tendencies are apparent from the beginning. Alexander's heart was lifted up, and his fall follows abruptly. His successors are condemned without exception. The fact that the Jews were subject to the Ptolemies for a full century is not even noted. For many Jews of the period the political issue of the day was whether to side with the Ptolemies or the Seleucids. Not so 1 Maccabees. For him any gentile domination is unacceptable.

Part One: The Persecution

1 MAC 1:11-40: THE PRELIMINARY EVENTS

¹¹In those days lawless men came forth from Israel, and misled many, saying, "Let us go and make a covenant with the Gentiles round about us, for since we separated from them many evils have come upon us." ¹²This proposal pleased them, ¹³and some of the people eagerly went to the king. He authorized them to observe the ordinances of the Gentiles. ¹⁴So they built a gymnasium in Jerusalem, according to Gentile custom, ¹⁵and removed the marks of circumcision, and abandoned the holy covenant. They

joined with the Gentiles and sold themselves to do evil. . .

²⁰After subduing Egypt, Antiochus returned in the one hundred and forty-third year. He went up against Israel and came to Jerusalem with a strong force. ²¹He arrogantly entered the sanctuary and took the golden altar, the lampstand for the light, and all its utensils. ²²He took also the table for the bread of the Presence, the cups for drink offerings, the bowls, the golden censers, the curtain, the crowns, and the gold decoration on the front of the temple; he stripped it all off. ²³He took the silver and the gold, and the costly vessels; he took also the hidden treasures which he found. ²⁴Taking them all, he departed to his own land.

He committed deeds of murder,
and spoke with great arrogance.
²⁵Israel mourned deeply in every community,
²⁶rulers and elders groaned,
maidens and young men became faint,
the beauty of the women faded.
²⁷Every bridegroom took up the lament;
she who sat in the bridal chamber was mourning.
²⁸Even the land shook for its inhabitants,
and all the house of Jacob was clothed with shame.
²⁹Two years later the king sent to the cities of Judah a chief collector of tribute, and he came to Jerusalem with a large force. ³⁰Deceitfully he spoke peaceable words to them, and they believed him; but he suddenly fell upon the city, dealt it a severe blow, and destroyed many people of Israel. ³¹He plundered the city, burned it with fire, and tore down its houses and its surrounding walls. ³²And they took captive the women and children, and seized the cattle. ³³Then they fortified the city of David with a great strong wall and strong towers, and it became their citadel. ³⁴And they stationed there a sinful people, lawless men. These strengthened their position; ³⁵they stored up arms

and food, and collecting the spoils of Jerusalem they
stored them there, and became a great snare.

³⁶It became an ambush against the sanctuary,
an evil adversary of Israel continually.
³⁷On every side of the sanctuary they shed innocent
blood;
they even defiled the sanctuary.
³⁸Because of them the residents of Jerusalem fled;
she became a dwelling of strangers;
she became strange to her offspring,
and her children forsook her.
³⁹Her sanctuary became desolate as a desert;
her feasts were turned into mourning,
her sabbaths into a reproach,
her honor into contempt.
⁴⁰Her dishonor now grew as great as her glory;
her exaltation was turned into mourning.

1 Maccabees passes very quickly over the events leading
up to the revolt. The struggle for the office of high priest,
which is described in 2 Maccabees, is not even mentioned. 1
Maccabees also omits any reference to Antiochus' second
expedition to Egypt, and his encounter with the Romans
there.

Despite the strong tendency of 1 Maccabees to present the
entire conflict as a struggle between Jews and gentiles, it is
apparent that it began with the actions of certain Jews.
These are described as "lawless men." Undoubtedly, personal ambition and gain were factors in their action. As we
shall see more clearly in 2 Maccabees, the conduct of the
men who acquired the high-priesthood by bribery, namely
Jason and Menelaus, was far from honorable. Yet the issues
were not so black and white as 1 Maccabees presents them.
The Hellenizers, those who favored acceptance of a Greek
way of life, undoubtedly saw their actions as a liberalization

and updating of Judaism. Throughout the Hellenistic world the Jews were regarded as strange and inhospitable because of the exclusivity of their religion. Many Jews who lived in the Greek-speaking world, in such centers as Alexandria in Egypt, learned to preserve their Jewish tradition in ways that down-played its differences from the surrounding culture. The reformers in Jerusalem must also have had some vision of Judaism as an integral part of the culture of the day.

The issue which is singled out in 1 Mac 1:14 is the building of a gymnasium. The significance of this institution was both practical and symbolic. On the one hand, it was a center for the diffusion of Greek customs and ideas. On the other hand, it was an institution which had no place in the Jewish tradition, and was associated with the worship of pagan gods. Moreover, the nudity involved in athletic exercises in antiquity was not only offensive to traditionalists. It caused Jews who participated in it to have their circumcision disguised by surgical operation, so that they would not be conspicuously different from the gentiles. In 1 Maccabees, removing the marks of circumcision is tantamount to abandoning the covenant. External signs become crucially important when the distinct identity of a people is at stake.

In 1 Mac 1:20-23 we are told how Antiochus plundered the temple in 169 BCE and carried off the golden altar and sacred vessels. The action may have had no more motivation than simple greed, and the financial needs of the king. It established Antiochus as another Nebuchadnezzar in the eyes of the Jews. 1 Mac 1:25-28 marks the occasion with a brief poetic passage, reminiscent of the laments for the fall of the temple.

The plunder of Jerusalem described in 1:29-35 is not so simply explained. It was carried out by Apollonius, who is said in 2 Mac 5:24 to be general of the Mysian mercenaries (1 Mac 1:29, "collector of tribute" is apparently a mistranslation from the Hebrew). This operation was not only an act of plunder, but involved the building of the citadel Akra and the setting up of a garrison. It is likely that this action was undertaken because the Hellenizing party had lost control in Jerusalem. The king may have perceived the Jews as being already in revolt, and sent Apollonius to restore his authority. If so, the subsequent persecution becomes more intelligible.

The erection of the Akra is again marked by a poetic passage in 1 Mac 1:36-40, again recalling the lamentations for the destruction of Jerusalem by the Babylonians.

1 MAC 1:41-64: THE PERSECUTION

[41]Then the king wrote to his whole kingdom that all should be one people, [42]and that each should give up his customs. [43]All the Gentiles accepted the command of the king. Many even from Israel gladly adopted his religion; they sacrificed to idols and profaned the sabbath. [44]And the king sent letters by messengers to Jerusalem and the cities of Judah; he directed them to follow customs strange to the land, [45]to forbid burnt offerings and sacrifices and drink offerings in the sanctuary, to profane sabbaths and feasts, [46]to defile the sanctuary and the priests, [47]to build altars and sacred precincts and shrines for idols, to sacrifice swine and unclean animals, [48]and to leave their sons uncircumcised. They were to make themselves abominable by everything unclean and profane, [49]so that they should forget the law and change all the ordinances. [50]"And whoever does not obey the command of the king shall die."

[51]In such words he wrote to his whole kingdom. And he appointed inspectors over all the people and commanded the cities of Judah to offer sacrifice, city by city. [52]Many of the people, every one who forsook the law, joined them, and they did evil in the land; [53]they drove Israel into hiding in every place of refuge they had.

⁵⁴Now on the fifteenth day of Chislev, in the one hundred and forty-fifth year, they erected a desolating sacrilege upon the altar of burnt offering. They also built altars in the surrounding cities of Judah, ⁵⁵and burned incense at the doors of the houses and in the streets. ⁵⁶The books of the law which they found they tore to pieces and burned with fire. ⁵⁷Where the book of the covenant was found in the possession of any one, or if any one adhered to the law, the decree of the king condemned him to death. ⁵⁸They kept using violence against Israel, against those found month after month in the cities. ⁵⁹And on the twenty-fifth day of the month they offered sacrifice on the altar which was upon the altar of burnt offering. ⁶⁰According to the decree, they put to death the women who had their children circumcised, ⁶¹and their families and those who circumcised them; and they hung the infants from their mothers' necks.

⁶²But many in Israel stood firm and were resolved in their hearts not to eat unclean food. ⁶³They chose to die rather than to be defiled by food or to profane the holy covenant; and they did die. ⁶⁴And very great wrath came upon Israel.

The persecution of Antiochus is represented as the arbitrary attempt of the king to impose uniformity on his subjects. In fact, there is no evidence that peoples other than the Jews were addressed in the king's edict. (The neighboring and related Samaritans may also have been involved.) 1 Maccabees may be attempting to maximize the evil of the king, or may be relating the persecution to the king's general promotion of Hellenism. It is apparent, however, that this persecution of Judaism was not an entirely new departure, but was the culmination of the chain of events initiated by the Hellenistic reform in Jerusalem itself.

Prior to the king's edict the conflict in Jerusalem might

possibly have been seen as one between a rigid and exclusive traditionalism and a new universalistic view of Judaism which was open to Greek culture. The edict, however, is itself rigidly exclusive of traditional Judaism. Jewish tradition and Hellenistic culture are now set up as mutually exclusive. The king is attempting to suppress the distinctive identity of the Jews, presumably because he saw it as a source of insubordination. He rightly perceived that their distinctive identity was rooted in their religious symbols.

The terms of the edict are specifically designed for the Jews. The issues are public sacrifice, use of the sanctuary, observance of the sabbath, circumcision and dietary laws. These are the externals of the religion. Antiochus does not attempt to convert the Jews to a new philosophy. His assault is directed to the visible symbols, on the assumption that without these things the religion can not survive. We do not know whether those who complied with the edict really intended to reject Judaism, or felt that the externals of the religion were dispensable. It is quite clear, however, that the Jews who resisted shared Antiochus' appreciation of the importance of symbols, and felt that the religion vitally needed them.

In December, 167 BCE, a "desolating sacrilege" was introduced into the temple. This was "the abomination that makes desolate" which we have met in Daniel, and which became a motif of the eschatological woes in the New Testament (Mark 13:14). The reference is to an altar which was superimposed on the altar of sacrifice, as is made clear in 1:59. Here as in the Book of Daniel the profanation of the temple is the greatest horror of all. Later Judaism would learn to live without the temple (as indeed the Jews in exile had lived without it in practice). Yet the danger to the temple symbolized most dramatically the threat to the people's existence. On both the communal and personal levels, this was a struggle of life and death.

1 MAC 2:1-28: THE ZEAL OF MATTATHIAS

2 In those days Mattathias the son of John, son of Simeon, a priest of the sons of Joarib, moved from Jerusalem and settled in Modein. ²He had five sons, John surnamed Gaddi, ³Simon called Thassi, ⁴Judas called Maccabeus, ⁵Eleazar called Avaran, and Jonathan called Apphus. ⁶He saw the blasphemies being committed in Judah and Jerusalem, ⁷and said,

"Alas! Why was I born to see this,
the ruin of my people, the ruin of the holy city,
and to dwell there when it was given over to the enemy,
the sanctuary given over to aliens?
⁸Her temple has become like a man without honor;
⁹her glorious vessels have been carried into captivity.
Her babes have been killed in her streets,
her youths by the sword of the foe.
¹⁰What nation has not inherited her palaces
and has not seized her spoils?
¹¹All her adornment has been taken away;
no longer free, she has become a slave.
¹²And behold, our holy place, our beauty,
and our glory have been laid waste;
the Gentiles have profaned it.
¹³Why should we live any longer?''

¹⁴And Mattathias and his sons rent their clothes, put on sackcloth and mourned greatly.

¹⁵Then the king's officers who were enforcing the apostasy came to the city of Modein to make them offer sacrifice. ¹⁶Many from Israel came to them; and Mattathias and his sons were assembled. ¹⁷Then the king's officers spoke to Mattathias as follows: "You are a leader, honored and great in this city, and supported by sons and brothers. ¹⁸Now be the first to come and do what the king commands, as all the Gentiles and the men of Judah and

those that are left in Jerusalem have done. Then you and your sons will be numbered among the friends of the king, and you and your sons will be honored with silver and gold and many gifts.''

[19]But Mattathias answered and said in a loud voice: "Even if all the nations that live under the rule of the king obey him, and have chosen to do his commandments, departing each one from the religion of his fathers, [20]yet I and my sons and my brothers will live by the covenant of our fathers. [21]Far be it from us to desert the law and the ordinances. [22]We will not obey the king's words by turning aside from our religion to the right hand or to the left.''

[23]When he had finished speaking these words, a Jew came forward in the sight of all to offer sacrifice upon the altar in Modein, according to the king's command. [24]When Mattathias saw it, he burned with zeal and his heart was stirred. He gave vent to righteous anger; he ran and killed him upon the altar. [25]At the same time he killed the king's officer who was forcing them to sacrifice, and he tore down the altar. [26]Thus he burned with zeal for the law, as Phinehas did against Zimri the son of Salu.

[27]Then Mattathias cried out in the city with a loud voice, saying: "Let every one who is zealous for the law and supports the covenant come out with me!'' [28]And he and his sons fled to the hills and left all that they had in the city.

1 Mac 2 introduces the heroes of the story, Mattathias and his sons. They had moved from Jerusalem to the village of Modein, presumably to avoid persecution. Here for the third time the author inserts a poetic lament for the ruin of people and city. This time the lament is on the lips of Mattathias. Again, the passage could have been written in reference to the destruction of Jerusalem by the Babylonians.

The poetic passages in 1 Mac 1 and 2 evoke the greatest crisis of Israel's past—the fall of Jerusalem, and specifically, of the temple. This event cast its shadow over post-exilic Judaism in much the same way that the Holocaust does over our own generation. Now the Jews were faced with the re-enactment of that great disaster. Mattathias and his sons mourn for what has happened, but they are not about to bow before it. Theirs is not the way of martyrdom, and their resistance is not passive.

The response of Mattathias to the king's officers is a ringing affirmation of the human right to independence. Even if all the nations obey the king, he and his sons would not. The essential issue here is self-determination. The merits of sabbath observance and circumcision are not debated in themselves. The point is that these are the customs of the Jewish people, handed down from their fathers. Fidelity to tradition is seen as a virtue in itself, and there is even an implication that pagan nations did wrong when they abandoned their own customs. Any people has a right to its own traditions. At no point do the Maccabees dwell on the finer points of the teaching of the prophets. They are not great teachers of ethics. The religion they fight to preserve is that which has shaped the customs of their people. In defending that religion they are defending their own dignity and self-respect.

The act of zeal

The piety of Mattathias finds expression when a Jew comes forward to offer sacrifice. He burns with zeal and slays the man upon the altar. His action is justified by reference to a paradigmatic story in the Old Testament. In Numbers 25, when an Israelite, Zimri the son of Salu, brings a Midianite woman into the camp, Phinehas, son of Eleazar, son of Aaron the priest, took a spear and pierced the couple together. By this act he is said to turn back the wrath of God, and he is given a covenant of peace and of perpetual priesthood. Zeal, then, after the model of Phinehas, is the righteous anger which endorses the use of violence for religious goals.

The ideal of zeal, portrayed in the biblical story of Phinehas and amplified in the story of the Maccabees, had a fateful history in the following centuries. It is from this background that the revolutionaries against Rome were called Zealots. (The name does not denote a well-defined party, but a political and religious attitude.) Their precedent has often been followed by Jews and Christians alike in subsequent centuries down to the present.

From a modern perspective, it seems easier to justify the action of Mattathias, who was resisting oppression, than that of the biblical Phinehas, who was extreme in his intolerance. The subsequent history of the Maccabees makes that distinction difficult to maintain. Once violence is admitted in the cause of a religion, it is difficult to draw the line with strictly defensive measures.

1 MAC 2:29-38: THE MARTYRS IN THE WILDERNESS

[29]Then many who were seeking righteousness and justice went down to the wilderness to dwell there, [30]they, their sons, their wives, and their cattle, because evils pressed heavily upon them. [31]And it was reported to the king's officers, and to the troops in Jerusalem the city of David, that men who had rejected the king's command had gone down to the hiding places in the wilderness. [32]Many pursued them, and overtook them; they encamped opposite them and prepared for battle against them on the sabbath day. [33]And they said to them, "Enough of this! Come out and do what the king commands, and you will live." [34]But they said, "We will not come out, nor will we do what the king commands and so profane the sabbath day." [35]Then

the enemy hastened to attack them. ³⁶But they did not answer them or hurl a stone at them or block up their hiding places, ³⁷for they said, "Let us all die in our innocence; heaven and earth testify for us that you are killing us unjustly." ³⁸So they attacked them on the sabbath, and they died, with their wives and children and cattle, to the number of a thousand persons.

Not all Jews took the militant line of the Maccabees. Many "who were seeking righteousness and justice" tried to avoid the conflict by withdrawing to the wilderness. It is not clear from this story whether these people were committed to non-violence, or, as rather appears from the story, were only strict observers of the law, which forbade them to fight on the sabbath. The sabbath posed an awkward problem for militant Jews throughout this period. On the one hand, both the Maccabean rebellion and the war against Rome were avowedly fought in defence of the law. Yet strict observance of the law would prevent them from defending themselves on the sabbath. So the choice was either to break the law which they were fighting to defend, or to let themselves be killed. (We hear of the same dilemma in the context of the war against Rome.) The Jews who had hidden in the wilderness made their choice, and died in their innocence.

Light is thrown on the mentality of these people by their dying protestation, calling on heaven and earth to testify for them. This appeal suggests another biblical paradigm, different from the Phinehas story. Deuteronomy 32 begins with an appeal to heaven and earth. Later in that chapter we read that the Lord says: "Vengeance is mine and recompense" for God avenges the blood of his servants and takes vengeance on his adversaries. By preserving their innocence these martyrs hoped to bring down a heavier vengeance on their enemies.

Further light is shed on this episode by the non-canonical

Testament of Moses (also called the Assumption of Moses)
which in its original form probably dates from Maccabean
times. There we hear of a man named Taxo, who took his
seven sons and resolved to go into a cave and die rather than
transgress the law, "for if we do this and die, our blood will
be avenged before the Lord." Then the kingdom of God
would be revealed before the whole earth.

The mentality of the martyrs in 1 Mac 2 and of Taxo in the
Testament of Moses is quite similar to that of the visions of
Daniel, and quite different from that of the Maccabees.
What is important here is the full observance of the law.
Vengeance is in the hands of God. We do not know whether
the martyrs in 1 Mac 2 expected to be vindicated in an after-
life, but by analogy with Daniel, the Testament of Moses and
2 Maccabees, they probably did. The pacifistic attitude in
the present is based on the assumption that God will act for
them, and also that the kingdom they hope to inherit is not
of this world. These expectations gave the martyrs an im-
pressive ability to act according to their consciences even in
the face of death.

1 MAC 2:39-48: THE REACTION OF MATTATHIAS

[39]When Mattathias and his friends learned of it, they
mourned for them deeply. [40]And each said to his
neighbor: "If we all do as our brethren have done and
refuse to fight with the Gentiles for our lives and our ordinances, they will quickly destroy us from the earth."
[41]So they made this decision that day: "Let us fight
against every man who comes to attack us on the sabbath
day; let us not all die as our brethren died in their hiding
places."

[42]Then there united with them a company of Hasideans, mighty warriors of Israel, every one who offered

himself willingly for the law. [43]And all who became
fugitives to escape their troubles joined them and rein-
forced them. [44]They organized an army, and struck down
sinners in their anger and lawless men in their wrath; the
survivors fled to the Gentiles for safety. [45]And Mattathias
and his friends went about and tore down the altars;
[46]they forcibly circumcised all the uncircumcised boys
that they found within the borders of Israel. [47]They
hunted down the arrogant men, and the work prospered
in their hands. [48]They rescued the law out of the hands of
the Gentiles and kings, and they never let the sinner gain
the upper hand.

The reaction of the Maccabees was frank and realistic. If
they continued to observe the sabbath strictly, there would
soon be no one left to observe the law at all. Better to break
one commandment that the others should be preserved. In
fact, the concern of the Maccabees is not primarily with the
preservation of the law, but with the preservation of the
Jewish people. This attitude should not be dismissed as cyni-
cal pragmatism. From the Maccabean viewpoint, the law is a
major factor in the identity of the people, but is not separable
from them. The people is ultimately more important than
the law. The sabbath was made for man, not man for the
sabbath. The Maccabean attitude also shows a fuller sense
of human responsibility for the outcome of the crisis.

The Maccabees are now joined by the Hasideans who are
described as mighty warriors. Contrary to what is often
stated in commentaries, there is no reason to assume that
this was the group from which the martyrs in the wilderness
came, or that the Book of Daniel reflects their views. There
is some reason to believe that they had already been active
before they united with the Maccabees. They may have been

already in revolt at the time Jerusalem was plundered by Apollonius. Later we find that these Hasideans are the group most willing to make peace, but nevertheless they are mighty warriors, and not in any way pacifistic.

The guerrilla warfare of Mattathias and his companions quickly moves beyond the purely defensive. Their zeal is directed against "lawless men," presumably those who co-operate with the policy of Hellenization. Their action includes forcible circumcision. Religious liberty is not the issue here but the triumph of traditional Judaism "within the borders of Israel." It is noteworthy that the terms "gen-tile" and "sinner" are used virtually interchangeably.

1 MAC 2:49-70: THE TESTAMENT OF MATTATHIAS

⁴⁹Now the days drew near for Mattathias to die, and he said to his sons: "Arrogance and reproach have now become strong; it is a time of ruin and furious anger. ⁵⁰Now, my children, show zeal for the law, and give your lives for the covenant of our fathers.

⁵¹"Remember the deeds of the fathers, which they did in their generations; and receive great honor and an everlasting name. ⁵²Was not Abraham found faithful when tested, and it was reckoned to him as righteousness? ⁵³Joseph in the time of his distress kept the command-ment, and became lord of Egypt. ⁵⁴Phinehas our father, because he was deeply zealous, received the covenant of everlasting priesthood. ⁵⁵Joshua, because he fulfilled the command, became a judge in Israel. ⁵⁶Caleb, because he testified in the assembly, received an inheritance in the land. ⁵⁷David, because he was merciful, inherited the throne of the kingdom for ever. ⁵⁸Elijah because of great zeal for the law was taken up into heaven. ⁵⁹Hananiah, Azariah, and Mishael believed and were saved from the

flame. ⁶⁰Daniel because of his innocence was delivered from the mouth of the lions.

⁶¹"And so observe, from generation to generation, that none who put their trust in him will lack strength. ⁶²Do not fear the words of a sinner, for his splendor will turn into dung and worms. ⁶³Today he will be exalted, but tomorrow he will not be found, because he has returned to the dust, and his plans will perish. ⁶⁴My children, be courageous and grow strong in the law, for by it you will gain honor.

⁶⁵"Now behold, I know that Simeon your brother is wise in counsel; always listen to him; he shall be your father. ⁶⁶Judas Maccabeus has been a mighty warrior from his youth; he shall command the army for you and fight the battle against the peoples. ⁶⁷You shall rally about you all who observe the law, and avenge the wrong done to your people. ⁶⁸Pay back the Gentiles in full, and heed what the law commands."

⁶⁹Then he blessed them, and was gathered to his fathers. ⁷⁰He died in the one hundred and forty-sixth year and was buried in the tomb of his fathers at Modein. And all Israel mourned for him with great lamentation.

The death-bed speech of Mattathias recalls the testament of Jacob, the father of Israel, in Genesis 49. Three main points are made:

First, the sons should give their lives for the covenant of the fathers. The warriors are no less prepared than the martyrs to lose their own lives.

Second, a catalogue of great names is recited to show that no one who puts his trust in God lacks strength. Prominent in the list are Phinehas and Elijah, the men of zeal. The list also includes Daniel and the three young men of the fiery furnace. While the Maccabees do not count on miraculous deliverance but are ready to lay down their lives, the memory of these stories can boost their courage. Fidelity under duress is the main trait emphasized in the list. Zeal is also noted as a virture. Oddly enough, David is said to have inherited the kingdom because he was merciful. This particular virtue does not receive much attention elsewhere in 1 Maccabees.

Third, in 2:65-68 Mattathias provides the quasi-official legitimation for the organization and program of the Maccabees. Judas is the general, designated by his father. His authority is still grounded in the Maccabean family. The battle is to be fought against the peoples and is designed to pay back the gentiles in full. Vengeance is in the hands of the Maccabees, not of God. The explicit nationalism of 1 Maccabees is apparent here. We will find some qualification of the animosity towards the gentiles in later chapters. It is also true that 1 Maccabees recognizes that there were renegade Jews. Yet the conflict is set up as one between the Jewish people and the gentiles. There is no appreciation here of Judaism as a religion transcending national bounds. On the contrary, Judaism here is the religious ideology which legitimates and sustains the Jewish people, in their quest not only for independence but also for power. This may not be the most attractive theology for the modern taste, but it highlights a major role that religion has always played, in every society. While we may suspect that the Maccabees were using their tradition rather than being guided by it, we must bear in mind that biblical material had always functioned in this way. The list of names mentioned by Mattathias (Joseph, Joshua, David) provided ample precedent for the close association of the God of Israel with the political fortunes of the Jewish people.

Part Two: The Career of Judas

1 MAC 3:1-9: THE GLORY OF HIS PEOPLE

3 Then Judas his son, who was called Maccabeus, took command in his place. ²All his brothers and all who had joined his father helped him; they gladly fought for Israel.

³He extended the glory of his people. Like a giant he put
on his breastplate;
he girded on his armor of war and waged battles,
protecting the host by his sword.
⁴He was like a lion in his deeds,
like a lion's cub roaring for prey.
⁵He searched out and pursued the lawless;
he burned those who troubled his people.
⁶Lawless men shrank back for fear of him;
all the evildoers were confounded; and deliverance
prospered by his hand.
⁷He embittered many kings,
but he made Jacob glad by his deeds,
and his memory is blessed for ever.
⁸He went through the cities of Judah;
he destroyed the ungodly out of the land;
thus he turned away wrath from Israel.
⁹He was renowned to the ends of the earth;
he gathered in those who were perishing.

I Mac 3 begins with a hymn in praise of Judas, the mighty warrior. The picture of the giant dressing for battle recalls the portrayal of the Divine Warrior in the Old Testament — e.g. Isa 59: 16-19 where Yahweh prepares for battle, glorious in his apparel. While the prophet looked to God as the mighty warrior, and the apocalyptic visionary looked to an angel such as Michael, 1 Maccabees looks to Judas. The human hero was not without precedent. Ben Sira (Ecclesiasticus) writing in the early part of the second century BCE sang the praises of the famous men of old. Among them was Joshua "a great savior of God's elect": "How glorious he was when he lifted his hands and stretched out his sword against the cities. . . for he waged the wars of the Lord" (Sir 46:2-3). Judas is the new Joshua, and much of the narrative is colored with motifs from the wars of the Lord in Joshua and Judges. The last verse of the hymn suggests even more. The one who is renowned to the ends of the earth and gathers in those who were perishing has some characteristics of a royal messiah. Compare Isa 11:10-11: "In that day the root of Jesse shall stand as an ensign to the peoples; him shall the nations seek, and his dwelling shall be glorious. In that day the Lord will extend his hand yet a second time to recover the remnant which is left of his people. . . " We will meet further messianic motifs in connection with the Maccabean house.

1 MAC 3:10-26: JUDAS' INITIAL VICTORIES

10But Apollonius gathered together Gentiles and a large force from Samaria to fight against Israel. 11When Judas learned of it, he went out to meet him, and he defeated and killed him. Many were wounded and fell, and the rest fled. 12Then they seized their spoils; and Judas took the sword of Apollonius, and used it in battle the rest of his life.

13Now when Seron, the commander of the Syrian army, heard that Judas had gathered a large compàny, including a body of faithful men who stayed with him and went out to battle, 14he said, "I will make a name for myself and win honor in the kingdom. I will make war on Judas and his companions, who scorn the king's command." 15And again a strong army of ungodly men went up with him to help him, to take vengeance on the sons of Israel.

[16]When he approached the ascent of Beth-horon, Judas went out to meet him with a small company. [17]But when they saw the army coming to meet them, they said to Judas, "How can we, few as we are, fight against so great and strong a multitude? And we are faint, for we have eaten nothing today." [18]Judas replied, "It is easy for many to be hemmed in by few, for in the sight of Heaven there is no difference between saving by many or by few. [19]It is not on the size of the army that victory in battle depends, but strength comes from Heaven. [20]They come against us in great pride and lawlessness to destroy us and our wives and our children, and to despoil us; [21]but we fight for our lives and our laws. [22]He himself will crush them before us; as for you, do not be afraid of them."

[23]When he finished speaking, he rushed suddenly against Seron and his army, and they were crushed before him. [24]They pursued them down the descent of Beth-horon to the plain; eight hundred of them fell, and the rest fled into the land of the Philistines. [25]Then Judas and his brothers began to be feared, and terror fell upon the Gentiles round about them. [26]His fame reached the king, and the Gentiles talked of the battles of Judas.

The first victory of Judas is over Apollonius, presumably the one who had plundered Jerusalem at the outbreak of the persecution. This is followed by the defeat of Seron, a Syrian general, at Beth-horon. The account emphasizes that the Jews were few and their enemies many. The motif is familiar from the historical books of the Old Testament. (Compare the words of Jonathan in 1 Sam 14:6: "nothing can hinder the Lord from saving by many or by few.") The most memorable illustration is that of Gideon in Judges 7, where Gideon is told to reduce his number, lest Israel say "My own hand has delivered me." Again, the fear that fell on the gentiles round about recalls the fear that fell on the nations after the Exodus, at the beginning of the conquest

(Exodus 15:15-16; Joshua 5:1). Despite the generally realistic tone of the account, the old theology of holy war is in the background here. The battle depends not on the size of the army but on the strength that comes from heaven. Such beliefs undoubtedly bolstered the courage of the guerrilla fighters. It also deepened the conviction that "God's on our side," and that the justice of Judas and his cause were guaranteed by his military success.

1 MAC 3:27-4:35: THE BATTLES OF EMMAUS AND BETH-ZUR

²⁷When King Antiochus heard these reports, he was greatly angered; and he sent and gathered all the forces of his kingdom, a very strong army. ²⁸And he opened his coffers and gave a year's pay to his forces, and ordered them to be ready for any need. ²⁹Then he saw that the money in the treasury was exhausted, and that the revenues from the country were small because of the dissension and disaster which he had caused in the land by abolishing the laws that had existed from the earlier days. ³⁰He feared that he might not have such funds as he had before for his expenses and for the gifts which he used to give more lavishly than preceding kings. ³¹He was greatly perplexed in mind, and determined to go to Persia and collect the revenues from those regions and raise a large fund.

³²He left Lysias, a distinguished man of royal lineage, in charge of the king's affairs from the river Euphrates to the borders of Egypt. ³³Lysias was also to take care of Antiochus his son until he returned. ³⁴And he turned over to Lysias half of his troops and the elephants, and gave him orders about all that he wanted done. As for the residents of Judea and Jerusalem, ³⁵Lysias was to send a force against them to wipe out and destroy the strength of Israel and the remnant of Jerusalem; he was to banish the

memory of them from the place, ³⁶settle aliens in all their territory, and distribute their land. ³⁷Then the king took the remaining half of his troops and departed from Antioch his capital in the one hundred and forty-seventh year. He crossed the Euphrates river and went through the upper provinces.

³⁸Lysias chose Ptolemy the son of Dorymenes, and Nicanor and Gorgias, mighty men among the friends of the king, ³⁹and sent with them forty thousand infantry and seven thousand cavalry to go into the land of Judah and destroy it, as the king had commanded. ⁴⁰So they departed with their entire force, and when they arrived they encamped near Emmaus in the plain. ⁴¹When the traders of the region heard what was said of them, they took silver and gold in immense amounts, and fetters, and went to the camp to get the sons of Israel for slaves. And forces from Syria and the land of the Philistines joined with them.

⁴²Now Judas and his brothers saw that misfortunes had increased and that the forces were encamped in their territory. They also learned what the king had commanded to do to the people to cause their final destruction. ⁴³But they said to one another, "Let us repair the destruction of our people, and fight for our people and the sanctuary." ⁴⁴And the congregation assembled to be ready for battle, and to pray and ask for mercy and compassion.

⁴⁵Jerusalem was uninhabited like a wilderness;
not one of her children went in or out.
The sanctuary was trampled down, and the sons of aliens
      held the citadel;
it was a lodging place for the Gentiles.
Joy was taken from Jacob;
the flute and the harp ceased to play.

⁴⁶So they assembled and went to Mizpah, opposite Jerusalem, because Israel formerly had a place of prayer in

Mizpah. [47]They fasted that day, put on sackcloth and sprinkled ashes on their heads, and rent their clothes. [48]And they opened the book of the law to inquire into those matters about which the Gentiles were consulting the images of their idols. [49]They also brought the garments of the priesthood and the first fruits and the tithes, and they stirred up the Nazirites who had completed their days; [50]and they cried aloud to Heaven, saying,

"What shall we do with these?
Where shall we take them?
[51]Thy sanctuary is trampled down and profaned,
and thy priests mourn in humiliation.
[52]And behold, the Gentiles are assembled against us to
destroy us;
thou knowest what they plot against us.
[53]How will we be able to withstand them,
if thou dost not help us?"

[54]Then they sounded the trumpets and gave a loud shout. [55]After this Judas appointed leaders of the people, in charge of thousands and hundreds and fifties and tens. [56]And he said to those who were building houses, or were betrothed, or were planting vineyards, or were faint-hearted, that each should return to his home, according to the law. [57]Then the army marched out and encamped to the south of Emmaus.

[58]And Judas said, "Gird yourselves and be valiant. Be ready early in the morning to fight with these Gentiles who have assembled against us to destroy us and our sanctuary. [59]It is better for us to die in battle than to see the misfortunes of our nation and of the sanctuary. [60]But as his will in heaven may be, so he will do."

4 Now Gorgias took five thousand infantry and a thousand picked cavalry, and this division moved out by night [2]to fall upon the camp of the Jews and attack them suddenly. Men from the citadel were his guides. [3]But Judas

heard of it, and he and his mighty men moved out to attack the king's force in Emmaus ⁴while the division was still absent from the camp. ⁵When Gorgias entered the camp of Judas by night, he found no one there, so he looked for them in the hills, because he said, "These men are fleeing from us."

⁶At daybreak Judas appeared in the plain with three thousand men, but they did not have armor and swords such as they desired. ⁷And they saw the camp of the Gentiles, strong and fortified, with cavalry round about it; and these men were trained in war. ⁸But Judas said to the men who were with him, "Do not fear their numbers or be afraid when they charge. ⁹Remember how our fathers were saved at the Red Sea, when Pharaoh with his forces pursued them. ¹⁰And now let us cry to Heaven, to see whether he will favor us and remember his covenant with our fathers and crush this army before us today. ¹¹Then all the Gentiles will know that there is one who redeems and saves Israel."

¹²When the foreigners looked up and saw them coming against them, ¹³they went forth from their camp to battle. Then the men with Judas blew their trumpets ¹⁴and engaged in battle. The Gentiles were crushed and fled into the plain, ¹⁵and all those in the rear fell by the sword. They pursued them to Gazara, and to the plains of Idumea, and to Azotus and Jamnia; and three thousand of them fell. ¹⁶Then Judas and his force turned back from pursuing them, ¹⁷and he said to the people, "Do not be greedy for plunder, for there is a battle before us; ¹⁸Gorgias and his force are near us in the hills. But stand now against our enemies and fight them, and afterward seize the plunder boldly."

¹⁹Just as Judas was finishing this speech, a detachment appeared, coming out of the hills. ²⁰They saw that their army had been put to flight, and that the Jews were burn-

ing the camp, for the smoke that was seen showed what
had happened. ²¹When they perceived this they were
greatly frightened, and when they also saw the army of
Judas drawn up in the plain for battle, ²²they all fled into
the land of the Philistines. ²³Then Judas returned to
plunder the camp, and they seized much gold and silver,
and cloth dyed blue and sea purple, and great riches. ²⁴On
their return they sang hymns and praises to Heaven, for
he is good, for his mercy endures for ever. ²⁵Thus Israel
had a great deliverance that day.

²⁶Those of the foreigners who escaped went and
reported to Lysias all that had happened. ²⁷When he
heard it, he was perplexed and discouraged, for things
had not happened to Israel as he had intended, nor had
they turned out as the king had commanded him. ²⁸But
the next year he mustered sixty thousand picked infan-
trymen and five thousand cavalry to subdue them. ²⁹They
came into Idumea and encamped at Beth-zur, and Judas
met them with ten thousand men.

³⁰When he saw that the army was strong, he prayed,
saying, "Blessed art thou, O Savior of Israel, who didst
crush the attack of the mighty warrior by the hand of thy
servant David, and didst give the camp of the Philistines
into the hands of Jonathan, the son of Saul, and of the
man who carried his armor. ³¹So do thou hem in this army
by the hand of thy people Israel, and let them be ashamed
of their troops and their cavalry. ³²Fill them with cowardice; melt the boldness of their strength; let them tremble in
their destruction. ³³Strike them down with the sword of
those who love thee, and let all who know thy name praise
thee with hymns.

³⁴Then both sides attacked, and there fell of the army of
Lysias five thousand men; they fell in action. ³⁵And when
Lysias saw the rout of his troops and observed the
boldness which inspired those of Judas, and how ready

they were either to live or to die nobly, he departed to Antioch and enlisted mercenaries, to invade Judea again with an even larger army.

The generals sent by Lysias pose a threat of far greater magnitude than that of the previous Syrian commanders, as can be seen by the threat to sell Jews into slavery. This threat is also reflected in 2 Mac 8, and had particularly deep-rooted associations for the Jews, in view of the biblical story of slavery in Egypt.

The Jews prepare for the battle at Mizpah. This episode echoes 1 Samuel 7, where the Israelites are gathered at Mizpah by Samuel to fast and confess their sins before a battle with the Philistines. The passage emphasizes the careful observance of the old traditions, including the consultation of the law, which had been outlawed by the king. Judas behaves like Moses in Deuteronomy, appointing his officers (compare Deut 1:15) and in accordance with the prescriptions of the Law of Moses in sending home those who were betrothed, engaged in building or planting, or faint-hearted (compare Deut 20:5-8). Judas is carefully portrayed as an exact observer of the law. Despite the agreement to fight on the sabbath in chap. 2, he keeps the intrusion on the sabbath to an minimum. All of this is by way of ensuring the support of God in the battle. At the same time, the poetic passages keep the desecrated temple in view as the ultimate motivating factor. The temple is the central symbol of the nation. Its desecration is the humiliation of the people, and it is better to die in battle than endure that humiliation. The gentiles are assembled to destroy not only the temple but also the Jews. What is at issue is the preservation of the nation.

The battle is decided by tactical manoeuvres. Judas eludes Gorgias' surprise attack, appears unexpectedly in the plain and catches the Syrian army divided. In typical biblical style, however, 1 Maccabees does not attribute the victory to such human factors but to the power of God. The victory at Emmaus is an act of God as surely as the crossing of the sea in Exodus. The battle at Beth-zur in 4:30-35 is similarly explained. Before the battle Judas asks God to give him victory as he gave it to David and Jonathan, by filling the enemy with cowardice.

The theology of victory

After the battles the Jews give praise to God. There is something ironic in the hymn that is sung in vs. 24—"for he is good, and his mercy endures forever" (Ps. 136). Mercy is manifested in military victory. True, the battles of Judas are still defensive ones, and his victories bring liberation to the Jews. Yet we must note the close identification of the divinity with the interests of a specific people.

The prayer before the battle of Beth-zur must strike us as even more ironic: "strike them down with the sword of those who love thee." It is assumed that the enemies of the Jews are the enemies of God. Love of God does not involve any desire for reconciliation with the enemy. 1 Maccabees' attitude towards the gentiles is the attitude of the psalmist: "I hate them with perfect hatred" (Ps. 139:22).

In all of this, 1 Maccabees was drawing on beliefs and assumptions which had a venerable history in the Old Testament, and would continue to figure prominently in Judaism and in Christianity alike. As we noted above, Judas is the new Joshua. The re-birth of the Jewish nation is conceived in ways that are similar to its original birth. God is known as the champion of the Jewish people. Their victory is taken as a sign of his power. It is probably true that the more profound parts of the biblical tradition were born out of the failures and set-backs of the Jewish people rather than out of their victories. Yet few peoples have been able to resist the assumption that their triumphs reflect the favor of divinity. The basic revelations of the Old Testament were precisely the "mighty acts of God" in the victories that brought Israel into being. If the claim for "acts of God" was justified in the case of Joshua, it is surely justified in the case of Judas too, but our better knowledge of the historical circumstances of the Maccabees allows us to see the difficulty and ambiguity involved in claiming that any human victories are "acts of God."

1 MAC 4:36-60: THE RE-CONSECRATION OF THE TEMPLE

[36]Then said Judas and his brothers, "Behold, our enemies are crushed; let us go up to cleanse the sanctuary and dedicate it." [37]So all the army assembled and they went up to Mount Zion. [38]And they saw the sanctuary desolate, the altar profaned, and the gates burned. In the courts they saw bushes sprung up as in a thicket, or as on one of the mountains. They saw also the chambers of the priests in ruins. [39]Then they rent their clothes, and mourned with great lamentation, and sprinkled themselves with ashes. [40]They fell face down on the ground, and sounded the signal on the trumpets, and cried out to Heaven. [41]Then Judas detailed men to fight against those in the citadel until he had cleansed the sanctuary.

[42]He chose blameless priests devoted to the law, [43]and they cleansed the sanctuary and removed the defiled stones to an unclean place. [44]They deliberated what to do about the altar of burnt offering, which had been profaned. [45]And they thought it best to tear it down, lest it bring reproach upon them, for the Gentiles had defiled it. So they tore down the altar, [46]and stored the stones in a convenient place on the temple hill until there should come a prophet to tell what to do with them. [47]Then they took unhewn stones, as the law directs, and built a new altar like the former one. [48]They also rebuilt the sanctuary and

the interior of the temple, and consecrated the courts.
⁴⁹They made new holy vessels, and brought the lampstand,
the altar of incense, and the table into the temple. ⁵⁰Then
they burned incense on the altar and lighted the lamps on
the lampstand, and these gave light in the temple. ⁵¹They
placed the bread on the table and hung up the curtains.
Thus they finished all the work they had undertaken.

⁵²Early in the morning on the twenty-fifth day of the
ninth month, which is the month of Chislev, in the one
hundred and forty-eighth year, ⁵³they rose and offered
sacrifice, as the law directs, on the new altar of burnt offerings which they had built. ⁵⁴At the very season and on
the very day that the Gentiles had profaned it, it was
dedicated with songs and harps and lutes and cymbals.
⁵⁵All the people fell on their faces and worshiped and
blessed Heaven, who had prospered them. ⁵⁶So they celebrated the dedication of the altar for eight days, and offered burnt offerings with gladness; they offered a sacrifice of deliverance and praise. ⁵⁷They decorated the front
of the temple with golden crowns and small shields; they
restored the gates and the chambers for the priests, and
furnished them with doors. ⁵⁸There was very great gladness among the people, and the reproach of the Gentiles
was removed.

⁵⁹Then Judas and his brothers and all the assembly of
Israel determined that every year at that season the days
of the dedication of the altar should be observed with
gladness and joy for eight days, beginning with the
twenty-fifth day of the month of Chislev.

⁶⁰At that time they fortified Mount Zion with high
walls and strong towers round about, to keep the Gentiles
from coming and trampling them down as they had done
before. ⁶¹And he stationed a garrison there to hold it. He
also fortified Beth-zur, so that the people might have a
stronghold that faced Idumea.

After his great victories in battle, Judas goes up to Mt. Zion. The historical sequence of events here conforms to an ancient pattern: compare Exodus 15, where, after the victory at the sea, we are told that God will bring in his people and plant them on his holy mountain. The sequence is natural enough. The desecration of the temple was a glaring eye-sore in the land. Its re-dedication symbolized the re-establishment of the Jewish people.

Throughout antiquity temples were thought to have central importance in the order of creation. The holy mountain was thought to be the navel of the earth, its center point, the point of connection between heaven and earth. The right maintenance of the temple was essential if there was to be right order in the world. In the Old Testament psalms we hear that Mt. Zion, the holy mountain, is the joy of all the earth. God is in its midst. So the Israelites need not fear "though the earth should change" and "the mountains shake in the heart of the sea" (Pss. 48 [47]; 46 [45]). When the temple lay desolate that assurance of security was gone. the work of Judas, then, was not only repeating the conquest of the land. In a sense it was repeating the work of creation, by restoring right order in place of chaos.

The entire sanctuary is built anew, faithfully following the instructions of the Torah (e.g. in the use of unhewn stones, compare Exod 20:25; Joshua 8:31). The stones of the old altar are stored "until there should come a prophet." There had been no authoritative prophets for many centuries, although various forms of prophecy always persisted. The present passage seems to point forward to the (distant) expectation of an eschatological prophet—a prophet like Moses (Deut 18:15) or Elijah (Mal 4:5). We will find a similar expression later when Simon is appointed high priest (14:41). It is evident that 1 Maccabees does not expect such an authoritative prophet soon. By contrast, the Dead Sea Scrolls predict the coming of a prophet, with the messiahs of

Aaron and Israel, to usher in the messianic age. In 1 Maccabees, however, the deliverance is brought about through the Maccabean family. It is still the work of God, but it is not overtly supernatural. The remoteness of the eschatological prophet goes hand in hand with the view that authority is given to the Maccabees for the present. There is no desire to see the present age come to an end. It is sufficient that it be transformed by Judas and his brothers.

The re-dedication of the temple is a major step in that transformation. It takes place in December 164 BCE "at the very season and on the very day that the gentiles had profaned it." The annual celebration of the feast, Hanukkah, marks the occasion as comparable to the major events of Israel's history, such as the Passover. It is the foundational event for a new order.

The fortification of Mt. Zion recalls the assurance of the psalmist: "within her citadels God has shown himself a sure defence" (Ps. 48 [47]: 3). We must note the realism of the Maccabees here. It is not enough to believe that God will protect Mt. Zion, although they surely believed that he would. It is also necessary to station a garrison there. Recent history had shown that God did not always protect it. The Maccabees believed that God helps those who help themselves.

1 MAC 5: GATHERING IN THE SCATTERED JEWS

5 When the Gentiles round about heard that the altar had been built and the sanctuary dedicated as it was before, they became very angry, ²and they determined to destroy the descendants of Jacob who lived among them. So they began to kill and destroy among the people. ³But Judas made war on the sons of Esau in Idumea, at Akrabattene, because they kept lying in wait for Israel. He dealt them a heavy blow and humbled them and despoiled them. ⁴He also remembered the wickedness of the sons of Baean, who were a trap and a snare to the people and ambushed them on the highways. ⁵They were shut up by him in their towers; and he encamped against them, vowed their complete destruction, and burned with fire their towers and all who were in them. ⁶Then he crossed over to attack the Ammonites, where he found a strong band and many people with Timothy as their leader. ⁷He engaged in many battles with them and they were crushed before him; he struck them down. ⁸He also took Jazer and its villages; then he returned to Judea.

⁹Now the Gentiles in Gilead gathered together against the Israelites who lived in their territory, and planned to destroy them. But they fled to the stronghold of Dathema, ¹⁰and sent to Judas and his brothers a letter which said, "The Gentiles around us have gathered together against us to destroy us. ¹¹They are preparing to come and capture the stronghold to which we have fled, and Timothy is leading their forces. ¹²Now then come and rescue us from their hands, for many of us have fallen, ¹³and all our brethren who were in the land of Tob have been killed; the enemy have captured their wives and children and goods, and have destroyed about a thousand men there."

¹⁴While the letter was still being read, behold, other messengers, with their garments rent, came from Galilee and made a similar report; ¹⁵they said that against them had gathered together men of Ptolemais and Tyre and Sidon and all Galilee of the Gentiles, "to annihilate us." ¹⁶When Judas and the people heard these messages, a great assembly was called to determine what they should do for their brethren who were in distress and were being attacked by enemies. ¹⁷Then Judas said to Simon his brother, "Choose your men and go rescue your brethren in Galilee; I and Jonathan my brother will go to Gilead."

¹⁸But he left Joseph, the son of Zechariah, and Azariah, a leader of the people, with the rest of the forces, in Judea to guard it; ¹⁹and he gave them this command, "Take charge of this people, but do not engage in battle with the Gentiles until we return. . . ."

²⁴Judas Maccabeus and Jonathan his brother crossed the Jordan and went three days' journey into the wilderness. ²⁵They encountered the Nabateans, who met them peaceably and told them all that had happened to their brethren in Gilead. . .

⁴⁵Then Judas gathered together all the Israelites in Gilead, the small and the great, with their wives and children and goods, a very large company, to go to the land of Judah. ⁴⁶So they came to Ephron. This was a large and very strong city on the road, and they could not go round it to the right or to the left; they had to go through it. ⁴⁷But the men of the city shut them out and blocked up the gates with stones. ⁴⁸And Judas sent them this friendly message, "Let us pass through your land to get to our land. No one will do you harm; we will simply pass by on foot." But they refused to open to him. ⁴⁹Then Judas ordered proclamation to be made to the army that each should encamp where he was. ⁵⁰So the men of the forces encamped, and he fought against the city all that day and all the night, and the city was delivered into his hands. ⁵¹He destroyed every male by the edge of the sword, and razed and plundered the city. Then he passed through the city over the slain.

⁵²And they crossed the Jordan into the large plain before Beth-shan. ⁵³And Judas kept rallying the laggards and encouraging the people all the way till he came to the land of Judah. ⁵⁴So they went up to Mount Zion with gladness and joy, and offered burnt offerings, because not one of them had fallen before they returned in safety.

⁵⁵Now while Judas and Jonathan were in Gilead and

Simon his brother was in Galilee before Ptolemais, [56]Joseph, the son of Zechariah, and Azariah, the commanders of the forces, heard of their brave deeds and of the heroic war they had fought. [57]So they said, "Let us also make a name for ourselves; let us go and make war on the Gentiles around us." [58]And they issued orders to the men of the forces that were with them, and they marched against Jamnia. [59]And Gorgias and his men came out of the city to meet them in battle. [60]Then Joseph and Azariah were routed, and were pursued to the borders of Judea; as many as two thousand of the people of Israel fell that day. [61]Thus the people suffered a great rout because, thinking to do a brave deed, they did not listen to Judas and his brothers. [62]But they did not belong to the family of those men through whom deliverance was given to Israel.

[63]The man Judas and his brothers were greatly honored in all Israel and among all the Gentiles, wherever their name was heard. [64]Men gathered to them and praised them.

[65]Then Judas and his brothers went forth and fought the sons of Esau in the land to the south. He struck Hebron and its villages and tore down its strongholds and burned its towers round about. [66]Then he marched off to go into the land of the Philistines, and passed through Marisa. [67]On that day some priests, who wished to do a brave deed, fell in battle, for they went out to battle unwisely. [68]But Judas turned aside to Azotus in the land of the Philistines; he tore down their altars, and the graven images of their gods he burned with fire; he plundered the cities and returned to the land of Judah.

The re-consecration of the temple is said to enrage the gentiles. We are reminded of the opposition of the neighboring peoples to the re-building of the temple after the exile, as recorded in the Book of Ezra. The temple was a public symbol of Jewish determination to maintain a distinctive presence in the region. The opposition of the gentiles to the temple is also an old motif, reflected in e.g. Ps. 48 [47]. In 1 Mac, however, the gentiles do not launch an attack directly against the temple, but threaten the vulnerable Jews in outlying areas.

The bulk of 1 Mac 5 is taken up with the campaigns of Judas and his brothers into Galilee and Gilead (east of the sea of Galilee). The gathering in of the Jews from these areas recalls the prophetic promises that the scattered sons of Israel would be brought back (Ezek 39:27; Jer 31:10: "He who scattered Israel will gather him"). The rescued Jews go up to Zion with gladness and joy, like the pilgrims in the Psalms. The eschatological promises find historical fulfillment at the hands of the Maccabees.

The campaigns also include punitive expeditions against such old foes as the Idumaeans and Ammonites. Judas deals peaceably with the Nabataeans and attempts to do likewise with the city of Ephron, but when the latter denies him passage he razes and plunders the city. We are reminded of Moses' encounter with the Amorites in Num 21:21-30. At no point is Judas represented as fighting a war of conquest. Yet his treatment of the gentiles is ruthless. Typically, he kills every male, and razes and plunders the city. There are echoes here of the ancient *herem* or "ban" —the regulation of holy war in the days of the conquest and Judges. The alleged destruction in ancient days was even more severe: at Jericho, the Israelites were said to have "utterly destroyed all in the city, both men and women, young and old, oxen, sheep and asses with the edge of the sword" (Joshua 6:21). Judas was probably not exceptional in his severity, by the standards of his time. Yet his conception of religion was such that it justified the slaughter of his enemies, beyond what was necessary for defensive purposes. We should note that the last excursion noted in this chapter, against Azotus in the land of the Philistines, is not for the purpose of rescuing Jews but of destroying pagan religion.

1 Maccabees never questions the justification for Judas' violence. His success is taken to show that God is with him. Moreover, he is God's elect in a special sense. This claim is highlighted in 1 Mac 5:55-62. Joseph and Azariah thought to win glory for themselves by making war on the gentiles. Their failure, however, is not explained primarily as a punishment for their ambition, but by the fact that "they did not belong to the family of those men through whom deliverance was given to Israel." We are left with the impression that the keys of the kingdom have been given to the Maccabean house.

We can well appreciate how the undoubted bravery and actual success of the Maccabees might inspire such trust in their followers. Yet modern history has taught us to be wary of such automatic justification of an individual or family. Subsequent generations of Jews would also have reason to question the divine election of the Maccabean house.

1 MAC 6:1-17: THE DEATH OF ANTIOCHUS EPIPHANES

6 King Antiochus was going through the upper provinces when he heard that Elymais in Persia was a city famed for its wealth in silver and gold. [2]Its temple was very rich, containing golden shields, breastplates, and weapons left there by Alexander, the son of Philip, the Macedonian king who first reigned over the Greeks. [3]So he came and tried to take the city and plunder it, but he could not, because his plan became known to the men of the city [4]and they withstood him in battle. So he fled and in great grief departed from there to return to Babylon.

[5]Then some one came to him in Persia and reported that the armies which had gone into the land of Judah had

been routed; ⁶that Lysias had gone first with a strong force, but had turned and fled before the Jews; that the Jews had grown strong from the arms, supplies, and abundant spoils which they had taken from the armies they had cut down; ⁷that they had torn down the abomination which he had erected upon the altar in Jerusalem; and that they had surrounded the sanctuary with high walls as before, and also Beth-zur, his city.

⁸When the king heard this news, he was astounded and badly shaken. He took to his bed and became sick from grief, because things had not turned out for him as he had planned. ⁹He lay there for many days, because deep grief continually gripped him, and he concluded that he was dying. ¹⁰So he called all his friends and said to them, "Sleep departs from my eyes and I am downhearted with worry. ¹¹I said to myself, 'To what distress I have come! And into what a great flood I now am plunged! For I was kind and beloved in my power.' ¹²But now I remember the evils I did in Jerusalem. I seized all her vessels of silver and gold; and I sent to destroy the inhabitants of Judah without good reason. ¹³I know that it is because of this that these evils have come upon me; and behold, I am perishing of deep grief in a strange land."

¹⁴Then he called for Philip, one of his friends, and made him ruler over all his kingdom. ¹⁵He gave him the crown and his robe and the signet, that he might guide Antiochus his son and bring him up to be king. ¹⁶Thus Antiochus the king died there in the one hundred and forty-ninth year. ¹⁷And when Lysias learned that the king was dead, he set up Antiochus the king's son to reign. Lysias had brought him up as a boy, and he named him Eupator.

The death of Antiochus is placed before the cleansing of the temple in 2 Maccabees. It now appears that he died in November or December of 164 BCE very shortly before the consecration. The news probably did not reach Jerusalem until afterwards. 1 Maccabees, however, wishes to dramatize the death of the great tyrant. His decline is attributed to frustration and disappointment, but especially to grief over what had happened in Jerusalem. He even feels remorse over his treatment of the Jews. This kind of moralizing fiction is common in ancient historiography and not peculiar to the Jews. 1 Maccabees is much more restrained than 2 Mac 9, which has the dying Antiochus express the desire to become a Jew. The moral of the story is obvious enough. Retribution is inevitable. The wicked cannot prosper in the end. No doubt, many historical examples of the unhappy deaths of tyrants could be collected, but the principle is by no means universal. The account of the death of Antiochus underlines the theological dimension of 1 Maccabees and also the nationalistic flavor of that theology. The sin of Antiochus is specifically his treatment of the Jews. There is a providential force which protects the interests of the Jewish people. Such a story evidently builds the confidence of a people and re-assures them in time of distress. It is a natural enough fantasy for people who have endured oppression. It is less easy to justify when it is taken as a dogma for all seasons.

1 MAC 6:18-63: THE FIRST DEFEAT

[18]Now the men in the citadel kept hemming Israel in around the sanctuary. They were trying in every way to harm them and strengthen the Gentiles. [19]So Judas decided to destroy them, and assembled all the people to besiege them. [20]They gathered together and besieged the citadel in the one hundred and fiftieth year; and he built siege towers and other engines of war. [21]But some of the garrison escaped from the siege and some of the ungodly Israelites joined them. [22]They went to the king and said,

"How long will you fail to do justice and to avenge our brethren? [23]We were happy to serve your father, to live by what he said and to follow his commands. [24]For this reason the sons of our people besieged the citadel and became hostile to us; moreover, they have put to death as many of us as they have caught, and they have seized our inheritances. [25]And not against us alone have they stretched out their hands, but also against all the lands on their borders. [26]And behold, today they have encamped against the citadel in Jerusalem to take it; they have fortified both the sanctuary and Beth-zur; [27]and unless you quickly prevent them, they will do still greater things, and you will not be able to stop them."

[28]The king was enraged when he heard this. He assembled all his friends, the commanders of his forces and those in authority. [29]And mercenary forces came to him from other kingdoms and from islands of the seas. [30]The number of his forces was a hundred thousand foot soldiers, twenty thousand horsemen, and thirty-two elephants accustomed to war. [31]They came through Idumea and encamped against Beth-zur, and for many days they fought and built engines of war; but the Jews sallied out and burned these with fire, and fought manfully.

[32]Then Judas marched away from the citadel and encamped at Beth-zechariah, opposite the camp of the king. [33]Early in the morning the king rose and took his army by a forced march along the road to Beth-zechariah, and his troops made ready for battle and sounded their trumpets. [34]They showed the elephants the juice of grapes and mulberries, to arouse them for battle. [35]And they distributed the beasts among the phalanxes; with each elephant they stationed a thousand men armed with coats of mail, and with brass helmets on their heads; and five hundred picked horsemen were assigned to each beast. [36]These took their position beforehand wherever the

beast was; wherever it went they went with it, and they never left it. ³⁷And upon the elephants were wooden towers, strong and covered; they were fastened upon each beast by special harness, and upon each were four armed men who fought from there, and also its Indian driver. ³⁸The rest of the horsemen were stationed on either side, on the two flanks of the army, to harass the enemy while being themselves protected by the phalanxes. ³⁹When the sun shone upon the shields of gold and brass, the hills were ablaze with them and gleamed like flaming torches.

⁴⁰Now a part of the king's army was spread out on the high hills, and some troops were on the plain, and they advanced steadily and in good order. ⁴¹All who heard the noise made by their multitude, by the marching of the multitude and the clanking of their arms, trembled, for the army was very large and strong. ⁴²But Judas and his army advanced to the battle, and six hundred men of the king's army fell. ⁴³And Eleazar, called Avaran, saw that one of the beasts was equipped with royal armor. It was taller than all the others, and he supposed that the king was upon it. ⁴⁴So he gave his life to save his people and to win for himself an everlasting name. ⁴⁵He courageously ran into the midst of the phalanx to reach it; he killed men right and left, and they parted before him on both sides. ⁴⁶He got under the elephant, stabbed it from beneath, and killed it; but it fell to the ground upon him and there he died. ⁴⁷And when the Jews saw the royal might and the fierce attack of the forces, they turned away in flight.

⁴⁸The soldiers of the king's army went up to Jerusalem against them, and the king encamped in Judea and at Mount Zion. ⁴⁹He made peace with the men of Beth-zur, and they evacuated the city, because they had no provisions there to withstand a siege, since it was a sabbatical year for the land. ⁵⁰So the king took Beth-zur and stationed a guard there to hold it. ⁵¹Then he encamped before the

sanctuary for many days. He set up siege towers, engines of war to throw fire and stones, machines to shoot arrows, and catapults. ⁵²The Jews also made engines of war to match theirs, and fought for many days. ⁵³But they had no food in storage, because it was the seventh year; those who found safety in Judea from the Gentiles had consumed the last of the stores. ⁵⁴Few men were left in the sanctuary, because famine had prevailed over the rest and they had been scattered, each to his own place.

⁵⁵Then Lysias heard that Philip, whom King Antiochus while still living had appointed to bring up Antiochus his son to be king, ⁵⁶had returned from Persia and Media with the forces that had gone with the king, and that he was trying to seize control of the government. ⁵⁷So he quickly gave orders to depart, and said to the king, to the commanders of the forces, and to the men, "We daily grow weaker, our food supply is scant, the place against which we are fighting is strong, and the affairs of the kingdom press urgently upon us. ⁵⁸Now then let us come to terms with these men, and make peace with them and with all their nation, ⁵⁹and agree to let them live by their laws as they did before; for it was on account of their laws which we abolished that they became angry and did all these things."

⁶⁰The speech pleased the king and the commanders, and he sent to the Jews an offer of peace, and they accepted it. ⁶¹So the king and the commanders gave them their oath. On these conditions the Jews evacuated the stronghold. ⁶²But when the king entered Mount Zion and saw what a strong fortress the place was, he broke the oath he had sworn and gave orders to tear down the wall all around. ⁶³Then he departed with haste and returned to Antioch. He found Philip in control of the city, but he fought against him, and took the city by force.

Up to this point, all Judas's ventures have met with success. The citadel Akra, in Jerusalem, had still withstood him, and he now applies himself to besieging it. He is not successful, however, and he suffers his first defeat at the hands of the Syrian relief forces.

Antiochus IV was succeeded by his son, Antiochus V, Eupator. (The title Eupator, meaning "nobly sired", may seem ironic from a Jewish viewpoint, but reflects the popularity of Antiochus Epiphanes.) The new king was a mere child. He had been brought up by Lysias, but the dying king had named another general, Philip, as guardian and regent. The young king, however, remains with Lysias and accompanies him on his expedition to Jerusalem.

In this campaign the Syrian army is equipped with elephants, the tanks of their day, and inflicts a clear defeat on Judas. 1 Maccabees offers no theological explanation for the defeat. In fact, the defeat is overshadowed by the heroic death of Eleazar, one of the Maccabean brothers. Presumably, the author did not feel that the loss of a few battles required theological explanation when the war as a whole was successful. He emphasizes the positive. Where divine support can be found, it is praised. Where the hand of God is unaccountably absent, he finds an inspiring example in the bravery of the Maccabees.

There is no claim of divine intervention in the siege of Jerusalem, and the eventual withdrawal of the Syrians is not hailed as a repetition of the deliverance from Sennacherib (although there may be some historical similarity between the two events). The acts of God in 1 Maccabees are those performed through the Maccabees, and the Maccabees achieved no deliverance here. Somewhat ironically, the weakness of the Jews is due to their observance of the sabbatical year, and also to their charity to the Jews brought in from Galilee and Gilead. Food is scarce. We may note here the indirect admission that observance of the law and charitable behavior do not, after all, ensure success, but can place one at a disadvantage. It must be said that on the whole the Maccabees had few illusions about this, as we have seen in chap. 2 above, where they decided to fight on the sabbath.

The deliverance of Jerusalem results from the rivalry between the Syrian generals, Lysias and Philip, and the consequent desire of Lysias to return home. The Maccabees are not mentioned in the peace negotiations. Their role in this rather embarrassing situation is quietly glossed over. The only lesson which 1 Maccabees salvages from this episode is the untrustworthiness of the Syrian king, who breaks his oath when he enters the city, although he apparently takes no action against the inhabitants.

In this chapter we see the first example of 1 Maccabees' treatment of a defeat. We cannot say that the book has a theology of defeat to complement its theology of victory. The theological implications of defeat are simply ignored. Yet the honesty of 1 Maccabees, in reporting these events in a matter-of-fact way enables us to see for ourselves that God did not always strengthen the sword of the Maccabees, even when they fought for the defence of their people.

1 MAC 7: 1-20: ALCIMUS AND THE HASIDEANS

7 In the one hundred and fifty-first year Demetrius the son of Seleucus set forth from Rome, sailed with a few men to a city by the sea, and there began to reign. ²As he was entering the royal palace of his fathers, the army seized Antiochus and Lysias to bring them to him. ³But when this act became known to him, he said, "Do not let me see their faces!" ⁴So the army killed them, and Demetrius took his seat upon the throne of his kingdom.

⁵Then there came to him all the lawless and ungodly men of Israel; they were led by Alcimus, who wanted to be

high priest. ⁶And they brought to the king this accusation against the people: "Judas and his brothers have destroyed all your friends, and have driven us out of our land. ⁷Now then send a man whom you trust; let him go and see all the ruin which Judas has brought upon us and upon the land of the king, and let him punish them and all who help them."

⁸So the king chose Bacchides, one of the king's friends, governor of the province Beyond the River; he was a great man in the kingdom and was faithful to the king. ⁹And he sent him, and with him the ungodly Alcimus, whom he made high priest; and he commanded him to take vengeance on the sons of Israel. ¹⁰So they marched away and came with a large force into the land of Judah; and he sent messengers to Judas and his brothers with peaceable but treacherous words. ¹¹But they paid no attention to their words, for they saw that they had come with a large force. ¹²Then a group of scribes appeared in a body before Alcimus and Bacchides to ask for just terms. ¹³The Hasideans were the first among the sons of Israel to seek peace from them, ¹⁴for they said, "A priest of the line of Aaron has come with the army, and he will not harm us." ¹⁵And he spoke peaceable words to them and swore this oath to them, "We will not seek to injure you or your friends." ¹⁶So they trusted him; but he seized sixty of them and killed them in one day, in accordance with the word which was written,

¹⁷"The flesh of thy saints and their blood
they poured out round about Jerusalem,
and there was none to bury them."

¹⁸Then the fear and dread of them fell upon all the people, for they said, "There is no truth or justice in them, for they have violated the agreement and the oath which they swore."

¹⁹Then Bacchides departed from Jerusalem and en-

camped in Beth-zaith. And he sent and seized many of the
men who had deserted to him, and some of the people,
and killed them and threw them into the great pit. [20]He
placed Alcimus in charge of the country and left with him
a force to help him; then Bacchides went back to the king.

From this point on, the internal struggles of the Seleucid
empire play an increasingly important part in the story. No
sooner have the Jews made peace with Antiochus V and
Lysias, than Demetrius, son of Seleucus (the predecessor of
Antiochus IV) arrives on the scene. His attitude towards the
Jews is not yet significantly different from that of the
previous Syrian kings. He attempts to side with the Hellenizing
party and put down the revolt.

The incident with Alcimus throws some interesting light
on the diversity of the Jewish resistance movement. The line
of priestly succession had been disrupted in the early years of
Antiochus Epiphanes and the Hellenistic reform. Menelaus,
whom 1 Maccabees doesn't deign to mention, but who will
figure prominently in 2 Maccabees, was not even a member
of the high priestly family. Alcimus, however, is "a priest of
the line of Aaron" and some Jews thought him an acceptable
high-priest. The Hasideans, who had joined Judas early on,
were now willing to lay down arms. Apparently their goal
was the re-establishment of an acceptable priesthood and
cult. Their assumption, that a legitimate priest would not
harm them, was rudely disappointed. As they might have
learned from the history of the Hellenistic reform, priestly
birth or office is no guarantee of character.

The Maccabees, by contrast, were not so naive "for they
saw that they had come with a large force." Military equipment reveals more about the true intentions than religious
professions. The disillusionment with the traditional priestly
line was now complete. The (inexact) quotation of Ps. 79
[78] in 1 Mac 7:16 throws us back again to the paradigm of

the destruction of Jerusalem which was invoked so often at
the beginning of the book.

1 MAC 7:21-50: THE DEFEAT OF NICANOR

²¹Alcimus strove for the high priesthood, ²²and all who
were troubling their people joined him. They gained con-
trol of the land of Judah and did great damage in Israel.
²³And Judas saw all the evil that Alcimus and those with
him had done among the sons of Israel; it was more than
the Gentiles had done. ²⁴So Judas went out into all the
surrounding parts of Judea, and took vengeance on the
men who had deserted, and he prevented those in the city
from going out into the country. ²⁵When Alcimus saw
that Judas and those with him had grown strong, and
realized that he could not withstand them, he returned to
the king and brought wicked charges against them.

²⁶Then the king sent Nicanor, one of his honored
princes, who hated and detested Israel, and he commanded
him to destroy the people. ²⁷So Nicanor came to
Jerusalem with a large force, and treacherously sent to
Judas and his brothers this peaceable message, ²⁸"Let there
be no fighting between me and you; I shall come with a
few men to see you face to face in peace." ²⁹So he came to
Judas, and they greeted one another peaceably. But the
enemy were ready to seize Judas. ³⁰It became known to
Judas that Nicanor had come to him with treacherous intent, and he was afraid of him and would not meet him
again. ³¹When Nicanor learned that his plan had been disclosed, he went out to meet Judas in battle near Caphar-
salama. ³²About five hundred men of the army of
Nicanor fell, and the rest fled into the city of David.

³³After these events Nicanor went up to Mount Zion. Some of the priests came out of the sanctuary, and some of the elders of the people, to greet him peaceably and to show him the burnt offering that was being offered for the king. ³⁴But he mocked them and derided them and defiled them and spoke arrogantly, ³⁵and in anger he swore this oath, "Unless Judas and his army are delivered into my hands this time, then if I return safely I will burn up this house." And he went out in great anger. ³⁶ Then the priests went in and stood before the altar and the temple, and they wept and said,

³⁷"Thou didst choose this house to be called by thy name,
   and to be for thy people a house of prayer and
supplication.

³⁸Take vengeance on this man and on his army,
   and let them fall by the sword;
   remember their blasphemies.
   and let them live no longer."

³⁹Now Nicanor went out from Jerusalem and encamped in Beth-horon, and the Syrian army joined him. ⁴⁰And Judas encamped in Adasa with three thousand men. Then Judas prayed and said, ⁴¹"When the messengers from the king spoke blasphemy, thy angel went forth and struck down one hundred and eighty-five thousand of the Assyrians. ⁴²So also crush this army before us today; let the rest learn that Nicanor has spoken wickedly against thy sanctuary, and judge him according to this wickedness." ⁴³So the armies met in battle on the thirteenth day of the month of Adar. The army of Nicanor was crushed, and he himself was the first to fall in the battle. ⁴⁴When his army saw that Nicanor had fallen, they threw down their arms and fled. ⁴⁵The Jews pursued them a day's journey, from Adasa as far as Gazara, and as they followed kept sounding the battle call on the trumpets. ⁴⁶And men came out of all the villages of Judea round

about, and they outflanked the enemy and drove them back to their pursuers, so that they all fell by the sword; not even one of them was left. [47]Then the Jews seized the spoils and the plunder, and they cut off Nicanor's head and the right hand which he had so arrogantly stretched out, and brought them and displayed them just outside Jerusalem. [48]The people rejoiced greatly and celebrated that day as a day of great gladness. [49]And they decreed that this day should be celebrated each year on the thirteenth day of Adar. [50]So the land of Judah had rest for a few days.

Jerusalem has again fallen from the hands of the Maccabees, but this time Judas already controls the countryside. At this point 1 Maccabees makes a noteworthy admission. Alcimus and those with him had done more evil than the gentiles. Yet these were Jews. The vengeance of Judas is now directed against his fellow-countrymen who had deserted. So when Nicanor is sent "to destroy the people" we recognize a simplification of the issue. Nicanor was still supporting one group of Jews against another. For 1 Maccabees, however, the Jewish people is for practical purposes identical with the supporters of the Maccabees. There is no pluralism here, but we must remember that Judas was no less tolerant than Alcimus and the Hellenizers. The choice was not between Maccabean Judaism and diversity, but between two mutually incompatible parties.

Nicanor is depicted in especially unfavorable terms. It is said that he hated Israel. He acts treacherously towards Judas and insolently towards the temple and the priests. Even though he had been sent to support Alcimus, he appears to have no sympathy for Jews of any stripe. The priests and elders who greet him are evidently loyal to Syria. The threat to destroy the temple, however, is quite intelligible as a measure against Judas, because of its symbolic importance for the Maccabees. The rebellious Jews would resent the destruction of the temple more than a loyalist priest like Alcimus. Nicanor, in short, is the typical "anti-terrorist" who uses more extreme terrorism to counter guerrilla warfare.

The defeat of Nicanor is presented as following directly on the prayer of the priests. The idea that anyone who profaned the temple would be struck down was understandably popular among the Jews. We will meet a greatly exaggerated illustration of the theme in the story of Heliodorus in 2 Maccabees. The prayer of Judas recalls the deliverance of Jerusalem from the Assyrians by the angel of the Lord. In the actual battle, however, there is no angel. God works through the sword of the Jews.

The chapter ends with unabashed gloating over Nicanor's severed head and hand, and the institution of a national festival. The display of the severed head may strike us as especially distasteful, but it is an integral part of the tactics of terror on both sides in this conflict. Judaism, as conceived by the Maccabees, is not an ascetic discipline or an ethical code. It embodies all that is necessary for the vitality of a people. Emotional satisfaction over the death of an enemy may not have been the noblest of sentiments but it was a natural one. The public display helped restore the morale of the people.

In the Book of Judges, we read after some episodes that the land had rest from its enemies for forty years (Judges 5:31; 8:28). After the defeat of Nicanor the land of Judah rests, but only for a few days.

1 MAC 8: THE TREATY WITH ROME

8 Now Judas heard of the fame of the Romans, that they were very strong and were well-disposed toward all who made an alliance with them, that they pledged friendship to those who came to them, ²and that they were very strong. Men told him of their wars and of the brave deeds which they were doing among the Gauls, how they had defeated them and forced them to pay tribute, ³and what they had done in the land of Spain to get control of the silver and gold mines there, ⁴and how they had gained control of the whole region by their planning and patience, even though the place was far distant from them. They also subdued the kings who came against them from the ends of the earth, until they crushed them and inflicted great disaster upon them; the rest paid them tribute every year. ⁵Philip, and Perseus king of the Macedonians, and the others who rose up against them, they crushed in battle and conquered. ⁶They also defeated Antiochus the Great, king of Asia, who went to fight against them with a hundred and twenty elephants and with cavalry and chariots and a very large army. He was crushed by them; ⁷they took him alive and decreed that he and those who should reign after him should pay a heavy tribute and give hostages and surrender some of their best provinces, ⁸the country of India and Media and Lydia. These they took from him and gave to Eumenes the king. ⁹The Greeks planned to come and destroy them, ¹⁰but this became known to them, and they sent a general against the Greeks and attacked them. Many of them were wounded and fell, and the Romans took captive their wives and children; they plundered them, conquered the land, tore down their strongholds, and enslaved them to this day. ¹¹The remaining kingdoms and islands, as many as ever opposed them, they destroyed and enslaved; ¹²but with their friends and those who rely on them they have kept friendship. They have subdued kings far and near, and as many as have heard of their fame have feared them. ¹³Those whom they wish to help and to make kings, they make kings, and those whom they wish they depose; and they have been greatly exalted. ¹⁴Yet for all this not one of them has put on a crown or worn purple as a mark of pride, [15]but they have built for themselves a senate chamber, and every day three hundred and twenty senators constantly deliberate concerning the people, to govern them well. [16]They trust one man each year to rule over them and to control all their land; they all heed the one man, and there is no envy or jealousy among them.

[17]So Judas chose Eupolemus the son of John, son of Accos, and Jason the son of Eleazar, and sent them to Rome to establish friendship and alliance, [18]and to free themselves from the yoke; for they saw that the kingdom of the Greeks was completely enslaving Israel. [19]They went to Rome, a very long journey; and they entered the senate chamber and spoke as follows: [20]"Judas, who is also called Maccabeus, and his brothers and the people of the Jews have sent us to you to establish alliance and peace with you, that we may be enrolled as your allies and friends." [21]The proposal pleased them, [22]and this is a copy of the letter which they wrote in reply, on bronze tablets, and sent to Jerusalem to remain with them there as a memorial of peace and alliance: [23]"May all go well with the Romans and with the nation of the Jews at sea and on land for ever, and may sword and enemy be far from them. [24]If war comes first to Rome or to any of their allies in all their dominion, [25]the nation of the Jews shall act as their allies wholeheartedly, as the occasion may indicate to them. [26]And to the enemy who makes war they shall not give or supply grain, arms, money, or ships, as Rome has decided; and they shall keep their obligations without receiving any return. [27]In the same way, if war comes first to the nation of the Jews, the Romans shall willingly act as their allies, as the occasion may indicate to them. [28]And to the enemy allies shall be given no grain, arms, money, or ships, as Rome has decided; and they shall keep these obligations and do so without deceit.

²⁹Thus on these terms the Romans make a treaty with the Jewish people. ³⁰If after these terms are in effect both parties shall determine to add or delete anything, they shall do so at their discretion, and any addition or deletion that they may make shall be valid.

³¹"And concerning the wrongs which King Demetrius is doing to them we have written to him as follows, 'Why have you made your yoke heavy upon our friends and allies the Jews? ³²If now they appeal again for help against you, we will defend their rights and fight you on sea and on land.'"

The authenticity of Judas' treaty with Rome has occasionally been questioned in modern scholarship, but for no good reason. The Romans had been active in the Near East since they had defeated Antiochus III in 190 BEC. In 168 they had given Antiochus Epiphanes an ultimatum and forced him to withdraw from Egypt. They had effectively weakened Antiochus V, but Demetrius (161 BCE) had become king over their opposition. Rome was still sufficiently remote so that Judas did not perceive it as a threat to Judaea. By contrast, the Ptolemies of Egypt and the Seleucids had a long history of dominion in the area. Judas was astute enough to realize the limits of nationalism. If Judaea was to emerge as a nation it would need allies on the international scene. True, there were many warnings in the prophets against entering into alliances with powers such as Egypt and Assyria, but there was also the precedent of Solomon, who freely built alliances with the surrounding peoples and brought the kingdom of Israel to the height of its power. From the Roman point of view, the Maccabees were worth encouraging as a nuisance to Demetrius. The Romans risked little in the treaty. Even if the concluding promise to defend the Jews was authentic (it is widely disputed), the Romans did not in fact act on it, and

Demetrius never seems to have taken the threat seriously. A full century would elapse before the Romans intervened actively in the affairs of Judaea.

The praise of the Romans in 8:1-16 is inspired primarily by their might and organization. This passage may reflect the thoughts of the author of 1 Maccabees rather than of Judas. The incidents referred to in 8:9-10 (the conquest of Corinth in 146 BCE) took place long after Judas' death. The suggestion that the Romans were only defending themselves against the Greeks is either naive or deliberate distortion. In addition to sheer power, the Romans are praised for fidelity to their friends, and for their subordination of personal ambition to the common interest. The naiveté of this praise may be due to unfamiliarity with the actual Romans. The passage mistakenly says that Rome was governed by one man, when in fact there were two consuls, and is slightly incorrect on the number of senators. Yet there is a striking admiration for the ruthless use of power, so long as it is not used against the Jewish people.

This chapter throws an interesting light on the attitude to gentiles in 1 Maccabees. As we have seen throughout the book there is an antithesis between Jews and gentiles. This applies, however, to gentiles who are perceived as a threat to Jewish identity, either by political and military pressure or by cultural infiltration. 1 Maccabees is not, however, adverse to finding foreign support for the Jews. We will find even more striking examples of this below in the career of Jonathan. Gentiles are bad in so far as they obstruct the Jewish nation. If they can be made to serve its purposes, so much the better. The author takes evident pride in the fact that the Maccabees were recognized by Rome, and boasts about its promise to help, even though it had never been acted upon. Unlike Daniel, which envisions the total destruction of the gentile kingdoms, 1 Maccabees has a long range political interest. The immediate enemies of Israel should be destroyed, but the ultimate goal is to become a nation on a par with others. This eagerness to show how the Jews can compare with other nations is also common in a number of non-canonical Jewish works from the second century.

The ambassadors to Rome were named Eupolemus and Jason. It is probable that the first man is identical with the Eupolemus who wrote a history of the Jewish kings, in Greek, a few years after the embassy. It is possible, though by no means certain, that the Jason in question is Jason of Cyrene, who wrote the history which is abbreviated in 2 Maccabees (also in Greek). In any case, it is remarkable that both men have Greek names. They must have been proficient in Greek if they were to serve as ambassadors to Rome. It appears then that there was not an absolute rift between Hellenizing Jews, who accepted Greek culture in some degree, and the Maccabees. No doubt there were moderate Hellenizers as well as extremists. For their part, the Maccabees did not reject all Greek culture. In fact, the later Hasmonean kings were thoroughly Hellenized.

In all of this we see the pragmatism both of Judas Maccabee and of the author of 1 Maccabees. Attitudes to gentiles and to foreign culture are not hard and fast. They may be adapted as the interests of the people demand. This pragmatism, in itself, is surely preferable to rigid principles, since it allows for the appreciation of changing circumstances. The wisdom of the embassy to Rome might be questioned in the light of subsequent history. When the Romans actively intervened in Jewish affairs the results were disastrous. In 161 BCE, however, the outcome was, at worst, harmless. The main effect of the treaty with Rome and of the report in 1 Maccabees, was to bolster Jewish self-esteem, and to lend status to the Maccabees as recognized leaders of the people despite the official status of Alcimus and the claims of Demetrius.

1 MAC 9:1-22: THE DEATH OF JUDAS

9 When Demetrius heard that Nicanor and his army had fallen in battle, he sent Bacchides and Alcimus into the land of Judah a second time, and with them the right wing of the army. [2]They went by the road which leads to Gilgal and encamped against Mesaloth in Arbela, and they took it and killed many people. [3]In the first month of the one hundred and fifty-second year they encamped against Jerusalem; [4]then they marched off and went to Berea with twenty thousand cavalry.

[5]Now Judas was encamped in Elasa, and with him were three thousand picked men. [6]When they saw the huge number of the enemy forces, they were greatly frightened, and many slipped away from the camp, until no more than eight hundred of them were left.

[7]When Judas saw that his army had slipped away and the battle was imminent, he was crushed in spirit, for he had no time to assemble them. [8]He became faint, but he said to those who were left, "Let us rise and go up against our enemies. We may be able to fight them." [9]But they tried to dissuade him, saying, "We are not able. Let us rather save our own lives now, and let us come back with our brethren and fight them; we are too few." [10]But Judas said, "Far be it from us to do such a thing as to flee from them. If our time has come, let us die bravely for our brethren, and leave no cause to question our honor."

[11]Then the army of Bacchides marched out from the camp and took its stand for the encounter. The cavalry was divided into two companies, and the slingers and the archers went ahead of the army, as did all the chief warriors. [12]Bacchides was on the right wing. Flanked by the two companies, the phalanx advanced to the sound of the trumpets; and the men with Judas also blew their trumpets. [13]The earth was shaken by the noise of the armies, and the battle raged from morning till evening.

¹⁴Judas saw that Bacchides and the strength of his army were on the right; then all the stouthearted men went with him, ¹⁵and they crushed the right wing, and he pursued them as far as Mount Azotus. ¹⁶When those on the left wing saw that the right wing was crushed, they turned and followed close behind Judas and his men. ¹⁷The battle became desperate, and many on both sides were wounded and fell. ¹⁸Judas also fell, and the rest fled.

¹⁹Then Jonathan and Simon took Judas their brother and buried him in the tomb of their fathers at Modein, ²⁰and wept for him. And all Israel made great lamentation for him; they mourned many days and said,

²¹"How is the mighty fallen,
the savior of Israel!"

²²Now the rest of the acts of Judas, and his wars and the brave deeds that he did, and his greatness, have not been recorded, for they were very many.

The ambassadors may not have returned before Judas met his death on the battlefield. Despite the boost provided by the recent victory over Nicanor, the Jews were disheartened when confronted by the huge army of Bacchides. The panic of the army recalls 1 Sam 13:5-7 when Saul's men hid themselves from the Philistines.

Judas's decision to fight was a questionable strategy, since defeat was imminent. There is no suggestion that he expected divine help (in marked contrast to 3:18 above, where he professed that heaven could save by few as well as by many). His motivation, according to vs. 10 is his honor. The gallant fight against the odds is emphasized over the disaster of defeat.

In view of the dominant role played by Judas up to this point, and the designation "savior of Israel," we might expect some theological reflection on his death. Yet, the death of the champion of the law is not perceived as a problem. In part this is due to the fact that the whole Maccabean house is the hero of the story. The death of Judas is not as great a disaster as it might seem, for his brother is there to carry on. Judas has played his part nobly, and must now leave the stage to another. 1 Maccabees does not raise the question of after-life, and certainly does not set any store by it. The after-life it treasures is the lasting good name. The salvation it seeks is not the personal salvation of the individual after death, but the communal salvation of family or people. Accordingly, Judas' death does not pose a crisis. Death is inevitable. When his time has come, the main thing is to die bravely.

In all of this 1 Maccabees stands in the mainstream of ancient Israelite thought, from Genesis to Ben Sira. It is in marked contrast to both Daniel and 2 Maccabees. 2 Maccabees 12: 43-45, pointedly argues that Judas believed in the resurrection, but has to infer it from his actions. If Judas did believe in after-life, the fact was apparently not well known. The lack of expectation for life after death is a significant factor in the pragmatic and realistic attitude of 1 Maccabees, which was probably also characteristic of the historical Maccabees.

There is no objective criterion by which we can decide whether the model of Judas is preferable to that proposed in the visions of Daniel. The martyrs of Daniel died with pure hands; Judas was a man of violence. Both withstood the oppressor. Judas had the more obvious achievement in the liberation of the Jews, but the long term impact is more difficult to judge.

The brief lament over Judas recalls David's lament for Saul and Jonathan. The title "savior of Israel" recalls the judges. The concluding reference to "the rest of the acts of Judas" copies a formula of the books of kings. Judas is given his place among the heroes of his people. His after-life is in the national heritage.

Part Three: The Career of Jonathan

1 MAC 9:23-73: THE RISE OF JONATHAN

²³After the death of Judas, the lawless emerged in all parts of Israel; all the doers of injustice appeared. ²⁴In those days a very great famine occurred, and the country deserted with them to the enemy. ²⁵And Bacchides chose the ungodly and put them in charge of the country. ²⁶They sought and searched for the friends of Judas and brought them to Bacchides, and he took vengeance on them and made sport of them. ²⁷Thus there was great distress in Israel, such as had not been since the time that prophets ceased to appear among them.

²⁸Then all the friends of Judas assembled and said to Jonathan, ²⁹"Since the death of your brother Judas there has been no one like him to go against our enemies and Bacchides, and to deal with those of our nation who hate us. ³⁰So now we have chosen you today to take his place as our ruler and leader, to fight our battle." ³¹And Jonathan at that time accepted the leadership and took the place of Judas his brother. . . .

⁴³When Bacchides heard of this, he came with a large force on the sabbath day to the banks of the Jordan. ⁴⁴And Jonathan said to those with him, "Let us rise up now and fight for our lives, for today things are not as they were before. ⁴⁵For look! the battle is in front of us and behind us; the water of the Jordan is on this side and on that, with marsh and thicket; there is no place to turn. ⁴⁶Cry out now to Heaven that you may be delivered from the hands of our enemies." ⁴⁷So the battle began, and Jonathan stretched out his hand to strike Bacchides, but he eluded him and went to the rear. ⁴⁸Then Jonathan and the men with him leaped into the Jordan and swam across

to the other side, and the enemy did not cross the Jordan to attack them. ⁴⁹And about one thousand of Bacchides' men fell that day.

⁵⁰Bacchides then returned to Jerusalem and built strong cities in Judea: the fortress in Jericho, and Emmaus, and Beth-horon, and Bethel, and Timnath, and Pharathon, and Tephon, with high walls and gates and bars. ⁵¹And he placed garrisons in them to harass Israel. ⁵²He also fortified the city of Beth-zur, and Gazara, and the citadel, and in them he put troops and stores of food. ⁵³And he took the sons of the leading men of the land as hostages and put them under guard in the citadel at Jerusalem.

⁵⁴In the one hundred and fifty-third year, in the second month, Alcimus gave orders to tear down the wall of the inner court of the sanctuary. He tore down the work of the prophets! ⁵⁵But he only began to tear it down, for at that time Alcimus was stricken and his work was hindered; his mouth was stopped and he was paralyzed, so that he could no longer say a word or give commands concerning his house. ⁵⁶And Alcimus died at that time in great agony. ⁵⁷When Bacchides saw that Alcimus was dead, he returned to the king, and the land of Judah had rest for two years.

⁵⁸Then all the lawless plotted and said, "See! Jonathan and his men are living in quiet and confidence. So now let us bring Bacchides back and he will capture them all in one night." ⁵⁹And they went and consulted with him. ⁶⁰He started to come with a large force, and secretly sent letters to all his allies in Judea, telling them to seize Jonathan and his men; but they were unable to do it, because their plan became known. ⁶¹And Jonathan's men seized about fifty of the men of the country who were leaders in this treachery, and killed them.

⁶²Then Jonathan with his men, and Simon, withdrew to

Beth-basi in the wilderness; he rebuilt the parts of it that had been demolished, and they fortified it. ⁶³When Bacchides learned of this, he assembled all his forces, and sent orders to the men of Judea. ⁶⁴Then he came and encamped against Beth-basi; he fought against it for many days and made machines of war.

⁶⁵But Jonathan left Simon his brother in the city, while he went out into the country; and he went with only a few men. ⁶⁶He struck down Odomera and his brothers and the sons of Phasiron in their tents. ⁶⁷Then he began to attack and went into battle with his forces; and Simon and his men sallied out from the city and set fire to the machines of war. ⁶⁸They fought with Bacchides, and he was crushed by them. They distressed him greatly, for his plan and his expedition had been in vain. ⁶⁹So he was greatly enraged at the lawless men who had counseled him to come into the country, and he killed many of them. Then he decided to depart to his own land.

⁷⁰When Jonathan learned of this, he sent ambassadors to him to make peace with him and obtain release of the captives. ⁷¹He agreed, and did as he said: and he swore to Jonathan that he would not try to harm him as long as he lived. ⁷²He restored to him the captives whom he had formerly taken from the land of Judah; then he turned and departed to his own land, and came no more into their territory. ⁷³Thus the sword ceased from Israel. And Jonathan dwelt in Michmash. And Jonathan began to judge the people, and he destroyed the ungodly out of Israel.

While Judas was presented as a new Joshua, Jonathan is modelled after the ancient Judges. This is most obvious at the end of chapter 9, when he dwells in Michmash and begins to judge the people. (Michmash was a village slightly north of Jerusalem, from which Jonathan son of Saul had driven the Philistines in 1 Sam 14.) The pattern of the Judges is also evident at the beginning. First, there is a great crisis, allegedly greater than any since authoritative prophecy had ceased in the early Persian period. This is surely an exaggeration, but it underlines the need for a savior, despite all that had been accomplished by Judas. Second, Jonathan is approached by the people and asked to be their leader. We may recall the manner in which Jephtah is approached in Judges 11. There are, of course, significant differences too. The spirit of the Lord does not fall on Jonathan, and his selection is due to the fact that he is a Maccabee. Yet he is given traditional status here by the allusions to the Judges. (There is another echo of Judges in 9:57, where the land has rest for two years.)

Jonathan at first operated as a hit-and-run guerrilla fighter. The only occasion on which he defeated Bacchides was when the latter attacked his fortress in the wilderness. Jonathan's success was due to the distraction and dissension of the Syrians. When Bacchides encountered a serious obstacle, he withdrew and made peace. Evidently Judaea was no longer worth a persistent effort. We also sense, in this and the following chapters, changing attitudes between Jews and Syrians. When Bacchides is thwarted by Jonathan, he is enraged at the Hellenizing Jews who had promised him an easy victory. The ideological bonds between the Jewish Hellenizers and the Syrians are no longer of primary importance. What matters now is expediency. Bacchides is not interested in spreading Hellenistic civilization, but in keeping the active opposition to a minimum. Conversely, we find Jonathan quite willing to deal with the Syrians, and in the following chapter, barter his loyalty for favors. The Hellenizing Jews are only of interest to the Syrians in so far as they provide access to control over Judaea. When they can no longer provide this, they cease to be a significant factor in the story.

The death of Alcimus conforms to a favorite theme of the Books of Maccabees: great sinners suffer appropriately in their death. The final actions of Alcimus, like so many crucial actions in this book, has to do with the temple. He tore down a wall, said to be the work of the prophets, presumably because the temple had been re-built after the exile under the leadership of Haggai and Zechariah. It is not clear exactly which wall was involved. It may have been a wall within the part of the temple reserved for Jews–e.g. between the court of the priests and the court of the Israelites. Alternatively, it may have been the wall which separated the court of the gentiles from the inner courts. This wall was so important that in the time of King Herod any foreigner who entered inside it was subject to the death penalty. If this was indeed the barrier which Alcimus sought to remove, then his action was symbolic not only of his own career but of the entire Hellenistic reform. It was in effect removing the distinction between Jew and gentile.

Other Jews after Alcimus would try to reduce or remove the distinction between Jew and gentile, most notably the apostle Paul in the New Testament (Gal 3:28). The context and motives were rather different, however. Paul, in effect, was launching a new religion which had its own distinctive identity, although it was not defined along the lines between Jew and Greek. Alcimus, in so far as we can tell, operated like his Hellenizing predecessors, for motives that were largely political. His treatment of the Hasideans who made peace with him, in chap. 7 above, does not suggest that he was inspired by any vision of universal harmony, whatever his conception of Jewish religion may have been.

After the death of Alcimus in 159 BCE the high-priesthood was left vacant for a time, and, in part as a result, the land has peace.

1 MAC 10: JONATHAN AND THE GENTILE KINGS

10 In the one hundred and sixtieth year Alexander Epiphanes, the son of Antiochus, landed and occupied Ptolemais. They welcomed him, and there he began to reign. ²When Demetrius the king heard of it, he assembled a very large army and marched out to meet him in battle. ³And Demetrius sent Jonathan a letter in peaceable words to honor him; ⁴for he said, "Let us act first to make peace with him before he makes peace with Alexander against us, ⁵for he will remember all the wrongs which we did to him and to his brothers and his nation." ⁶So Demetrius gave him authority to recruit troops, to equip them with arms, and to become his ally; and he commanded that the hostages in the citadel should be released to him.

⁷Then Jonathan came to Jerusalem and read the letter in the hearing of all the people and of the men in the citadel. ⁸They were greatly alarmed when they heard that the king had given him authority to recruit troops. ⁹But the men in the citadel released the hostages to Jonathan, and he returned them to their parents.

¹⁰And Jonathan dwelt in Jerusalem and began to rebuild and restore the city. ¹¹He directed those who were doing the work to build the walls and encircle Mount Zion with squared stones, for better fortification; and they did so.

¹²Then the foreigners who were in the strongholds that Bacchides had built fled; ¹³each left his place and departed to his own land. ¹⁴Only in Beth-zur did some remain who had forsaken the law and the commandments, for it served as a place of refuge.

¹⁵Now Alexander the king heard of all the promises which Demetrius had sent to Jonathan, and men told him of the battles that Jonathan and his brothers had fought, of the brave deeds that they had done, and of the troubles

that they had endured. [16]So he said, "Shall we find another such man? Come now, we will make him our friend and ally." [17]And he wrote a letter and sent it to him, in the following words:

[18]"King Alexander to his brother Jonathan, greeting. [19]We have heard about you, that you are a mighty warrior and worthy to be our friend. [20]And so we have appointed you today to be the high priest of your nation; you are to be called the king's friend" (and he sent him a purple robe and a golden crown) "and you are to take our side and keep friendship with us."

[21]So Jonathan put on the holy garments in the seventh month of the one hundred and sixtieth year, at the feast of tabernacles, and he recruited troops and equipped them with arms in abundance. [22]When Demetrius heard of these things he was grieved and said, [23]"What is this that we have done? Alexander has gotten ahead of us in forming a friendship with the Jews to strengthen himself. [24]I also will write them words of encouragement and promise them honor and gifts, that I may have their help." [25]So he sent a message to them in the following words: "King Demetrius to the nation of the Jews, greeting. [26]Since you have kept your agreement with us and have continued your friendship with us, and have not sided with our enemies, we have heard of it and rejoiced. [27]And now continue still to keep faith with us, and we will repay you with good for what you do for us. [28]We will grant you many immunities and give you gifts. . . ."

[46]When Jonathan and the people heard these words, they did not believe or accept them, because they remembered the great wrongs which Demetrius had done in Israel and how he had greatly oppressed them. [47]They favored Alexander, because he had been the first to speak peaceable words to them, and they remained his allies all his days.

⁴⁸Now Alexander the king assembled large forces and encamped opposite Demetrius. ⁴⁹The two kings met in battle, and the army of Demetrius fled, and Alexander pursued him and defeated them. ⁵⁰He pressed the battle strongly until the sun set, and Demetrius fell on that day.

⁵¹Then Alexander sent ambassadors to Ptolemy king of Egypt with the following message: ⁵²(Since I have returned to my kingdom and have taken my seat on the throne of my fathers, and established my rule—for I crushed Demetrius and gained control of our country; ⁵³I met him in battle, and he and his army were crushed by us, and we have taken our seat on the throne of his kingdom—⁵⁴now therefore let us establish friendship with one another; give me now your daughter as my wife, and I will become your son-in-law, and will make gifts to you and to her in keeping with your position. . . . "

⁵⁷So Ptolemy set out from Egypt, he and Cleopatra his daughter, and came to Ptolemais in the one hundred and sixty-second year. ⁵⁸Alexander the king met him, and Ptolemy gave him Cleopatra his daughter in marriage, and celebrated her wedding at Ptolemais with great pomp, as kings do.

⁵⁹Then Alexander the king wrote to Jonathan to come to meet him. ⁶⁰So he went with pomp to Ptolemais and met the two kings; he gave them and their friends silver and gold and many gifts, and found favor with them. ⁶¹A group of pestilent men from Israel, lawless men, gathered together against him to accuse him; but the king paid no attention to them. ⁶²The king gave orders to take off Jonathan's garments and to clothe him in purple, and they did so. ⁶³The king also seated him at his side; and he said to his officers, "Go forth with him into the middle of the city and proclaim that no one is to bring charges against him about any matter, and let no one annoy him for any reason." ⁶⁴And when his accusers saw the honor

that was paid him, in accordance with the proclamation, and saw him clothed in purple, they all fled. ⁶⁵Thus the king honored him and enrolled him among his chief friends, and made him general and governor of the province. ⁶⁶And Jonathan returned to Jerusalem in peace and gladness.

⁶⁷In the one hundred and sixty-fifth year Demetrius the son of Demetrius came from Crete to the land of his fathers. ⁶⁸When Alexander the king heard of it, he was greatly grieved and returned to Antioch. ⁶⁹And Demetrius appointed Apollonius the governor of Coele-syria, and he assembled a large force and encamped against Jamnia. Then he sent the following message to Jonathan the high priest:

⁷⁰"You are the only one to rise up against us, and I have become a laughingstock and reproach because of you. Why do you assume authority against us in the hill country? ⁷¹If you now have confidence in your forces, come down to the plain to meet us, and let us match strength with each other there, for I have with me the power of the cities. ⁷²Ask and learn who I am and who the others are that are helping us. Men will tell you that you cannot stand before us, for your fathers were twice put to flight in their own land. ⁷³And now you will not be able to withstand my cavalry and such an army in the plain, where there is no stone or pebble, or place to flee."

⁷⁴When Jonathan heard the words of Apollonius, his spirit was aroused. He chose ten thousand men and set out from Jerusalem, and Simon his brother met him to help him. ⁷⁵He encamped before Joppa, but the men of the city closed its gates, for Apollonius had a garrison in Joppa. ⁷⁶So they fought against it, and the men of the city became afraid and opened the gates, and Jonathan gained possession of Joppa. ⁷⁷When Apollonius heard of it, he mustered three thou-

sand cavalry and a large army, and went to Azotus as though he were going farther. At the same time he advanced into the plain, for he had a large troop of cavalry and put confidence in it. [78]Jonathan pursued him to Azotus, and the armies engaged in battle. [79]Now Apollonius had secretly left a thousand cavalry behind them. [80]Jonathan learned that there was an ambush behind him, for they surrounded his army and shot arrows at his men from early morning till late afternoon. [81]But his men stood fast, as Jonathan commanded, and the enemy's horses grew tired.

[82]Then Simon brought forward his force and engaged the phalanx in battle (for the cavalry was exhausted); they were overwhelmed by him and fled, [83]and the cavalry was dispersed in the plain. They fled to Azotus and entered Beth-dagon, the temple of their idol, for safety. [84]But Jonathan burned Azotus and the surrounding towns and plundered them; and the temple of Dagon, and those who had taken refuge in it he burned with fire. [85]The number of those who fell by the sword, with those burned alive, came to eight thousand men.

[86]Then Jonathan departed from there and encamped against Askalon, and the men of the city came out to meet him with great pomp. [87]And Jonathan and those with him returned to Jerusalem with much booty. [88]When Alexander the king heard of these things, he honored Jonathan still more; [89]and he sent to him a golden buckle, such as it is the custom to give to the kinsmen of kings. He also gave him Ekron and all its environs as his possession.

1 Mac 10 marks the transition of the Maccabees from a state of rebellion to being a significant power in the political struggles of the Near East. Up to this point they had not succeeded in gaining firm control over Jerusalem and Judaea, but their enemies had not been able to crush them either. Now,

when two rivals were claiming the Syrian throne, Jonathan
was able to play them off against each other and become
master of the Jewish territory.

The pragmatic character of the Maccabees is evident in
Jonathan's ready acceptance of favors from the gentile
kings. He does not dispute Demetrius' authority to em-
power him to recruit troops. Evidently Jonathan could raise
troops without the king's permission, but there is no defiance here. Instead, he uses the authority of the king to get
control of Jerusalem. If he then abandons Demetrius for
Alexander Balas, the reason is not only that Demetrius has
previously afflicted the Jews. Alexander makes him a better
offer, and one that confers greater honor on Jonathan
himself, by appointing him high priest. Now the Maccabees
did not belong to the line of legitimate high priests, any
more than the renegade Menelaus (Alcimus may have had a
better claim to the office). When Jonathan accepts the high
priesthood from a king whose own legitimacy was disputed,
he was manifestly not concerned with restoring traditional
religion, but with securing his own power. It is possible that
the usurpation of the high priesthood by the Maccabees was
the occasion for the breaking off of the sect that built the
community of Qumran by the Dead Sea. Many scholars
hold that either Jonathan or his successor Simon is the
"Wicked Priest" who appears in the Scrolls (in the commentary on Habbakuk) as the arch-enemy of the Sect.

The success of Jonathan undoubtedly benefited the
Jewish people. Demetrius endeavored to win back Jonathan
by remitting taxes and granting various favors to the Jews.
We are told that Jonathan did not trust him. Yet this lack of
trust only became apparent when Jonathan had found a better patron in Alexander. Alexander's own pedigree could
scarcely inspire great trust in the Jews - he was son of Antiochus Epiphanes. For the present, however, he offered the
better prospects.

Jonathan does not press for complete independence at this point. Such a strategy might have lost him his leverage. Accordingly, the antithesis of Jews and gentiles recedes in this part of the story. Jonathan does not scorn the gentiles when they dress him in purple and make him general and governor. In all of this, there is remarkable flexibility on Jonathan's part, to a degree which we might not have anticipated at the beginning of the revolt. Evidently the Maccabees were no religious purists.

Yet the campaigns of Jonathan in the service of the gentile king are presented here as if they were a crusade against paganism. 1 Maccabees carefully notes the destruction of the temple of Dagon, and those who had taken refuge in it. By any standards this action was sacrilegious. Throughout antiquity, temples were respected as places of asylum. Both the temple and the region (from Joppa to Ascalon), however, had ancient associations with the Philistines (see e.g. 1 Sam 1-5). Jonathan's ruthless action is in no way criticized here. Perhaps the echoes of the Philistine wars are taken as justification, or the fact that the temple is pagan is adequate warrant. It is apparent, however, that at this point Jonathan is rather selective in his opposition to paganism. He does not hesitate to accept the honors of the king.

The chapter concludes with the acquisition of Ekron, as a gift from Alexander. The expansion of the Jewish territories has begun.

1 MAC 11: THE JEWS AND THE DYNASTIC STRUGGLES

[13] Then Ptolemy entered Antioch and put on the crown of Asia. Thus he put two crowns upon his head, the crown of Egypt and that of Asia. [14]Now Alexander the king was in Cilicia at that time, because the people of that region were in revolt. [15]And Alexander heard of it and came against him in battle. Ptolemy marched out and met him

with a strong force, and put him to flight. ¹⁶So Alexander fled into Arabia to find protection there, and King Ptolemy was exalted. ¹⁷And Zabdiel the Arab cut off the head of Alexander and sent it to Ptolemy. ¹⁸But King Ptolemy died three days later, and his troops in the strongholds were killed by the inhabitants of the strongholds. ¹⁹So Demetrius became king in the one hundred and sixty-seventh year.

²⁰In those days Jonathan assembled the men of Judea to attack the citadel in Jerusalem, and he built many engines of war to use against it. ²¹But certain lawless men who hated their nation went to the king and reported to him that Jonathan was besieging the citadel. ²²When he heard this he was angry, and as soon as he heard it he set out and came to Ptolemais; and he wrote Jonathan not to continue the siege, but to meet him for a conference at Ptolemais as quickly as possible.

²³When Jonathan heard this, he gave orders to continue the siege; and he chose some of the elders of Israel and some of the priests, and put himself in danger, ²⁴for he went to the king at Ptolemais, taking silver and gold and clothing and numerous other gifts. And he won his favor. ²⁵Although certain lawless men of his nation kept making complaints against him, ²⁶the king treated him as his predecessors had treated him; he exalted him in the presence of all his friends. ²⁷He confirmed him in the high priesthood and in as many other honors as he had formerly had, and made him to be regarded as one of his chief friends. ²⁸Then Jonathan asked the king to free Judea and the three districts of Samaria from tribute, and promised him three hundred talents. ²⁹The king consented, and wrote a letter to Jonathan about all these things...

⁴¹Now Jonathan sent to Demetrius the king the request that he remove the troops of the citadel from Jerusalem, and the troops in the strongholds; for they kept fighting

against Israel. ⁴²And Demetrius sent this message to
Jonathan, "Not only will I do these things for you and
your nation, but I will confer great honor on you and your
nation, if I find an opportunity. ⁴³Now then you will do
well to send me men who will help me, for all my troops
have revolted." ⁴⁴So Jonathan sent three thousand
stalwart men to him at Antioch, and when they came to
the king, the king rejoiced at their arrival.

⁴⁵Then the men of the city assembled within the city, to
the number of a hundred and twenty thousand, and they
wanted to kill the king. ⁴⁶But the king fled into the palace.
Then the men of the city seized the main streets of the city
and began to fight. ⁴⁷So the king called the Jews to his aid,
and they all rallied about him and then spread out
through the city; and they killed on that day as many as a
hundred thousand men. ⁴⁸They set fire to the city and
seized much spoil on that day, and they saved the king.
⁴⁹When the men of the city saw that the Jews had gained
control of the city as they pleased, their courage failed
and they cried out to the king with this entreaty, ⁵⁰"Grant
us peace, and make the Jews stop fighting against us and
our city." ⁵¹And they threw down their arms and made
peace. So the Jews gained glory in the eyes of the king and
of all the people in his kingdom, and they returned to
Jerusalem with much spoil.

⁵²So Demetrius the king sat on the throne of his kingdom, and the land was quiet before him. ⁵³But he broke
his word about all that he had promised; and he became
estranged from Jonathan and did not repay the favors
which Jonathan had done him, but oppressed him greatly.

⁵⁴After this Trypho returned, and with him the young
boy Antiochus, who began to reign and put on the crown.
⁵⁵All the troops that Demetrius had cast off gathered
around him, and they fought against Demetrius, and he
fled and was routed. ⁵⁶And Trypho captured the elephants and gained control of Antioch. ⁵⁷Then the young

Antiochus wrote to Jonathan, saying, "I confirm you in the high priesthood and set you over the four districts and make you one of the friends of the king." [58]And he sent him gold plate and a table service, and granted him the right to drink from gold cups and dress in purple and wear a gold buckle. [59]Simon his brother he made governor from the Ladder of Tyre to the borders of Egypt.

[60]Then Jonathan set forth and traveled beyond the river and among the cities, and all the army of Syria gathered to him as allies. When he came to Askalon, the people of the city met him and paid him honor. [61]From there he departed to Gaza, but the men of Gaza shut him out. So he besieged it and burned its suburbs with fire and plundered them. [62]Then the people of Gaza pleaded with Jonathan, and he made peace with them, and took the sons of their rulers as hostages and sent them to Jerusalem. And he passed through the country as far as Damascus.

[63]Then Jonathan heard that the officers of Demetrius had come to Kadesh in Galilee with a large army, intending to remove him from office. [64]He went to meet them, but left his brother Simon in the country. [65]Simon encamped before Beth-zur and fought against it for many days and hemmed it in. [66]Then they asked him to grant them terms of peace, and he did so. He removed them from there, took possession of the city, and set a garrison over it.

[67]Jonathan and his army encamped by the waters of Gennesaret. Early in the morning they marched to the plain of Hazor, [68]and behold, the army of the foreigners met him in the plain; they had set an ambush against him in the mountains, but they themselves met him face to face. [69]Then the men in ambush emerged from their places and joined battle. [70]All the men with Jonathan fled; not one of them was left except Mattathias the son of Absalom and Judas the son of Chalphi, commanders of the forces of the army. [71]Jonathan rent his garments and put

> dust on his head and prayed. [72]Then he turned back to the
> battle against the enemy and routed them, and they fled.

The campaign of Ptolemy against Alexander was of interest to 1 Maccabees because it brought about the fall of Alexander in 145 BCE. 1 Maccabees has a completely positive attitude towards Alexander, the patron of Jonathan, and blames this war completely on the Ptolemy. By contrast, Josephus, the Jewish historian writing at the end of the first century CE, claims that Ptolemy came to help Alexander but that the latter acted treacherously towards him. The facts of the case are in doubt. The Ptolemy in question was Ptolemy VI Philometor, an important figure in Jewish history of the period. Onias IV, the son of the last legitimate high priest, and himself the legitimate heir to the office, had fled to Egypt, entered the service of Philometor, and risen to a prominent position in the Egyptian army. Philometor had permitted him to build a temple at Leontopolis in Egypt, which was something of a scandal since Jewish law permitted only the central temple in Jerusalem. We can imagine that the author of 1 Maccabees, who admired the Maccabean high priests, may have been less than enthusiastic about the patron of Onias. Ptolemy died of wounds received in the battle with Alexander.

Demetrius II was conciliatory towards Jonathan. He released the Jews from taxes, confirmed the grants previously made to them, and even promised to disband the troops in the citadel Akra. In return, Jonathan sent three thousand men to Antioch to help put down a revolt. Jewish mercenaries were widespread in the ancient world and well trusted for their loyalty. In Antioch, they were evidently ruthless in suppressing the revolt. The presence of Jewish soldiers putting down a revolt in Antioch is a far cry from the original war of liberation of the Maccabees. Expediency has become the sole principle of Jonathan's actions.

There was need for considerable flexibility in the struggles of the Seleucid empire. Demetrius did not keep his promise to disband the Akra garrison, and instead oppressed Jonathan, presumably because he was becoming too powerful. Then the general Trypho arrived on the scene with Antiochus VI, the young son of Alexander Balas, who was only 3 or 4 years old. This child-king was now set up as a rival to Demetrius II. In view of his good relationship with Alexander, Jonathan was naturally well disposed to Antiochus. The transfer of allegiance was made firm when Antiochus gained control of Antioch and confirmed Jonathan as high priest. The favor of the Maccabees was further ensured by appointing Simon to a governorship too.

The Maccabees could now use their official Syrian appointments to tighten control over their territories. The chapter ends with a victory over forces of Demetrius near Hazor in northern Israel. The Jews are at first defeated, but when Jonathan prays, the enemy is routed. The narrative here recalls Joshua 7, where Joshua similarly rends his clothes and prays after an initial defeat at Ai. Unlike the story of Joshua, 1 Maccabees does not suggest that defeat was due to the sin of the Jews - it was simply the result of an ambush. In 1 Maccabees, defeats do not bear theological explanations, but victories do. If Jonathan prevailed after his prayer, it must have been by the help of God. The enemy in this episode is referred to as "foreigners." Despite the fact that Jonathan and his followers are taking active part in the inner struggles of the Seleucid empire the author still wishes to give the impression that we are dealing with a war of Jews against gentiles, in which God is commited to the Jewish side.

1 MAC 12:1-23: JEWS AND SPARTANS

12 Now when Jonathan saw that the time was favorable for him, he chose men and sent them to Rome to confirm and renew the friendship with them. ²He also sent letters to the same effect to the Spartans and to other places. ³So

they went to Rome and entered the senate chamber and
said, "Jonathan the high priest and the Jewish nation
have sent us to renew the former friendship and alliance
with them." ⁴And the Romans gave them letters to the
people in every place, asking them to provide for the envoys safe conduct to the land of Judah.

⁵This is a copy of the letter which Jonathan wrote to the
Spartans: ⁶"Jonathan the high priest, the senate of the
nation, the priests, and the rest of the Jewish people to
their brethren the Spartans, greeting. ⁷Already in time
past a letter was sent to Onias the high priest from Arius,
who was king among you, stating that you are our
brethren, as the appended copy shows. ⁸Onias welcomed
the envoy with honor, and received the letter, which contained a clear declaration of alliance and friendship.
⁹Therefore, though we have no need of these things, since
we have as encouragement the holy books which are in
our hands, ¹⁰we have undertaken to send to renew our
brotherhood and friendship with you, so that we may not
become estranged from you, for considerable time has
passed since you sent your letter to us. ¹¹We therefore
remember you constantly on every occasion, both in our
feasts and on other appropriate days, at the sacrifices
which we offer and in our prayers, as it is right and proper
to remember brethren. ¹²And we rejoice in your glory.
¹³But as for ourselves, many afflictions and many wars
have encircled us; the kings round about us have waged
war against us. ¹⁴We were unwilling to annoy you and our
other allies and friends with these wars, ¹⁵for we have the
help which comes from Heaven for our aid; and we were
delivered from our enemies and our enemies were humbled.
¹⁶We therefore have chosen Numenius the son of Antiochus and Antipater the son of Jason, and have sent
them to Rome to renew our former friendship and alliance with them. ¹⁷We have commanded them to go also to

you and greet you and deliver to you this letter from us concerning the renewal of our brotherhood. ¹⁸And now please send us a reply to this."

¹⁹This is a copy of the letter which they sent to Onias: ²⁰Arius, king of the Spartans, to Onias the high priest, greeting. ²¹It has been found in writing concerning the Spartans and the Jews that they are brethren and are of the family of Abraham. ²²And now that we have learned this, please write us concerning your welfare; ²³we on our part write to you that your cattle and your property belong to us, and ours belong to you. We therefore command that our envoys report to you accordingly."

Just as Judas had sent an embassy to Rome, so now did Jonathan. The purpose was presumably to gain recognition and status rather than actual aid. Jonathan had by now had time to perceive that the Romans would not rush to intervene on the side of the Jews.

On this occasion Jonathan also sent an embassy to Sparta, affirming the brotherhood of Spartans and Jews. The authenticity of the various letters cited in connection with this embassy has been debated at length. According to 1 Maccabees, King Arius I of Sparta had written to the high priest Onias I of Jerusalem early in the third century BCE, claiming that the Jews and Spartans were both descended from Abraham. Such a letter could possibly have been written but there is no apparent reason why the Spartans would have taken this initiative. This letter may well be a fiction, although it may have been forged before the time of Jonathan. The legend that the Spartans and Jews were related was certainly older than Maccabean times. According to 2 Mac 5:9, the ousted high priest Jason fled to Sparta "in hope of finding protection because of their kinship." Jewish writers of the Hellenistic age often concocted fanciful genealogies, to build connections between Judaism and

Greek culture. According to one Cleodemus Malchas, the sons of Abraham by Keturah migrated to Libya (Cyrene) and there joined with Heracles (the Greek demi-god) in a campaign. Heracles then allegedly married the daughter of Aphras, one of the sons of Abraham. Aphras also gave his name to Africa, while another son of Abraham, Asshur, gave his name to Assyria. The work of Cleodemus is obviously not history but fanciful speculation. The legend of the relationship between Jews and Spartans probably originated in such speculation. It was strengthened by the fact that the Spartans like the Jews had strict laws, a venerated law-giver (Lycurgus) and a reputation for inhospitality.

There is no reason to doubt that Jonathan sent an embassy to Sparta (perhaps en route to Rome). The Spartans were allies of Rome, and Rome had intervened to crush the Achaean league when it threatened Sparta (146 BCE). A link with Sparta might enhance the Jews in the eyes of Rome. Whether the letter preserved in 1 Maccabees is authentic, is another matter. The tone is less than diplomatic ("though we have no need of these things" [12:9]) and the boast that "we have the help which comes from Heaven for our aid" is scarcely appropriate in correspondence of this sort. Both these remarks are quite in line with the theology of 1 Maccabees. It is possible that the author has re-touched the letter, or has supplied what Jonathan *should* have written.

Once again, this diplomatic activity shows how rapidly the Maccabees learned to move in the world of Hellenistic diplomacy. The envoys, Numenius son of Antiochus and Antipater son of Jason, bear distinctly Hellenistic names, but then already in the next generation the heir of the Maccabees John Hyrcanus would have a Greek name beside his Jewish one. The Maccabees did not reject all Hellenism, and Hellenized Jews could still be found in their service.

If the opening formula is accurate, Jonathan, with the council and priests would seem to lay claim to considerable independence. Jonathan still operated within the context of the Seleucid monarchy, but his actions in establishing diplomatic contacts with Rome and Sparta were surely paving the way for the day when he could dispense with the Syrian overlords, although the shadow of Rome might itself be more difficult to shake off.

The letter to the Spartans makes another breach in the simple dichotomy between Jews and gentiles. It may well be that the dichotomy was more characteristic of the author of 1 Maccabees than it was of the Maccabees themselves. In any case, the pragmatic spirit of the Maccabees could not be restrained by such fixed categories. Success in the Hellenistic world required alliances with other powers, and the Jews would attempt to use these alliances for their own best advantage.

1 MAC 12:24-53: THE CAPTURE OF JONATHAN

³⁹Then Trypho attempted to become king of Asia and put on the crown, and to raise his hand against Antiochus the king. ⁴⁰He feared that Jonathan might not permit him to do so, but might make war on him, so he kept seeking to seize and kill him, and he marched forth and came to Beth-shan. ⁴¹Jonathan went out to meet him with forty thousand picked fighting men, and he came to Beth-shan. ⁴²When Trypho saw that he had come with a large army, he was afraid to raise his hand against him. ⁴³So he received him with honor and commended him to all his friends, and he gave him gifts and commanded his friends and his troops to obey him as they would himself. ⁴⁴Then he said to Jonathan, "Why have you wearied all these people when we are not at war? ⁴⁵Dismiss them now to their homes and choose for yourself a few men to stay with you, and come with me to Ptolemais. I will hand it over to you as well as the other strongholds and the remaining

troops and all the officials, and will turn round and go
home. For that is why I am here.''

⁴⁶Jonathan trusted him and did as he said; he sent away
the troops, and they returned to the land of Judah. ⁴⁷He
kept with himself three thousand men, two thousand of
whom he left in Galilee, while a thousand accompanied
him. ⁴⁸But when Jonathan entered Ptolemais, the men of
Ptolemais closed the gates and seized him, and all who
had entered with him they killed with the sword.

⁴⁹Then Trypho sent troops and cavalry into Galilee and
the Great Plain to destroy all Jonathan's soldiers. ⁵⁰But
they realized that Jonathan had been seized and had
perished along with his men, and they encouraged one
another and kept marching in close formation, ready for
battle. ⁵¹When their pursuers saw that they would fight
for their lives, they turned back. ⁵²So they all reached the
land of Judah safely, and they mourned for Jonathan and
his companions and were in great fear; and all Israel
mourned deeply. ⁵³And all the nations round about them
tried to destroy them, for they said, "They have no leader
or helper. Now therefore let us make war on them and
blot out the memory of them from among men.''

Jonathan was still loyal to Antiochus and his general
Trypho. Yet it was at the hands of the latter that he met his
death. He had now become powerful enough so that he was
a serious obstacle to Trypho's ambitions. Jonathan may
have mistrusted the general at first (he approached him with
a large army) but he was easily won over by flattery. Presumably he was not aware of Trypho's designs on Antiochus.
Then when Trypho got him with only a small force in
Ptolemais, he seized him.

Jonathan ultimately fell victim to the intrigues and shift-
ing loyalties amid which he had manoeuvred successfully for
twenty years. To be sure, he was more honorable than many,

and was consistently loyal to Alexander Balas and his son
Antiochus VI. This in itself was ironic, since they were
directly descended from Antiochus Epiphanes. Yet there is
no doubt that Jonathan's success was due to his opportunism, and his willingness to ally himself with anyone as expediency demanded. In the end his fall was due to the fact that
he had risen too high, and, in the particular circumstances,
to an error of opportunistic judgment. As in the case of
Judas, there is no theological reflection on Jonathan's fall.
Though success in battle might be due to his prayer, failure
does not require explanation. In the scheme of 1 Maccabees,
it is time for Jonathan to leave the stage to Simon.

The chapter ends on a note of crisis. The nations rise up
against the Jews to destroy them. We can see by now that
this is a vast over-simplification of the complex political alliances of the day, but 1 Maccabees wishes to evoke the recurring crises of the book of Judges. It is assumed that a people
is helpless before its enemies if it has no leader or savior. The
stage is set for the advent of Simon.

Part Four: The Career of Simon

1 MAC 13: THE RISE OF SIMON

13 Simon heard that Trypho had assembled a large army
to invade the land of Judah and destroy it, ²and he saw
that the people were trembling and fearful. So he went up
to Jerusalem, and gathering the people together ³he encouraged them, saying to them, "You yourselves know
what great things I and my brothers and the house of my
father have done for the laws and the sanctuary; you
know also the wars and the difficulties which we have
seen. ⁴By reason of this all my brothers have perished for

the sake of Israel, and I alone am left. ⁵And now, far be it from me to spare my life in any time of distress, for I am not better than my brothers. ⁶But I will avenge my nation and the sanctuary and your wives and children, for all the nations have gathered together out of hatred to destroy us."

⁷The spirit of the people was rekindled when they heard these words, ⁸and they answered in a loud voice, "You are our leader in place of Judas and Jonathan your brother. ⁹Fight our battles, and all that you say to us we will do." ¹⁰So he assembled all the warriors and hastened to complete the walls of Jerusalem, and he fortified it on every side. ¹¹He sent Jonathan the son of Absalom to Joppa, and with him a considerable army; he drove out its occupants and remained there.

¹²Then Trypho departed from Ptolemais with a large army to invade the land of Judah, and Jonathan was with him under guard. ¹³And Simon encamped in Adida, facing the plain. ¹⁴Trypho learned that Simon had risen up in place of Jonathan his brother, and that he was about to join battle with him, so he sent envoys to him and said, ¹⁵"It is for the money that Jonathan your brother owed the royal treasury, in connection with the offices he held, that we are detaining him. ¹⁶Send now a hundred talents of silver and two of his sons as hostages, so that when released he will not revolt against us, and we will release him."

¹⁷Simon knew that they were speaking deceitfully to him, but he sent to get the money and the sons, lest he arouse great hostility among the people, who might say, ¹⁸"Because Simon did not send him the money and the sons, he perished." ¹⁹So he sent the sons and the hundred talents, but Trypho broke his word and did not release Jonathan.

²⁰After this Trypho came to invade the country and

destroy it, and he circled around by the way to Adora. But Simon and his army kept marching along opposite him to every place he went. ²¹Now the men in the citadel kept sending envoys to Trypho urging him to come to them by way of the wilderness and to send them food. ²²So Trypho got all his cavalry ready to go, but that night a very heavy snow fell, and he did not go because of the snow. He marched off and went into the land of Gilead. ²³When he approached Baskama, he killed Jonathan, and he was buried there. ²⁴Then Trypho turned back and departed to his own land.

²⁵And Simon sent and took the bones of Jonathan his brother, and buried him in Modein, the city of his fathers. ²⁶All Israel bewailed him with great lamentation, and mourned for him many days. ²⁷And Simon built a monument over the tomb of his father and his brothers; he made it high that it might be seen, with polished stone at the front and back. ²⁸He also erected seven pyramids, opposite one another, for his father and mother and four brothers. ²⁹And for the pyramids he devised an elaborate setting, erecting about them great columns, and upon the columns he put suits of armor for a permanent memorial, and beside the suits of armor carved ships, so that they could be seen by all who sail the sea. ³⁰This is the tomb which he built in Modein, it remains to this day.

³¹Trypho dealt treacherously with the young king Antiochus; he killed him ³²and became king in his place, putting on the crown of Asia; and he brought great calamity upon the land. ³³But Simon built up the strongholds of Judea and walled them all around, with high towers and great walls and gates and bolts, and he stored food in the strongholds. ³⁴Simon also chose men and sent them to Demetrius the king with a request to grant relief to the country, for all that Trypho did was to plunder. ³⁵Demetrius the king sent him a favorable reply to this request,

and wrote him a letter as follows, [36]"King Demetrius to Simon, the high priest and friend of kings, and to the elders and nation of the Jews, greeting. [37]We have received the gold crown and the palm branch which you sent, and we are ready to make a general peace with you and to write to our officials to grant you release from tribute. [38]All the grants that we have made to you remain valid, and let the strongholds that you have built be your possession. [39]We pardon any errors and offenses committed to this day, and cancel the crown tax which you owe; and whatever other tax has been collected in Jerusalem shall be collected no longer. [40]And if any of you are qualified to be enrolled in our bodyguard, let them be enrolled, and let there be peace between us."

[41]In the one hundred and seventieth year the yoke of the Gentiles was removed from Israel, [42]and the people began to write in their documents and contracts, "In the first year of Simon the great high priest and commander and leader of the Jews."

[43]In those days Simon encamped against Gazara and surrounded it with troops. He made a siege engine, brought it up to the city, and battered and captured one tower. [44]The men in the siege engine leaped out into the city, and a great tumult arose in the city. [45]The men in the city, with their wives and children, went up on the wall with their clothes rent, and they cried out with a loud voice, asking Simon to make peace with them; [46]they said, "Do not treat us according to our wicked acts but according to your mercy." [47]So Simon reached an agreement with them and stopped fighting against them. But he expelled them from the city and cleansed the houses in which the idols were, and then entered it with hymns and praise. [48]He cast out of it all uncleanness, and settled in it men who observed the law. He also strengthened its fortifications and built in it a house for himself.

⁴⁹The men in the citadel at Jerusalem were prevented from going out to the country and back to buy and sell. So they were very hungry, and many of them perished from famine. ⁵⁰Then they cried to Simon to make peace with them, and he did so. But he expelled them from there and cleansed the citadel from its pollutions. ⁵¹On the twenty-third day of the second month, in the one hundred and seventy-first year, the Jews entered it with praise and palm branches, and with harps and cymbals and stringed instruments, and with hymns and songs, because a great enemy had been crushed and removed from Israel. ⁵²And Simon decreed that every year they should celebrate this day with rejoicing. He strengthened the fortifications of the temple hill alongside the citadel, and he and his men dwelt there. ⁵³And Simon saw that John his son had reached manhood, so he made him commander of all the forces, and he dwelt in Gazara.

Simon is immediately recognized as the heir to his brother. The emphasis falls on the family, which is on its way to becoming a dynasty. They are said to fight "for the laws and the sanctuary" and so they do, but, as we have seen, these are only aspects of the fight for aggrandisement of the people and the Maccabees as their leaders. If Simon's offer to take over the leadership is presented as a self-sacrificial act, we know that this is true, but that it is by no means free of self-interest. Typically 1 Maccabees suggests that all the nations are about to destroy the Jews and the sanctuary. We may recall the rebellion of the nations against Yahweh and his anointed in Psalm 2. Here Simon takes over the role of the Lord's anointed. The dynastic implications are strengthened by the erection of the family tomb in Modein.

The murder of Jonathan is followed by the murder of the young king Antiochus, showing the treacherous character of Trypho. Demetrius II had also proven unreliable, but

Simon readily turns to him now, and the king, faced with the threat posed by Trypho, willingly accepts him. Simon succeeds to the high-priesthood, and thus makes the breach with the traditional priestly line all the more permanent.

The concessions won by Simon at this point surpassed those made to his brothers and amounted to an acknowledgement of Jewish independence. So, in 1 Mac 13:41 we read that in 142 BCE the yoke of the gentiles was removed from Israel, and Jews began to date events from the accession of Simon. Demetrius, of course, had little power in the region in any case, and Trypho had temporarily departed. Simon, however, undertook to give substance to the grant by building up the fortresses of Judaea. He also dislodged the hostile garrisons in Gazara and the Akra citadel in Jerusalem. The importance of the latter event can hardly be exaggerated. The Akra had withstood the Jews for fully quarter of a century. Besides the practical nuisance of a hostile garrison in Jerusalem, its symbolic significance was great. It represented the dominion of the Syrians over the most sacred Jewish place. The conquest of the citadel was appropriately marked by ritual purification. It is to Simon's credit that he engaged in no slaughter of the occupants of either Gazara or the Akra. More clearly than in the case of Jonathan or even Judas, Simon is characterized by religious interests. He cleanses the houses where there were idols and settles in Gazara "men who observed the law." Even in these cases it is difficult to draw a line between religious and nationalistic fervor. The worship of idols was symbolic of foreign rule. Observance of the Jewish law was a gesture of Jewish independence.

1 MAC 14:1-15: SIMON'S REIGN AS A MESSIANIC AGE

14   In the one hundred and seventy-second year Demetrius the king assembled his forces and marched into Media to secure help, so that he could make war against Trypho. ²When Arsaces the king of Persia and Media heard that Demetrius had invaded his territory, he sent one of his commanders to take him alive. ³And he went and defeated the army of Demetrius, and seized him and took him to Arsaces, who put him under guard.

⁴The land had rest all the days of Simon.

He sought the good of his nation; his rule was pleasing to them,

as was the honor shown him, all his days.

⁵To crown all his honors he took Joppa for a harbor,

and opened a way to the isles of the sea.

⁶He extended the borders of his nation,

and gained full control of the country.

⁷He gathered a host of captives;

he ruled over Gazara and Beth-zur and the citadel,

and he removed its uncleanness from it;

and there was none to oppose him.

⁸They tilled their land in peace;

the ground gave its increase,

and the trees of the plains their fruit.

⁹Old men sat in the streets;

they all talked together of good things;

and the youths donned the glories and garments of war.

¹⁰He supplied the cities with food,

and furnished them with the means of defense,

till his renown spread to the ends of the earth.

¹¹He established peace in the land,

and Israel rejoiced with great joy.

¹²Each man sat under his vine and his fig tree,

and there was none to make them afraid.

¹³No one was left in the land to fight them,

and the kings were crushed in those days.

¹⁴He strengthened all the humble of his people;

he sought out the law,

and did away with every lawless and wicked man.
¹⁵He made the sanctuary glorious,
    and added to the vessels of the sanctuary.

Hitherto in 1 Maccabees we have often read that the land
rested for a short period. Now we read that it had rest all the
days of Simon. We shall see that there is considerable exaggeration in this claim, although the respite was longer than
at any time since the Maccabean rebellion began. For the
first time in this period, no alien stronghold was left in Judaea.
Moreover, Simon was able to enlarge the territories of the
Jews and get a sea-port in Joppa. The portrayal of Simon's
reign draws heavily on the Old Testament prophets. Zechariah
had predicted that "Old men and old women shall sit again
in the streets of Jerusalem, each with staff in hand for very
age" and that "there shall be a sowing of peace; the vine
shall yield its fruit, and ground shall give its increase"
(Zech 8:4, 12). Leviticus had also promised that the land
would yield its increase (26:4) and a similar prophecy is
found in Ezekiel 34:27. Micah had spoken of a time when
"they shall sit every man under his vine and under his fig·
tree, and none shall make them afraid" (4:4). The era of
peace described here is unparalleled in the history of Israel
except for the reign of Solomon, the builder of the temple.
Appropriately, Simon also makes the temple glorious. The
entire passage is reminiscent of the prayer for the king in Ps.
72 [71], which relates the prosperity of the land to the justice
of the king and prays for the subjugation of the kings of the
earth and the extension of the boundaries of the land. As all
nations would call the king blessed, so Simon's fame would
spread to the ends of the earth.

If Simon's reign has the character of a messianic age, it
does not for that reason mark the end of history. The eschatology of 1 Maccabees is realized eschatology. The promises
are fulfilled in the Maccabean family. The vision of peace
and prosperity is no longer a utopian dream of an ideal

future. It is claimed as the achievement of the Maccabees.
True, the age of peace doesn't last indefinitely, but it
demonstrates the potential of the Maccabean dynasty.

1 MAC 14:16-24: INTERNATIONAL RECOGNITION

[16]It was heard in Rome, and as far away as Sparta, that
Jonathan had died, and they were deeply grieved. [17]When
they heard that Simon his brother had become high priest
in his place, and that he was ruling over the country and
the cities in it, [18]they wrote to him on bronze tablets to
renew with him the friendship and alliance which they
had established with Judas and Jonathan his brothers.
[19]And these were read before the assembly in Jerusalem.

[20]This is a copy of the letter which the Spartans sent:
"The rulers and the city of the Spartans to Simon the high
priest and to the elders and the priests and the rest of the
Jewish people, our brethren, greeting. [21]The envoys who
were sent to our people have told us about your glory and
honor, and we rejoiced at their coming. [22]And what they
said we have recorded in our public decrees, as follows,
Numenius the son of Antiochus and Antipater the son of
Jason, envoys of the Jews, have come to us to renew their
friendship with us. [23]It has pleased our people to receive
these men with honor and to put a copy of their words in
the public archives, so that the people of the Spartans may
have a record of them. And they have sent a copy of this to
Simon the high priest."

[24]After this Simon sent Numenius to Rome with a large
gold shield weighing a thousand minas, to confirm the
alliance with the Romans.

Like his brother before him, Simon makes contact with
Rome and Sparta. It is not apparent here whether Simon
sent the same delegates on a new embassy. More probably,
they only returned from the mission initiated by Jonathan

after Simon had come to power. Simon does send Numenius back to Rome with a gift for the Romans. The gift amounted to approximately 15,000 ounces or 450 kilograms of gold, a very substantial gift from a small nation, and signified the earnestness of the Jews in their approach to Rome. We find in 15:15-24 that the Romans accepted the gift and informed the peoples of the region of their support for the Jews. All of this was designed to build status both in Judaea and among the surrounding peoples. Simon was well aware that Judaea had not become independent of international relations. In the context of 1 Mac 14 the dealings with Rome and Sparta show how Simon's fame reached to the ends of the earth.

1 MAC 14:25-49: THE EDICT OF THE PEOPLE

²⁵When the people heard these things they said, "How shall we thank Simon and his sons? ²⁶For he and his brothers and the house of his father have stood firm; they have fought and repulsed Israel's enemies and established its freedom." ²⁷So they made a record on bronze tablets and put it upon pillars on Mount Zion.

This is a copy of what they wrote: "On the eighteenth day of Elul, in the one hundred and seventy-second year, which is the third year of Simon the great high priest, ²⁸in Asaramel, in the great assembly of the priests and the people and the rulers of the nation and the elders of the country, the following was proclaimed to us:

²⁹"Since wars often occurred in the country, Simon the son of Mattathias, a priest of the sons of Joarib, and his brothers, exposed themselves to danger and resisted the enemies of their nation, in order that their sanctuary and the law might be preserved; and they brought great glory to their nation. ³⁰Jonathan rallied the nation, and became their high priest, and was gathered to his people. ³¹And when their enemies decided to invade their country and

lay hands on their sanctuary, ³²then Simon rose up and fought for his nation. He spent great sums of his own money; he armed the men of his nations' forces and paid them wages. ³³He fortified the cities of Judea, and Beth-zur on the borders of Judea, where formerly the arms of the enemy had been stored, and he placed there a garrison of Jews. ³⁴He also fortified Joppa, which is by the sea, and Gazara, which is on the borders of Azotus, where the enemy formerly dwelt. He settled Jews there, and provided in those cities whatever was necessary for their restoration.

³⁵"The people saw Simon's faithfulness and the glory which he had resolved to win for his nation, and they made him their leader and high priest, because he had done all these things and beause of the justice and loyalty which he had maintained toward his nation. He sought in every way to exalt his people. ³⁶And in his days things prospered in his hands, so that the Gentiles were put out of the country, as were also the men in the city of David in Jerusalem, who had built themselves a citadel from which they used to sally forth and defile the environs of the sanctuary and do great damage to its purity. ³⁷He settled Jews in it, and fortified it for the safety of the country and of the city, and built the walls of Jerusalem higher.

³⁸"In view of these things King Demetrius confirmed him in the high priesthood, ³⁹and he made him one of the king's friends and paid him high honors. ⁴⁰For he had heard that the Jews were addressed by the Romans as friends and allies and brethren, and that the Romans had received the envoys of Simon with honor.

⁴¹"And the Jews and their priests decided that Simon should be their leader and high priest for ever, until a trustworthy prophet should arise, ⁴²and that he should be governor over them and that he should take charge of the sanctuary and appoint men over its tasks and over the

country and the weapons and the strongholds, and that he should take charge of the sanctuary, [43]and that he should be obeyed by all, and that all contracts in the country should be written in his name, and that he should be clothed in purple and wear gold.

[44]And none of the people or priests shall be permitted to nullify any of these decisions or to oppose what he says, or to convene an assembly in the country without his permission, or to be clothed in purple or put on a gold buckle. [45]Whoever acts contrary to these decisions or nullifies any of them shall be liable to punishment.

[46]And all the people agreed to grant Simon the right to act in accord with these decisions. [47]So Simon accepted and agreed to be high priest, to be commander and ethnarch of the Jews and priests, and to be protector of them all. [48]And they gave orders to inscribe this decree upon bronze tablets, to put them up in a conspicuous place in the precincts of the sanctuary, [49]and to deposit copies of them in the treasury, so that Simon and his sons might have them.

The elevation of Simon is completed by the edict of the people, declaring him high priest, ethnarch and commander for life. The acclaim of the people is important, since hitherto the high priesthood of the Maccabees rested only on the appointments by pagan kings. Given the proclamation by the people, the Maccabees must now be regarded as legitimate high priests.

The reason for the proclamation is simply gratitude for all that the Maccabees had done for the nation. The listing of these deeds recalls the recitation of the mighty acts of Yahweh in the context of covenant renewal in a passage like Joshua 24. Here the mighty deeds are those of Simon, and it is to him that gratitude is directed. He is especially praised for winning glory for his nation, but also for his justice, loyalty and faithfulness. The proclamation reads like a fitting conclusion to the story of the Maccabees. While they had not been religiously scrupulous and they had fought with the ruthlessness of their day, there was no doubt that they had "repulsed Israel's enemies and established its freedom" (14:26). The glory of the people is reflected in the fact that they were addressed by the Romans as friends and allies, however empty that rhetoric may have been. The edict evidently recognizes that the honors conferred by Demetrius were wrung from him by the new status of the Jews.

To appreciate the extent of Simon's achievement we must bear in mind that this was the first time since the Babylonian exile that the Jews could claim to be an independent people. Small wonder then that they thought a definitive turning point had come.

Simon was proclaimed high priest forever, until a trustworthy prophet should arise. As we have seen above (chap. 4), the coming of the prophet would be an eschatological event, so the appointment was, in effect, forever. Moreover, all power was concentrated in Simon's hands. There is no reason to doubt the essential authenticity of the edict.

1 Mac 14 might seem to be a suitable conclusion for the book. The hymnic praise of Simon balances the praise of Judas in 1 Mac 3. The appointment of Simon has a ring of finality which is almost comparable to the election of the Davidic house. (This comparison becomes more realistic in view of the actual development of the Maccabean or Hasmonean dynasty.) Yet the book does not conclude on this lofty plateau. In continuing the story down to the time of John Hyrcanus the author provided an important perspective on the development of this near-messianic era.

1 MAC 15:1-16:10: THE RENEWED SYRIAN THREAT

15 Antiochus, the son of Demetrius the king, sent a letter from the islands of the sea to Simon, the priest and ethnarch of the Jews, and to all the nation; ²its contents were as follows: "King Antiochus to Simon the high priest and ethnarch and to the nation of the Jews, greeting. ³Whereas certain pestilent men have gained control of the kingdom of our fathers, and I intend to lay claim to the kingdom so that I may restore it as it formerly was, and have recruited a host of mercenary troops and have equipped warships, ⁴and intend to make a landing in the country so that I may proceed against those who have destroyed our country and those who have devastated many cities in my kingdom, ⁵now therefore I confirm to you all the tax remissions that the kings before me have granted you, and release from all the other payments from which they have released you. ⁶I permit you to mint your own coinage as money for your country, ⁷and I grant freedom to Jerusalem and the sanctuary. All the weapons which you have prepared and the strongholds which you have built and now hold shall remain yours. ⁸Every debt you owe to the royal treasury and any such future debts shall be canceled for you from henceforth and for all time. ⁹When we gain control of our kingdom, we will bestow great honor upon you and your nation and the temple, so that your glory will become manifest in all the earth."

¹⁰In the one hundred and seventy-fourth year Antiochus set out and invaded the land of his fathers. All the troops rallied to him, so that there were few with Trypho. ¹¹Antiochus pursued him, and he came in his flight to Dor, which is by the sea; ¹²for he knew that troubles had converged upon him, and his troops had deserted him. ¹³So Antiochus encamped against Dor, and with him were a hundred and twenty thousand warriors and eight thousand cavalry. ¹⁴He surrounded the city, and the ships joined battle from the sea; he pressed the city hard from land and sea, and permitted no one to leave or enter it.

¹⁵Then Numenius and his companions arrived from Rome, with letters to the kings and countries, in which the following was written: ¹⁶"Lucius, consul of the Romans, to King Ptolemy, greeting. ¹⁷The envoys of the Jews have come to us as our friends and allies to renew our ancient friendship and alliance. They had been sent by Simon the high priest and by the people of the Jews, ¹⁸and have brought a gold shield weighing a thousand minas. ¹⁹We therefore have decided to write to the kings and countries that they should not seek their harm or make war against them and their cities and their country, or make alliance with those who war against them. ²⁰And it has seemed good to us to accept the shield from them. ²¹Therefore if any pestilent men have fled to you from their country, hand them over to Simon the high priest, that he may punish them according to their law."

²²The consul wrote the same thing to Demetrius the king and to Attalus and Ariarathes and Arsaces, ²³and to all the countries, and to Sampsames, and to the Spartans, and to Delos, and to Myndos, and to Sicyon, and to Caria, and to Samos, and to Pamphylia and to Lycia, and to Halicarnassus, and to Rhodes, and to Phaselis, and to Cos, and to Side, and to Aradus and Gortyna and Cnidus and Cyprus and Cyrene. ²⁴They also sent a copy of these things to Simon the high priest.

²⁵Antiochus the king besieged Dor anew, continually throwing his forces against it and making engines of war; and he shut Trypho up and kept him from going out or in. ²⁶And Simon sent to Antiochus two thousand picked men, to fight for him, and silver and gold and much military equipment. ²⁷But he refused to receive them, and he broke all the agreements he formerly had made with Simon, and became estranged from him. ²⁸He sent to him Athenobius, one of his friends, to confer with him, saying, "You hold control of Joppa and Gazara and the

citadel in Jerusalem; they are cities of my kingdom. ²⁹You have devastated their territory, you have done great damage in the land, and you have taken possession of many places in my kingdom. ³⁰Now then, hand over the cities which you have seized and the tribute money of the places which you have conquered outside the borders of Judea; ³¹or else give me for them five hundred talents of silver, and for the destruction that you have caused and tribute money of the cities, five hundred talents more. Otherwise we will come and conquer you."

³²So Athenobius the friend of the king came to Jerusalem and when he saw the splendor of Simon, and the sideboard with its gold and silver plate, and his great magnificence, he was amazed. He reported to him the words of the king, ³³but Simon gave him this reply: "We have neither taken foreign land nor seized foreign property, but only the inheritance of our fathers, which at one time had been unjustly taken by our enemies. ³⁴Now that we have the opportunity, we are firmly holding the inheritance of our fathers. ³⁵As for Joppa and Gazara, which you demand, they were causing great damage among the people and to our land; for them we will give a hundred talents." Athenobius did not answer him a word, ³⁶but returned in wrath to the king and reported to him these words and the splendor of Simon and all that he had seen. And the king was greatly angered.

³⁷Now Trypho embarked on a ship and escaped to Orthosia. ³⁸Then the king made Cendebeus commander-in-chief of the coastal country, and gave him troops of infantry and cavalry. ³⁹He commanded him to encamp against Judea, and commanded him to build up Kedron and fortify its gates, and to make war on the people; but the king pursued Trypho. ⁴⁰So Cendebeus came to Jamnia and began to provoke the people and invade Judea and take the people captive and kill them. ⁴¹He built up Kedron and stationed there horsemen and troops, so that

they might go out and make raids along the highways of Judea, as the king had ordered him.

16 John went up from Gazara and reported to Simon his father what Cendebeus had done. ²And Simon called in his two older sons Judas and John, and said to them: "I and my brothers and the house of my father have fought the wars of Israel from our youth until this day, and things have prospered in our hands so that we have delivered Israel many times. ³But now I have grown old, and you by His mercy are mature in years. Take my place and my brother's, and go out and fight for our nation, and may the help which comes from Heaven be with you."

⁴So John chose out of the country twenty thousand warriors and horsemen, and they marched against Cendebeus and camped for the night in Modein. ⁵Early in the morning they arose and marched into the plain, and behold, a large force of infantry and horsemen was coming to meet them; and a stream lay between them. ⁶Then he and his army lined up against them. And he saw that the soldiers were afraid to cross the stream, so he crossed over first; and when his men saw him, they crossed over after him. ⁷Then he divided the army and placed the horsemen in the midst of the infantry, for the cavalry of the enemy were very numerous. ⁸And they sounded the trumpets, and Cendebeus and his army were put to flight, and many of them were wounded and fell; the rest fled into the stronghold. ⁹At that time Judas the brother of John was wounded, but John pursued them until Cendebeus reached Kedron, which he had built. ¹⁰They also fled into the towers that were in the fields of Azotus, and John burned it with fire and about two thousand of them fell. And he returned to Judea safely.

The peace of Simon's reign was interrupted by the arrival in 138 BCE of Antiochus VII Sidetes, the younger brother of Demetrius II (who had been captured by the Parthians). Antiochus confirmed the concessions which had been made to the Jews by previous Seleucid kings. Apparently he did not include in this the places Simon had taken by force, Joppa, Gazara and the Akra citadel in Jerusalem. When he had gained the upper hand over Trypho, he rejected Simon's offer of assistance and demanded compensation for the places Simon had taken, and also the tribute of the territories Simon had captured outside Judaea.

There is no suggestion that Antiochus intended to re-conquer all the territory held by Simon, but he was asserting that the Jews only had a right to whatever territories were formally granted to them by the Seleucids. Simon makes a distinction. He affirms the right of the Jews to recover "the inheritance of our fathers" which had been unjustly taken from them. At the same time he concedes that Joppa and Gazara were cities over which Antiochus had some rights, but points out that they were causing damage to the people. In offering to pay one-tenth of the sum demanded, Simon was conceding some justification to Antiochus' demand, but also offering a compromise. Yet, the smallness of the offer was inevitably taken as an act of defiance.

Simon may have been emboldened by the letters of the Romans, publicly declaring their support and friendship. He was also confident in his own strength. Perhaps the key statement in Simon's reply to Antiochus was: "Now that we have the opportunity, we are firmly holding the inheritance of our fathers." Ultimately more important than the justification for holding the various places was the ability to hold them. Simon's confidence was justified. Even though he was too old to fight, his sons won a decisive victory, and John Hyrcanus distinguished himself. Admittedly, this was not the end of the matter, since Antiochus later, after Simon's death, forced Hyrcanus to accept his conditions. (Antiochus gave back the cities in return for the payment of tribute, probably because he was pressured to do so by Rome.)

This entire episode shows that the young Jewish state was by no means secure. Only when Antiochus Sidetes was killed in a campaign against the Parthians could the Jews begin to feel confident of their independence.

The inclusion of this episode adds a note of caution after the euphoric account of Simon in chap. 14. The peace achieved by the Maccabees was temporary and fragile, and was always dependent on the international situation for its continuance. Despite the appeals to the help that comes from heaven, that help never removed them from the constraints of their political environment and the fluctuating power of their neighbors.

1 MAC 16:11-24: THE DEATH OF SIMON

[11]Now Ptolemy the son of Abubus had been appointed governor over the plain of Jericho, and he had much silver and gold, [12]for he was son-in-law of the high priest. [13]His heart was lifted up; he determined to get control of the country, and made treacherous plans against Simon and his sons, to do away with them. [14]Now Simon was visiting the cities of the country and attending to their needs, and he went down to Jericho with Mattathias and Judas his sons, in the one hundred and seventy-seventh year, in the eleventh month, which is the month of Shebat. [15]The son of Abubus received them treacherously in the little stronghold called Dok, which he had built; he gave them a great banquet, and hid men there. [16]When Simon and his sons were drunk, Ptolemy and his men rose up, took their weapons, and rushed in against Simon in the banquet hall, and they killed him and his two sons and some of his servants. [17]So he committed an act of great treachery and returned evil for good.

[18]Then Ptolemy wrote a report about these things and sent it to the king, asking him to send troops to aid him and to turn over to him the cities and the country. [19]He

sent other men to Gazara to do away with John; he sent letters to the captains asking them to come to him so that he might give them silver and gold and gifts; [20]and he sent other men to take possession of Jerusalem and the temple hill. [21]But some one ran ahead and reported to John at Gazara that his father and brothers had perished, and that "he has sent men to kill you also." [22]When he heard this, he was greatly shocked; and he seized the men who came to destroy him and killed them, for he had found out that they were seeking to destroy him.

[23]The rest of the acts of John and his wars and the brave deeds which he did, and the building of the walls which he built, and his achievements, [24]behold, they are written in the chronicles of his high priesthood, from the time that he became high priest after his father.

Like all his brothers, Simon met a violent death. He and two of his sons were treacherously murdered by Simon's own son-in-law, Ptolemy, the son of Abubus. (It is of interest that such a Hellenistic name should be found among the relatives of the high priest at this time). Ptolemy aspired to seize power himself. Simon's death was not only violent, but also ignominious, as he and his sons were drunk.

1 Maccabees bases no theological reflection on the death of Simon. If a Syrian king had died in this way, he would surely have been said to be punished by God. Yet the very inclusion of this episode modifies the impact of the book. The great eulogy of Simon in 1 Mac 14 is put in perspective.

1 Maccabees notes only the treachery of Ptolemy, and then moves rapidly to show how John survived. We might say that John was lucky to escape the fate of his father and brothers. The author would surely have seen in these events evidence of God's providential care for the Maccabean house.

The book contains no concluding reflections. It ends with

the formulaic language of the Books of Kings, on how the rest of the deeds of John are written in the chronicles of the high priesthood. The author probably composed his work during John's lifetime. In a sense, this ending is fitting. The plateau of Jewish independence had been reached with Simon. Beyond that, no end is envisaged. The high priesthood and virtual monarchy are passed on in the Maccabean family. There will still be problems, but the new order has been established.

First Maccabees in Retrospect

1 MACCABEES is a far more detailed historical source than Daniel. It is undeniably more limited as a work of literature or of theology. While Daniel abounds in vivid paradigms and metaphors—the fiery furnace, the lion's den, the beasts from the sea—1 Maccabees is preoccupied with historical data. The only paradigm which stands out clearly is that of Mattathias slaying the apostate Jew at the altar—a paradigmatic act which is itself based on the biblical story of Phinehas. In this case we may feel some ambivalence about the propriety of the model.

The Maccabean brothers are themselves paradigmatic figures, who can clearly serve as models in similar situations. Their example inspired many in the struggles against Rome in the first and early second centuries CE. We can also appreciate their relevance for modern Israel, and even, perhaps, for Christian liberation movements in Latin America or elsewhere. The problem is not in seeing how the example of the Maccabees could be applied, but in deciding whether it should be.

Here, more obviously than in Daniel, religion is an instrument of political ideology. We have seen repeatedly how the successes of the Maccabees are attributed to the hand of God, but their failures are passed over discreetly. There is an unqualified endorsement of the Maccabean house, and of the people whom they lead. The conviction that God is with them gives the people confidence in their struggle. It does not make their conduct very obviously different from that of other people. True, they observe the law and venerate the temple, but the law is not absolute, and exceptions can be made when the need arises. More fundamentally, both the temple and the law were cherished because they symbolized the distinctive identity of the Jewish people. The advancement of the people is the primary concern. As we have seen at various points, this advancement cannot be completely categorized as a liberation movement. It extends to the developing power of the Jewish state. 1 Maccabees is not a manifesto for the liberation of all oppressed peoples. It is an account of one people's acquisition of power.

1 Maccabees is a far less idealistic book than Daniel. Despite the persistent antithesis of Jews and gentiles, the heroes of the book repeatedly compromise with gentile rulers. The Maccabees emerge as pragmatists. They have some absolutes. They refrain from idolatry and are devoted to the temple, but on the whole they are remarkably flexible. In the end, they must be judged by what they accomplished. This was something less than the utopia of 1 Mac 14, but it certainly enhanced the freedom and self-respect of the Jewish people.

It is somewhat ironic that 1 Maccabees was not included in the Jewish canon. It may be that the canon was essentially closed before it was written. It may also be that popular veneration of the family declined under the reigns of their successors. Some pious Jews, such as the Essenes of Qumran, would evidently have rejected the view of Judaism proposed here.

The inclusion of 1 Maccabees in the Catholic canon adds an interesting perspective to the collection of scripture. The book addresses the religious problems of political power much more directly than the more visionary books do. The wise leaders in Daniel "leave the fighting to God" and work to preserve purity despite the prevailing political structures. Yet it is inevitable that some people exercise power in the society. The Maccabees represent religion through the exercise of power, instead of through avoidance. Their religion consequently loses much of its purity, but they must be credited with a vigorous sense of human responsibility. The society they produced may not have been as deeply informed by religious principles as the pietists would wish, but at least they achieved some practical improvements in the conditions of the present, rather than wait for the ideal state which may never come.

The model of the Maccabees was itself a reapplication of old biblical models such as those of Phinehas, Joshua and the Judges. The close identification of God with the interests of one particular people and its rulers has ample precedent in the stories of the Conquest and in the Royal Psalms. It is a model which remains attractive to any people that has suffered oppression. Its recourse to violence cannot in itself disqualify this model as a religious course of action. There may be times when it is justified and necessary.

The dangers inherent in the model are all too apparent. The unqualified endorsement of a particular family is an invitation to the abuse of power. Violence breeds more violence and the violent deaths of the Maccabean brothers contains a lesson which should not be ignored. Moreover, the success of such a model is heavily dependent on the circumstances of the particular time and place. Policies that worked well against the Seleucids brought sheer disaster when used against the Romans.

Perhaps the greatest shortcoming of the religious

ideology of 1 Maccabees is that it only accounts for victories and not for failures. Belief that God is on your side may encourage the soldier, but it does not in itself guarantee victory. Sooner or later defeat and failure require a religious explanation too if religion is really to help people cope with the vicissitudes of life.

SECOND MACCABEES

Second Maccabees:
Introduction

2 MACCABEES covers the course of events leading up to the persecution by Antiochus Epiphanes, the persecution itself, and the Maccabean revolt down to the victory over Nicanor in 161 BCE. There is thus considerable overlap with 1 Maccabees, especially in 2 Mac 8-15 and 1 Mac 3-7. Yet the overall impression of the two books is quite different. In place of the sober narrative of 1 Maccabees, 2 Maccabees presents a vivid and emotional account. Miraculous and supernatural occurrences are freely interspersed in the story. Perhaps the most obvious and best known aspect of the book is the heavy concentration on the deaths of the martyrs, which is evidently designed to move and inspire, rather than simply inform. Because of these features, the historical value of 2 Maccabees has often been doubted, and it has been conventional to characterize 1 Maccabees as "historical" but 2 Maccabees as "religious." Such a contrast, however, is far too simple. We have seen that 1 Maccabees is shaped by its own theology and ideology. While 2 Maccabees is more obviously theological in character, it is also of considerable importance as an historical source.

The composition of 2 Maccabees
2 Maccabees is not an original work but is a summary of

a five volume work by one Jason of Cyrene. The summary is introduced at 2:19 as "the story of Judas Maccabeus and his brothers, and the purification of the great temple, and the dedication of the altar, and further the wars against Antiochus Epiphanes and his son Eupator, and the appearances which came from heaven. . ." In fact the story extends beyond Antiochus V Eupator to Demetrius I, but we do not need to suppose that this was an addition to Jason's work as it is still within the career of Judas.

The abbreviator (or Epitomator, as he is often called, from the Greek *epitome,* summary) compares his task to that of the decorator of a house, so we may assume that he has also undertaken some embellishment of the story. The preface in 2:19-32 and the conclusion in 15:37-39 are evidently from his hand, as likewise are the editorial comments in 6:12-17 and probably also those in 4:17 and 5:17-20.

Whether the summary includes narrative material which was not in Jason's work is more difficult to say. Some scholars regard 2 Mac 7, the story of the seven brothers, as an independent composition which may have been inserted by a third party after the work of the abbreviator. There are various reasons for this suggestion: differences in style, the fact that the brothers are brought before the king although he was not present in Jerusalem, the lack of reference to the temple in this chapter. As we shall see in the commentary, this story is evidently a legend and was probably originally an independent story. Yet it fits in so well with the theology of 2 Maccabees that we must assume it was included by the abbreviator. Whether it was also included in Jason's history is less clear. It is noteworthy that the summary description of Jason's work in 2:19-22 (which we have quoted above), makes no reference to the deaths of the martyrs, although they play a crucial part in the story. It is possible that chapter 7 was added by the abbreviator as part of the work of embellishment, but we cannot exclude the possibility that it was already contained in Jason's work.

Scholars have also suspected that the death-bed letter of Antiochus Ephiphanes in 9:18-27 is an embellishment which was not found in Jason's work. The letter is preceded by a fantastic account of the king's repentance, and his alleged intention to convert to Judaism. The letter itself, however, has none of this blatant Jewish character, and may.well be an authentic letter or an adaptation of one.

In addition to this disputed letter in chapter 9, 2 Maccabees includes six other letters. Two of these stand as a preface to the book in 1:1-2:18, and are not part of the summary. We shall return to them below when we discuss the date of composition. The other four, in chapter 11, are substantially authentic letters, although they are out of order and out of context.

This discussion of the composition is of significance for our understanding of 2 Maccabees in two respects. First, while the author of the book as we now have it, was not, on his own admission (2:28) concerned with the exact details, he was adapting a lengthy and rather comprehensive historical work. Second, the book as we now have it is an integral document in its own right. We can no longer be sure whether the story of the seven brothers or the death-bed letter of Antiochus Epiphanes were part of Jason's work, and we cannot profitably discuss the theological perspective of the original history. The abbreviator has taken the material supplied by Jason and given it his own theological stamp.

The date of composition

Jason of Cyrene may well have been an eyewitness of the events he recorded. He probably wrote his history not too long after the last events he recorded—that is, shortly after 160 BCE. In view of his enthusiasm both for Onias III, the last legitimate high priest, and for Judas Maccabee, he probably wrote before the Maccabees usurped the high priesthood (Jonathan became high priest in 152 BCE). The suggestion that Jason was a contemporary of Judas Maccabee is supported by the casual reference in 4:11 to Eupolemus, who went on the mission to Rome (cf. 1 Mac 8:17), and who is presumed to be well known to the readers. The fact that Eupolemus' companion on the mission to Rome was named Jason is intriguing, although the identification with Jason of Cyrene is no more than a possibility.

The main clue to the date of Second Maccabees in its present form is found in the letters which are pre-fixed to the book. There is wide agreement that the first of these letters, 2 Mac 1:1-9, is an authentic letter, urging the Jews of Egypt to celebrate the festival of Hanukkah. This letter is dated to 124 BCE in 1:9 (the one hundred and eighty-eighth year). The summary of Jason's history is appended to this letter to provide an explanation and motivation for the celebration. It is plausible to assume that the summary was made for this occasion, although we can not, of course, be certain. It does not follow that the abbreviator's main concern was to persuade the Jews of Egypt to celebrate Hanukkah. His work has its own theological message over and above the support it could lend to the letter to Egypt.

The first letter refers, in 1:7, to an earlier letter in 143 BCE. This earlier letter is not preserved. There is, however, a second, lengthy, letter in 1:10-2:18, which is ostensibly sent from "those in Jerusalem and those in Judea and the senate and Judas" shortly before the original re-consecration of the temple in 164 BCE, but after the death of Antiochus Epiphanes. This letter is generally regarded as inauthentic. It is doubtful whether the king's death was known in Jerusalem before the re-consecration of the temple. Moreover, the Senate was still loyal to Menelaus in 164 BCE. There is little agreement, however, as to the real date of this letter. Many scholars think it is a later insertion in 2 Maccabees, perhaps from the first century BCE. It cannot be the work of the abbreviator, since the account of the king's death is contradictory to that in 2 Mac 9. It may, however, be an older letter which was incorporated in 2 Maccabees in 124 BCE. While it was not written before the actual re-consecration in 164 BCE, it may conceivably have been written before the annual celebration of Hanukkah at some later point. The letter is not formally dated, and the name of Judas may have been inserted through a misunderstanding. It must be said that the provenance of this second letter is the most obscure of all the questions regarding the composition of 2 Maccabees.

Historical value

Despite the inclusion of fantastic and legendary stories, 2 Maccabees is an important historical source. It is the main source of information on the internal strife in Jerusalem which led up to the persecution of Antiochus Epiphanes and is far more illuminating than the terse and oversimplified account of 1 Maccabees on this period. 2 Maccabees correctly places the death of Antiochus Epiphanes before the purification of the temple. The order is reversed in 1 Maccabees. 2 Maccabees shows a detailed knowledge of the institutions of the Seleucid empire. Even when it becomes melodramatic and legendary, it remains within the conventions of Hellenistic history writing. 2 Maccabees is often described as "tragic" or (rather infelicitously) "pathetic" history writing because of its persistent appeal to the emotions. Yet this emotional quality is typical of most Hellenistic history writing, even of a leading historian such as Polybius, who criticizes others for being too emotional. Also the appeals to the supernatural were by no means uncommon in Hellenistic historians. This is not to say that the miraculous episodes in 2 Maccabees must be regarded as historical, but that they are compatible with conventions of ancient history writing, and should not detract from the credibility of the genuine historical information provided by 2 Maccabees.

2 Maccabees is not always reliable in its historical data. Apart from the obvious legendary episodes, such as the

death-bed conversion of Antiochus Epiphanes, we have
noted that the letters in chapter 11 are jumbled. Some other
historical details are also loosely handled—e.g. Timothy is
killed in 10:37 but reappears, alive and active, in 12:2. (It is
unlikely that there were two Timothys in question.) Yet
despite its aberrations, 2 Maccabees is now recognized as a
much more valuable historical source than was thought by
scholars of earlier generations.

Theological and political perspective

2 Maccabees has often been viewed as a propaganda document for the Jerusalem temple. Such a function would be
highly compatible with the introductory letter urging the
Jews in Egypt to celebrate Hanukkah, the feast of the purification of the temple. In fact, 2 Maccabees is structured as
the account of a series of attacks on the temple and its defence: 2 Mac 3; 4:1-10:9 and 10:10-15:36. The first of these is
"the episode of Heliodorus and the protection of the
treasury" (3:40). The second is the persecution of Antiochus
Epiphanes and culminates with the re-dedication of the temple. The third is concerned with the continued attacks on
Jewish territory and ends with the defeat of Nicanor, from
which time it is said that "the city has been in the possession
of the Hebrews" (2 Mac 15:37).

Yet the interest in the temple must be seen in perspective:
"the Lord did not choose the nation for the sake of the holy
place, but the place for the sake of the nation" (5:19). As in 1
Maccabees, the Jewish people is of primary importance.
The temple is a symbol of the covenant. It shares in the misfortunes and glories of the people. The destiny of the people, in turn, is bound up with the covenant, and the people's
fidelity to the law. So the attack of Heliodorus fails because
"the laws were very well observed because of the piety of the
high priest Onias" (3:1). The attack of Antiochus Epiphanes
succeeds for a time because "they were involved in many

sins" (5:18). When the tide eventually turns, it is due in part to the virtue and prowess of Judas Maccabee, but it is also due to the blood of the martyrs which has been shed.

At this point 2 Maccabees diverges from 1 Maccabees, with which it shares the respect for the temple and fidelity to the covenant. We have seen that 1 Maccabees was highly pragmatic, and thoroughly committed to the Maccabean family. When God saves his people, he does so through his chosen human instruments, the Maccabees. There are no direct, miraculous, supernatural interventions in 1 Maccabees. Since it is up to the Jews and specifically the Maccabees to provide for themselves, it is even necessary to make an exception to the law and fight on the sabbath. This exception is not noted in 2 Maccabees. Instead the emphasis is on full devotion to the law, even unto death. In this respect, 2 Maccabees stands closer to Daniel. Like Daniel too, 2 Maccabees provides the underpinning for martyrdom with the belief in resurrection—a belief which was notably lacking in 1 Maccabees.

2 Maccabees, then has a rather more idealistic view of the covenant than 1 Maccabees. Yet it shows no reservations in its support for Judas. In this respect it differs from Daniel, which practically ignores the armed revolt and expects salvation from heaven. The support for Judas must be seen in perspective. The role of the supernatural is much more clearly emphasized than was the case in 1 Maccabees. The rest of the Maccabean family is passed over in silence. True, since the narrative deals with the career of Judas, there is little occasion to speak of Jonathan and Simon, although the heroic death of Eleazar is curiously ignored at 2 Mac 13:15. Most striking, however, is the omission of Mattathias, who is not even mentioned. In the perspective of 2 Maccabees the power of God is not committed to a chosen family, but to those who keep the law. Judas is characterized in 14:6 as the leader of the Hasideans, the pious Jews who had joined the

Maccabeans somewhat belatedly, according to 1 Mac 2, and who were eager to make peace when Alcimus was appointed high priest. It is tempting to suppose that 2 Maccabees reflects the viewpoint of these Hasideans, marked by devotion to the law and to the traditional priesthood, but we do not know enough about the Hasideans to make such a claim with any confidence.

The theology of 2 Maccabees is one of intense devotion to the law. Death, even suicide, in the case of Razis in chapter 14, is desirable in defence of the law. The rewards of loyalty are possession of the city and temple for the Jewish people and resurrection for the individual. There is no claim here of higher revelation, as in Daniel. The revelation that has been given in the law of Moses is sufficient.

For the modern reader 2 Maccabees combines the problems of Daniel and 1 Maccabees. On the one hand there is the question of martyrdom, and even of suicide. Was such sacrifice of life necessary or justified? And do the Maccabean martyrs provide a paradigm to be imitated? On the other hand, there is the violence, sometimes vengeful, of Judas against his "barbarian" enemies. On the latter point it should be said that 2 Maccabees is by no means simplistic in its contrast of Jews and gentiles. The entire work, in style, form and language is steeped in Greek culture. Some Greeks are sympathetic to the Jews. Even Antiochus Epiphanes has a death-bed conversion. The Jews do not reject pagan rule, but only its abuses, and are shown as good peace-loving citizens. There is no war to the death between Greek and Jew. Yet the book has its nationalistic dimension too. God is the God of the Jews, who fights for his people and his city.

2 Maccabees does not provide simple paradigms which can be recommended for all situations, any more than did Daniel or 1 Maccabees. Its significance to-day is that it raises certain questions, and proposes some responses, which were not the only religious responses in antiquity or now. The

questions concern religious idealism and political reality, the choice of absolute values in the face of death, the power and the danger of the visionary's confidence in the supernatural and the miraculous. 2 Maccabees provides an occasion to reflect on these questions. We should not expect it to provide definitive answers.

SECOND MACCABEES: COMMENTARY

Introductory Material

2 MAC 1:1-9: THE FIRST LETTER

1 The Jewish brethren in Jerusalem and those in the land of Judea.

To their Jewish brethren in Egypt,

Greeting, and good peace.

²May God do good to you, and may he remember his covenant with Abraham and Isaac and Jacob, his faithful servants. ³May he give you all a heart to worship him and to do his will with a strong heart and a willing spirit. ⁴May he open your heart to his law and his commandments, and may he bring peace. ⁵May he hear your prayers and be reconciled to you, and may he not forsake you in time of evil. ⁶We are now praying for you here.

⁷In the reign of Demetrius, in the one hundred and sixty-ninth year, we Jews wrote to you, in the critical distress which came upon us in those years after Jason and his company revolted from the holy land and the kingdom ⁸and burned the gate and shed innocent blood. We besought the Lord and we were heard, and we offered sacrifice and cereal offering, and we lighted the lamps

and we set out the loaves. ⁹And now see that you keep the feast of booths in the month of Chislev, in the one hundred and eighty-eighth year.

The purpose of the introductory letter is to invite the Jews of Egypt to join in celebrating the feast of Hanukkah, as a gesture of Jewish unity. The letter does not imply that there had been any disunity between Egyptian Jewry and the homeland. Onias IV, son of Onias III the last legitimate high priest, had fled to Egypt and had been permitted by the Ptolemy to build a temple at Leontopolis. This temple was in defiance of Jewish law which prohibited any temple outside of Jerusalem. Yet there is no evidence that the temple of Onias was ever a rival to that of Jerusalem or that there was any suggestion that Egyptian Judaism would break off from the homeland in any way. The letter prefixed to 2 Maccabees was necessary because the festival of Hanukkah had not become current in the Diaspora, not because there was any regional schism.

The brief letter gives a clear indication of the religious values of those who sent it. Two points stand out. First is the covenant with Abraham, Isaac and Jacob. This ancient covenant is the basis for the unity of the scattered branches of Judaism. Second, membership within this covenant is assured by worshipping God and keeping his commandments. Keeping his commandments is in itself a sign of God's favor and assurance of help in time of need. The experience of the persecution under Antiochus with its eventual deliverance, is taken as evidence of God's fidelity to the covenant, and cause for celebration.

We may sense here at the outset part of the problem involved in 2 Maccabees and also in any theology of history which attempts to infer a pattern from particular events. In the case of the Maccabean revolt, the Jews who were faithful to the traditional covenant were rewarded with success. It does not follow that every time a people in distress besought the Lord, he would answer them. We can understand, however, how the Jews who had experienced the rebellion and its outcome might think that success was determined by virtue. This theology is reminiscent of the Deuteronomic theology of the OT. Its weakness lies in the rather facile correlation of virtue and success, which was penetratingly criticized in the Book of Job. Its strength lies in the self-critical stance which does not blame misfortunes simply on the wickedness of foreigners but looks for the problems within the people itself. 2 Maccabees gives the most penetrating analysis of the responsibility of Jews for the events which culminated in the persecution of Antiochus Epiphanes.

The Second Letter

2 MAC 1:10-17: THE DEATH OF ANTIOCHUS

[10]Those in Jerusalem and those in Judea and the senate and Judas, To Aristobulus, who is of the family of the anointed priests, teacher of Ptolemy the king, and to the Jews in Egypt,

Greeting, and good health.

[11]Having been saved by God out of grave dangers we thank him greatly for taking our side against the king. [12]For he drove out those who fought against the holy city. [13]For when the leader reached Persia with a force that seemed irresistible, they were cut to pieces in the temple of Nanea by a deception employed by the priests of Nanea. [14]For under pretext of intending to marry her, Antiochus came to the place together with his friends, to secure most of its treasures as a dowry. [15]When the priests of the temple of Nanea had set out the treasures and Antiochus had come with a few men inside the wall of the sacred precinct, they closed the temple as soon as he entered it.

¹⁶Opening the secret door in the ceiling, they threw stones and struck down the leader and his men, and dismembered them and cut off their heads and threw them to the people outside. ¹⁷Blessed in every way be our God, who has brought judgment upon those who have behaved impiously.

The first episode in the second letter is also Deuteronomic in theology and also introduces a theme which will recur throughout 2 Maccabees - tyrants are punished in their death. The actual account given here of the death of Antiochus Epiphanes contradicts even the account given in 2 Mac 9. Antiochus IV was not killed in the raid on the temple but died shortly afterwards. Antiochus III had been killed in a raid on a temple. Jews in Jerusalem or Egypt may not have had precise knowledge of the manner of the king's death.

The Aristobulus addressed at the beginning of the letter is presumably the Jewish Alexandrian philosopher who wrote an allegorical commentary on the Torah, of which fragments survived. His name is used here because he was one of the most famous Jews in Egypt in the mid-second century BCE.

2 MAC 1:18-2:18: THE LEGEND OF THE FIRE

¹⁸Since on the twenty-fifth day of Chislev we shall celebrate the purification of the temple, we thought it necessary to notify you, in order that you also may celebrate the feast of booths and the feast of the fire given when Nehemiah, who built the temple and altar, offered sacrifices.

¹⁹For when our fathers were being led captive to Persia, the pious priests of that time took some of the fire of the altar and secretly hid it in the hollow of a dry cistern, where they took such precautions that the place was

unknown to any one. [20]But after many years had passed, when it pleased God, Nehemiah, having been commissioned by the king of Persia, sent the descendants of the priests who had hidden the fire to get it. And when they reported to us that they had not found fire but thick liquid, he ordered them to dip it out and bring it. [21]And when the materials for the sacrifices were presented, Nehemiah ordered the priests to sprinkle the liquid on the wood and what was laid upon it. [22]When this was done and some time had passed and the sun, which had been clouded over, shone out, a great fire blazed up, so that all marveled. [23]And while the sacrifice was being consumed, the priests offered prayer—the priests and every one. Jonathan led, and the rest responded, as did Nehemiah. [24]The prayer was to this effect:

"O Lord, Lord God, Creator of all things, who art awe-inspiring and strong and just and merciful, who alone art King and art kind, [25]who alone art bountiful, rescue Israel from every evil, who didst choose the fathers and consecrate them, [26]accept this sacrifice on behalf of all thy people Israel and preserve thy portion and make it holy. [27]Gather together our scattered people, set free those who are slaves among the Gentiles, look upon those who are rejected and despised, and let the Gentiles know that thou art our God. [28]Afflict those who oppress and are insolent with pride. [29]Plant thy people in thy holy place, as Moses said."

[30]Then the priests sang the hymns. [31]And when the materials of the sacrifice were consumed, Nehemiah ordered that the liqud that was left should be poured upon large stones. [32]When this was done, a flame blazed up; but when the light from the altar shone back, it went out. [33]When this matter became known, and it was reported to the king of the Persians that, in the place where the exiled priests had hidden the fire, the liquid had appeared with

which Nehemiah and his associates had burned the materials of the sacrifice, [34]the king investigated the matter, and enclosed the place and made it sacred. [35]And with those persons whom the king favored he exchanged many excellent gifts. [36]Nehemiah and his associates called this "nephthar," which means purification, but by most people it is called naphtha.

2 One finds in the records that Jeremiah the prophet ordered those who were being deported to take some of the fire, as has been told, [2]and that the prophet after giving them the law instructed those who were being deported not to forget the commandments of the Lord, nor to be led astray in their thoughts upon seeing the gold and silver statues and their adornment. [3]And with other similar words he exhorted them that the law should not depart from their hearts.

[4]It was also in the writing that the prophet, having received an oracle, ordered that the tent and the ark should follow with him, and that he went out to the mountain where Moses had gone up and had seen the inheritance of God. [5]And Jeremiah came and found a cave, and he brought there the tent and the ark and the altar of incense, and he sealed up the entrance. [6]Some of those who followed him came up to mark the way, but could not find it. [7]When Jeremiah learned of it, he rebuked them and declared: "The place shall be unknown until God gathers his people together again and shows his mercy. [8]And then the Lord will disclose these things, and the glory of the Lord and the cloud will appear, as they were shown in the case of Moses, and as Solomon asked that the place should be specially consecrated."

[9]It was also made clear that being possessed of wisdom Solomon offered sacrifice for the dedication and completion of the temple. [10]Just as Moses prayed to the Lord, and fire came down from heaven and devoured the sacri-

fices, so also Solomon prayed, and the fire came down and consumed the whole burnt offerings. ¹¹And Moses said, "They were consumed because the sin offering had not been eaten." ¹²Likewise Solomon also kept the eight days.

¹³The same things are reported in the records and in the memoirs of Nehemiah, and also that he founded a library and collected the books about the kings and prophets, and the writings of David, and letters of kings about votive offerings. ¹⁴In the same way Judas also collected all the books that had been lost on account of the war which had come upon us, and they are in our possession. ¹⁵So if you have need of them, send people to get them for you.

¹⁶Since, therefore, we are about to celebrate the purification, we write to you. Will you therefore please keep the days? ¹⁷It is God who has saved all his people, and has returned the inheritance to all, and the kingship and priesthood and consecration, ¹⁸as he promised through the law. For we have hope in God that he will soon have mercy upon us and will gather us from everywhere under heaven into his holy place, for he has rescued us from great evils and has purified the place.

The long digression on "the fire given when Nehemiah, who built the temple and altar," is obviously legendary in character. To begin with, Nehemiah did not build the temple. He re-built the walls of Jerusalem, but the temple had been re-built by Zerubabbel about 70 years before Nehemiah. Moreover, the Jews had not been taken captive to Persia but to Babylon. The story provides a pseudo-etymology for *naphtha* (petroleum), which can not be justified philologically. The story of the hiding of the fire and its association with Nehemiah and Jeremiah has no historical basis.

This legend is inserted at the beginning of 2 Maccabees for two reasons. First, it is apparent from 1:18 that a "feast of the fire" was celebrated in conjunction with Hanukkah. (The "feast of booths" here refers to Hanukkah and presumably implies that Hanukkah is comparable to the great feast of Tabernacles or Succoth). We know little about this celebration. Apparently it was not familiar to the Jews of Egypt, as the letter has to explain it to them. We do not know how widely it was ever celebrated or how long it survived. The most obvious purpose of the legend is to provide a rationale for this celebration.

More important than the historical curiosity of this celebration is the second purpose of the legend—to establish and strengthen the sense of divine approval for the temple. The fire hidden before the exile makes for continuity between Solomon's temple and that of the post-exilic era. The sense of continuity with the past is underlined by the references to Moses and Solomon in 2 Mac 2:9-12. The names of Nehemiah and Jeremiah were also illustrious. The legend wishes to suggest that the worship of the temple in the second century BCE is the worship of Solomon, Nehemiah and Jeremiah, and therefore proper, and worthy of confidence. The miraculous preservation of the fire indicates the approval of God.

This legend arose because some Jews in the post-exilic period had doubts as to whether the restored temple had the same status as the old one. These doubts must have been especially acute in the second century BCE, when the temple had been profaned, not only by the Syrians, but by the illegitimate Jewish high priests. Even the Maccabees did not belong to the traditional priestly line. Hence the compiler of 2 Maccabees in its final form wished to include any material which would restore confidence in the temple.

From a modern critical viewpoint, this legend scarcely inspires confidence in anything. It requires a considerable will to believe on the part of the reader. Even in antiquity, this story can only have been effective with people who were predisposed to believe in the sanctity of the Jerusalem temple.

That sanctity derived in part from the antiquity of the temple and of the rituals performed there. While the legend of the fire had no historical basis, there was undeniable continuity between the temple of the Hellenistic age and the worship of the times of Nehemiah, Jeremiah and even Solomon. However far-fetched its details, the legend reminded the Jews of the real antiquity of their religion. The real message of the story lay in its appeal for fidelity to the religion of the fathers.

Fidelity to tradition involved also fidelity to the specific place, Jerusalem, however that fidelity might be expressed. The importance of the place, we might say the "turf," is shown in the prayer of Nehemiah in 2 Mac 1:24-29: "Gather together our scattered people. . . plant thy people in thy holy place." The concrete particularism of Jewish faith has often seemed scandalous to Christians. Yet it is doubtful whether Christianity, or any other religion, could survive long without specific concrete symbols, and without some "turf," some special place to give orientation to the people. The temple symbolized the unity and the distinct identity of the Jewish people. True, history would show that it was not an indispensible symbol, but Jerusalem and the land of Israel have always had tremendous symbolic and psychological importance for Judaism. The legend of the fire expresses and affirms the importance of the sacred place.

Christians, who do not find their basic identity in Judaism may have some difficulty in fully appreciating the specifically Jewish symbols. They can at least appreciate the light this legend throws on the nature of the religious tradition which is also part of the Christian heritage. The religion envisaged in the second letter of 2 Maccabees is one which organizes the lives of the people by giving them a sense that they belong to an ancient tradition and have a sacred place. It enables them to feel that they belong to something lasting, and something which derives significance from the approval of God. For a people largely scattered among the gentiles, the traditions and the place provide a sense of security and self-worth. It is important to realize that such a sense of security and identity is a vital part of religion, and is a necessary underpinning for the loftier ethical concerns.

The concluding paragraphs of the letter highlight some other crucial components of the Jewish tradition. Nehemiah is said to have collected the books about the kings and prophets, and Judas Maccabee likewise collected "the books which had been lost." Many scholars believe that Judas Maccabee played a significant part in forming the canon of the Hebrew scriptures. It is noteworthy that the collection of scriptures was undertaken at a time of crisis, when the Jewish people was re-assembling its resources and re-organizing in the face of a threat. The scriptures have played an even more fundamental role in the preservation of Jewish identity than have the temple and the land. We should note that the emphasis here is not on the content of the books collected by Judas. The point is that there is a collection of representative books, and all Jews should have them. The scriptures, like the temple, are a symbol of unity and identity.

The letter concludes with the renewed appeal to join in the celebration of Hanukkah. We can now better appreciate the significance of the festival. It celebrates not only the triumph of the Maccabees but the persistence and survival of the Jewish religion. As such it is a fitting preface for 2 Maccabees, no matter when it was added to the book. 2 Maccabees too is more than the account of an historical episode. It is an affirmation that the Jewish religion can overcome the most severe crisis and provide enduring resources for fulfilment in life.

2 MAC 2:19-32: THE ABBREVIATOR'S PREFACE

[19]The story of Judas Maccabeus and his brothers, and the purification of the great temple, and the dedication of

the altar, [20]and further the wars against Antiochus Epiphanes and his son Eupator, [21]and the appearances which came from heaven to those who strove zealously on behalf of Judaism, so that though few in number they seized the whole land and pursued the barbarian hordes, [22]and recovered the temple famous throughout the world and freed the city and restored the laws that were about to be abolished, while the Lord with great kindness became gracious to them—[23]all this, which has been set forth by Jason of Cyrene in five volumes, we shall attempt to condense into a single book. [24]For considering the flood of numbers involved and the difficulty there is for those who wish to enter upon the narratives of history because of the mass of material, [25]we have aimed to please those who wish to read, to make it easy for those who are inclined to memorize, and to profit all readers. [26]For us who have undertaken the toil of abbreviating, it is no light matter but calls for sweat and loss of sleep, [27]just as it is not easy for one who prepares a banquet and seeks the benefit of others. However, to secure the gratitude of many we will gladly endure the uncomfortable toil, [28]leaving the responsibility for exact details to the compiler, while devoting our effort to arriving at the outlines of the condensation. [29]For as the master builder of a new house must be concerned with the whole construction, while the one who undertakes its painting and decoration has to consider only what is suitable for its adornment, such in my judgment is the case with us. [30]It is the duty of the original historian to occupy the ground and to discuss matters from every side and to take trouble with details, [31]but the one who recasts the narrative should be allowed to strive for brevity of expression and to forego exhaustive treatment. [32]At this point therefore let us begin our narrative, adding only so much to what has already been said; for it is foolish to lengthen the preface while cutting short the history itself.

We have already commented on the translator's preface in the Introduction to 2 Maccabees. It highlights the importance of the temple in the story and also the role of the supernatural in the success of the Maccabees. It is apparent that the abbreviator has undertaken some embellishment, over and above the narrative of Jason, but this preface provides little guidance for distinguishing between the two authors. The work as we have it must be taken to reflect the theology of the abbreviator.

Part One: The First Assault on the Temple

2 MAC 3: THE LEGEND OF HELIODORUS

3 While the holy city was inhabited in unbroken peace and the laws were very well observed because of the piety of the high priest Onias and his hatred of wickedness, ²it came about that the kings themselves honored the place and glorified the temple with the finest presents, ³so that even Seleucus, the king of Asia, defrayed from his own revenues all the expenses connected with the service of the sacrifices. ⁴But a man named Simon, of the tribe of Benjamin, who had been made captain of the temple, had a disagreement with the high priest about the administration of the city market; ⁵and when he could not prevail over Onias he went to Apollonius of Tarsus, who at that time was governor of Coelesyria and Phoenicia. ⁶He reported to him that the treasury in Jerusalem was full of untold sums of money, so that the amount of the funds could not be reckoned, and that they did not belong to the account of the sacrifices, but that it was possible for them to fall under the control of the king. ⁷When Apollonius met the king, he told him of the money about which he had been informed. The king chose Heliodorus, who was in charge of his affairs, and sent him with commands to effect the removal of the aforesaid money. ⁸Heliodorus at once set out on his journey, ostensibly to make a tour of inspection of the cities of Coelesyria and Phoenicia, but in fact to carry out the king's purpose.

⁹When he had arrived at Jerusalem and had been kindly welcomed by the high priest of the city, he told about the disclosure that had been made and stated why he had come, and he inquired whether this really was the situation. ¹⁰The high priest explained that there were some deposits belonging to widows and orphans, ¹¹and also some money of Hyrcanus, son of Tobias, a man of very prominent position, and that it totaled in all four hundred talents of silver and two hundred of gold. To such an extent the impious Simon had misrepresented the facts. ¹²And he said that it was utterly impossible that wrong should be done to those people who had trusted in the holiness of the place and in the sanctity and inviolability of the temple which is honored throughout the whole world. ¹³But Heliodorus, because of the king's commands which he had, said that this money must in any case be confiscated for the king's treasury. ¹⁴So he set a day and went in to direct the inspection of these funds.

There was no little distress throughout the whole city. ¹⁵The priests prostrated themselves before the altar in their priestly garments and called toward heaven upon him who had given the law about deposits, that he should keep them safe for those who had deposited them. ¹⁶To see the appearance of the high priest was to be wounded at heart, for his face and the change in his color disclosed the anguish of his soul. ¹⁷For terror and bodily trembling had come over the man, which plainly showed to those who looked at him the pain lodged in his heart. ¹⁸People also hurried out of their houses in crowds to make a general supplication because the holy place was about to be brought into contempt. [19]Women, girded with sackcloth under their breasts, thronged the streets. Some of the maidens who were kept indoors ran together to the gates, and some to the walls, while others peered out of the windows. [20]And holding up their hands to heaven, they all made entreaty. [21]There was something pitiable in the prostration of the whole populace and the anxiety of the high priest in his great anguish.

[22]While they were calling upon the Almighty Lord that he would keep what had been entrusted safe and secure for those who had entrusted it, [23]Heliodorus went on with what had been decided. [24]But when he arrived at the treasury with his bodyguard, then and there the Sovereign of spirits and of all authority caused so great a manifestation that all who had been so bold as to accompany him were astounded by the power of God, and became faint with terror. [25]For there appeared to them a magnificently caparisoned horse, with a rider of frightening mien, and it rushed furiously at Heliodorus and struck at him with its front hoofs. Its rider was seen to have armor and weapons of gold. [26]Two young men also appeared to him, remarkably strong, gloriously beautiful and splendidly dressed, who stood on each side of him and scourged him continuously, inflicting many blows on him. [27]When he suddenly fell to the ground and deep darkness came over him, his men took him up and put him on a stretcher [28]and carried him away, this man who had just entered the aforesaid treasury with a great retinue and all his bodyguard but was now unable to help himself; and they recognized clearly the sovereign power of God. [29]While he lay prostrate, speechless because of the divine intervention and deprived of any hope of recovery, [30]they praised the Lord who had acted marvelously for his own place. And the temple, which a little while before was full of fear

and disturbance, was filled with joy and gladness, now
that the Almighty Lord had appeared.

[31]Quickly some of Heliodorus' friends asked Onias to
call upon the Most High and to grant life to one who was
lying quite at his last breath. [32]And the high priest, fearing
that the king might get the notion that some foul play had
been perpetrated by the Jews with regard to Heliodorus,
offered sacrifice for the man's recovery. [33]While the high
priest was making the offering of atonement, the same
young men appeared again to Heliodorus, dressed in the
same clothing, and they stood and said, "Be very grateful
to Onias the high priest, since for his sake the Lord has
granted you your life. [34]And see that you, who have been
scourged by heaven, report to all men the majestic power
of God." Having said this they vanished.

[35]Then Heliodorus offered sacrifice to the Lord and
made very great vows to the Savior of his life, and having
bidden Onias farewell, he marched off with his forces to
the king. [36]And he bore testimony to all men of the deeds
of the supreme God, which he had seen with his own eyes.
[37]When the king asked Heliodorus what sort of person
would be suitable to send on another mission to Jerusalem, he replied, [38]"If you have any enemy or plotter
against your government, send him there, for you will get
him back thoroughly scourged, if he escapes at all, for
there certainly is about the place some power of God.
[39]For he who has his dwelling in heaven watches over that
place himself and brings it aid, and he strikes and destroys
those who come to do it injury." [40]This was the outcome
of the episode of Heliodorus and the protection of the
treasury.

2 Maccabees 3 is a blend of historical information and
pious legend.

Unlike 1 Maccabees, 2 Maccabees does not locate the

origin of the crisis immediately in the actions of Antiochus Epiphanes, but rather in the tensions within the Jewish community which were present already under Seleucus IV. For most of the Hellenistic period Jerusalem had been subject to the Ptolemies of Egypt. It had passed into the control of the Seleucids at the beginning of the second century BCE. Some Jews, however, were still sympathetic to the Ptolemies. The most prominent of these was Hyrcanus, son of Joseph, son of Tobias, who appears in our narrative at 2 Mac 3:11. This Hyrcanus had deposited money in the Jerusalem temple. The dispute about the temple funds must, then, be seen as political in nature. The fact that the pro-Egyptian Hyrcanus could keep his funds in the temple cast some suspicion on the loyalty of the high priest Onias. We can also see that Simon, the "captain of the temple," was prepared to exploit the situation, to increase his own power and influence at the expense of Onias. This kind of political infighting became a crucial factor in the events of the following years.

2 Maccabees brings its own political perspective to the story. The high priest, Onias, is above reproach, and is not suspected of any political motivation. He welcomes Heliodorus kindly, and, when the latter is stricken down, intercedes on his behalf. He is anxious to avoid the impression that there was any foul play by the Jews. Onias is represented as a man devoted to the temple and the law, who is a faithful subject of the king. 2 Maccabees does not regard Jewish independence as of crucial importance. What matters most is the observance of the law. It is doubtful whether Onias was as politically innocent as he is represented here. His portrayal is determined by the theology of 2 Maccabees rather than by the facts of history.

The chapter opens with the assertion that the city was at peace, and the temple was honored by the gentiles, because of the piety of the high priest. The high priest is a representative figure, but he must be seen in perspective. The peaceful situation results from the fact that the policies of a pious priest are followed by the people. The actions of the priest cannot be divorced from those of the people. Later, when the priesthood is corrupted, God's favor can be restored by the actions of Judas and the martyrs. The fortunes of the people are determined not only by the priesthood, but by the general observance of the law.

Undoubtedly, 2 Maccabees is naive when it suggests that peace and prosperity follow the observance of the law. This doctrine follows the Deuteronomic theology of the Old Testament, which had already been subjected to a penetrating critique in the Book of Job. We should note however that 2 Maccabees holds this doctrine in a somewhat flexible way. The sufferings of the martyrs are not viewed as punishment for their own sins, even if they do result from the sins of others. Besides it is true that the upheavals in the time of Antiochus Epiphanes were caused in large part by the attempt of the Hellenizing Jews to overthrow the traditional laws. The policies of Onias III may well have involved less risk of conflict with the king, or of strife within the people. Yet we must recognize that 2 Maccabees here is concerned to expound a theological message rather than to report history. The message is that Jews ought to concentrate on observing the law rather than engage in political opportunism. The claim that good observance resulted in peace in the time of Onias supplies motivation for this message. As we shall see, it is not the deepest motivation for observation of the law to be found in 2 Maccabees, but is rather a supplementary consideration, which is of some importance.

The climax of the chapter is the miraculous way in which Heliodorus is prevented from entering the city. The account conforms to a type of story which was widespread in the Hellenistic age, telling of the epiphany or apparition of a deity in defence of a city. A number of such epiphanies can be found in the Lindos Chronicle, an inscription dating from

99 BCE. A close parallel is found in the Third Book of Maccabees, where Ptolemy Philopator attempts to enter the temple but is scourged by God "so that he lay on the ground powerless and paralyzed in all his members" (3 Mac 2:22). The account in 3 Maccabees is apparently modelled on that of 2 Maccabees to some degree. A biblical precedent for this kind of story can be found in Isa 37:36 and 2 Kings 19:35, in the destruction of Sennacherib, when "the angel of the Lord went forth and slew a hundred and eighty five thousand in the camp of the Assyrians."

We may take it that Heliodorus made an attempt or threatened to enter the temple, and for some reason failed to do so. We cannot expect to extract the details of what happened from a legend of this sort. The story is designed to inspire awe and wonder and to strengthen the conviction that "he who has his dwelling in heaven watches over that place himself." We are reminded of the faith of the Psalmist: "God is in the midst of her, she shall not be moved" (Ps. 46 [45]:5). History had shown, however, that God did not always rescue Jerusalem and that she could in fact be moved, or at least her inhabitants could be moved to Babylon. 2 Maccabees adapts the traditional theology by making the divine protection contingent on the observance of the laws (below 5:18). This form of the belief is less prone to falsification, since observance of the laws is seldom perfect. In fact, the temple was successfully profaned by Antiochus Epiphanes and again, in the Roman era, by Pompey in 63 BCE and decisively by the destruction of 70 CE.

The miraculous character of the deliverance here must be seen in conjunction with the other apparitions later in the book. The author's lively belief in supernatural protection was no doubt strengthened by the eventual success of the Maccabean revolt and the re-purification of the temple. These developments can of course be explained in terms of disintegration of the Seleucid kingdom. Yet they were due to circumstances which lay outside the power of the Maccabees or of the Jewish people as a whole, and so could be seen as the work of God. This conviction, that the success of the Jewish people was due to a power which was more than human, is symbolically expressed in the story of Heliodorus.

The legendary character of the story is especially obvious at the end, where Heliodorus bears testimony to all men of the deeds of the supreme God. This was the Heliodorus who shortly afterwards murdered Seleucus IV. His conversion to the supreme God was, presumably, short-lived. In fact, 2 Maccabees repeatedly has pagans express their admiration for Judaism and even confess the God of Israel. The death-bed conversion of Antiochus Epiphanes in chapter 9 is an even less plausible instance. The author of 2 Maccabees was evidently concerned for the status of Judaism in the Hellenistic world. It is doubtful that the alleged conversion of Heliodorus would have impressed many gentiles, but it was a reassuring fantasy for the Jews.

Part Two: The Hellenistic Reform and the Persecution

2 MAC 4: THE CORRUPTION OF THE PRIESTHOOD

4 The previously mentioned Simon, who had informed about the money against his own country, slandered Onias, saying that it was he who had incited Heliodorus and had been the real cause of the misfortune. ²He dared to designate as a plotter against the government the man who was the benefactor of the city, the protector of his fellow countrymen, and a zealot for the laws. ³When his hatred progressed to such a degree that even murders were committed by one of Simon's approved agents, ⁴Onias recognized that the rivalry was serious and that Apollonius, the son of Menestheus and governor of Coele-syria and Phoenicia, was intensifying the malice of Simon. ⁵So he betook himself to the king, not accusing his fellow citizens but having in view the welfare, both public and private, of all the people. ⁶For he saw that without the king's attention public affairs could not again reach a peaceful settlement, and that Simon would not stop his folly.

⁷When Seleucus died and Antiochus who was called Epiphanes succeeded to the kingdom, Jason the brother of Onias obtained the high priesthood by corruption, ⁸promising the king at an interview three hundred and sixty talents of silver and, from another source of revenue, eighty talents. ⁹In addition to this he promised to pay one hundred and fifty more if permission were given to establish by his authority a gymnasium and a body of youth for it, and to enrol the men of Jerusalem as citizens of Antioch. ¹⁰When the king assented and Jason came to office, he at once shifted his countrymen over to the Greek way of life. ¹¹He set aside the existing royal concessions to the Jews, secured through John the father of Eupolemus, who went on the mission to establish friendship and alliance with the Romans; and he destroyed the lawful ways of living and introduced new customs contrary to the law. ¹²For with alacrity he founded a gymnasium right under the citadel, and he induced the noblest of the young men to wear the Greek hat. ¹³There was such an extreme of Hellenization and increase in the adoption of foreign ways because of the surpassing wickedness of Jason, who was ungodly and no high priest, ¹⁴that the priests were no longer intent upon their service at the altar. Despising the sanctuary and neglecting the sacrifices, they hastened to take part in the unlawful proceed-

ings in the wrestling arena after the call to the discus, [15]disdaining the honors prized by their fathers and putting the highest value upon Greek forms of prestige. [16]For this reason heavy disaster overtook them, and those whose ways of living they admired and wished to imitate completely became their enemies and punished them. [17]For it is no light thing to show irreverence to the divine laws—a fact which later events will make clear.

[18]When the quadrennial games were being held at Tyre and the king was present, [19]the vile Jason sent envoys, chosen as being Antiochian citizens from Jerusalem, to carry three hundred silver drachmas for the sacrifice to Hercules. Those who carried the money, however, thought best not to use it for sacrifice, because that was inappropriate, but to expend it for another purpose. [20]So this money was intended by the sender for the sacrifice to Hercules, but by the decision of its carriers it was applied to the construction of triremes.

[21]When Apollonius the son of Menestheus was sent to Egypt for the coronation of Philometor as king, Antiochus learned that Philometor had become hostile to his government, and he took measures for his own security. Therefore upon arriving at Joppa he proceeded to Jerusalem. [22]He was welcomed magnificently by Jason and the city, and ushered in with a blaze of torches and with shouts. Then he marched into Phoenicia.

[23]After a period of three years Jason sent Menelaus, the brother of the previously mentioned Simon, to carry the money to the king and to complete the records of essential business. [24]But he, when presented to the king, extolled him with an air of authority, and secured the high priesthood for himself, outbidding Jason by three hundred talents of silver. [25]After receiving the king's orders he returned, possessing no qualification for the high priesthood, but having the hot temper of a cruel tyrant

and the rage of a savage wild beast. ²⁶So Jason, who after supplanting his own brother was supplanted by another man, was driven as a fugitive into the land of Ammon. ²⁷And Menelaus held the office, but he did not pay regularly any of the money promised to the king. ²⁸When Sostratus the captain of the citadel kept requesting payment, for the collection of the revenue was his responsibility, the two of them were summoned by the king on account of this issue. ²⁹Menelaus left his own brother Lysimachus as deputy in the high priesthood, while Sostratus left Crates, the commander of the Cyprian troops.

³⁰While such was the state of affairs, it happened that the people of Tarsus and of Mallus revolted because their cities had been given as a present to Antiochus, the king's concubine. ³¹So the king went hastily to settle the trouble, leaving Andronicus, a man of high rank, to act as his deputy. ³²But Menelaus, thinking he had obtained a suitable opportunity, stole some of the gold vessels, of the temple and gave them to Andronicus; other vessels as it happened, he had sold to Tyre and the neighboring cities. ³³When Onias became fully aware of these acts he publicly exposed them, having first withdrawn to a place of sanctuary at Daphne near Antioch. ³⁴Therefore Menelaus, taking Andronicus aside, urged him to kill Onias. Andronicus came to Onias, and resorting to treachery offered him sworn pledges and gave him his right hand, and in spite of his suspicion persuaded Onias to come out from the place of sanctuary; then, with no regard for justice, he immediately put him out of the way. ³⁵For this reason not only Jews, but many also of other nations, were grieved and displeased at the unjust murder of the man. ³⁶When the king returned from the region of Cilicia, the Jews in the city appealed to him with regard to the unreasonable murder of Onias, and the Greeks shared

their hatred of the crime. ³⁷Therefore Antiochus was grieved at heart and filled with pity, and wept because of the moderation and good conduct of the deceased; ³⁸and inflamed with anger, he immediately stripped off the purple robe from Andronicus, tore off his garments, and led him about the whole city to that very place where he had committed the outrage against Onias, and there he dispatched the bloodthirsty fellow. The Lord thus repaid him with the punishment he deserved.

³⁹When many acts of sacrilege had been committed in the city by Lysimachus with the connivance of Menelaus, and when report of them had spread abroad, the populace gathered against Lysimachus, because many of the gold vessels had already been stolen. ⁴⁰And since the crowds were becoming aroused and filled with anger, Lysimachus armed about three thousand men and launched an unjust attack, under the leadership of a certain Auranus, a man advanced in years and no less advanced in folly. ⁴¹But when the Jews became aware of Lysimachus' attack, some picked up stones, some blocks of wood, and others took handfuls of the ashes that were lying about, and threw them in wild confusion at Lysimachus and his men. ⁴²As a result, they wounded many of them, and killed some, and put them all to flight; and the temple robber himself they killed close by the treasury.

⁴³Charges were brought against Menelaus about this incident. ⁴⁴When the king came to Tyre, three men sent by the senate presented the case before him. ⁴⁵But Menelaus, already as good as beaten, promised a substantial bribe to Plotemy son of Dorymenes to win over the king. ⁴⁶Therefore Ptolemy, taking the king aside into a colonnade as if for refreshment, induced the king to change his mind. ⁴⁷Menelaus, the cause of all the evil, he acquitted of the charges against him, while he sentenced to death those unfortunate men, who would have been freed un-

condemned if they had pleaded even before Scythians.
⁴⁸And so those who had spoken for the city and the
villages and the holy vessels quickly suffered the unjust
penalty. ⁴⁹ Therefore even the Tyrians, showing their
hatred of the crime, provided magnificently for their
funeral. ⁵⁰But Menelaus, because of the cupidity of those
in power, remained in office, growing in wickedness, having become the chief plotter against his fellow citizens.

2 Maccabees 4 moves rapidly through three major
developments. First, because of the continued plotting of
Simon, the high priest Onias went to the king. His mission
was aborted when Seleucus IV was murdered. Second,
Jason, the brother of Onias, now offered the king a substantial sum of money and had himself appointed high priest. He
proceeded to introduce the so-called Hellenistic reform in
Jerusalem. Third, Jason was in turn outbid for the priesthood by Menelaus, a brother of Simon, who was not even a
member of the high priestly family. Menelaus eventually
had Onias murdered.

The Mission of Onias

It is significant that the high priest Onias attempted to
settle his problems in Jerusalem by appealing to the Seleucid
king. At no point does Onias appear as a revolutionary,
and 2 Maccabees indignantly rejects any suggestion that he
was a plotter against the government. The insistence that
he was "not accusing his fellow citizens" seems forced. He
surely was accusing them, but as the legitimate high priest
he was only acting in defence of the *status quo*.

Jason as high priest

The rise of Jason involved more than the corruption of the
high priesthood. Jason undertook a radical reform of the
Jewish way of life. The gymnasium and the "body of youth"

were the basic institutions of Greek education. There has been extensive debate as to just what is meant by the enrolment of the men of Jerusalem as citizens of Antioch (literally "to enrol the Antiochenes in Jerusalem."). There is no record that Jerusalem was renamed Antioch, so that its citizens could be called Antiochenes. It is debated whether the Antiochenes in Jerusalem were citizens of a distinct community within the city or members of a larger Antiochene republic on the model of Rome. It is probable that in any case Jason's action disenfranchised many people who had been citizens of Jerusalem under Jewish law, and concentrated political power in the hands of his own supporters.

Jason's action may have been motivated to a considerable degree by personal ambition. He may also, however, have had a genuine desire to bring Jerusalem into line with Hellenistic civilization. There is nothing to suggest that Jason repudiated Judaism. He continued to function as high priest. The Judaism he sought was one fully compatible with a Hellenistic life style. Other Jews in the Diaspora, especially in Alexandria, were more successful in striking a balance between Jewish tradition and the culture of the day. Jason's reform was vitiated by the political intrigue which brought it about.

The actual transformation described in 2 Mac 4:12-17 is not so much a repudiation of the Jewish law as a shift of values. True, the "royal concessions" made by Antiochus III and mentioned in 4:11 had made the Torah the law of the land. This status was now revoked. More basic, however, was the change in values represented by the gymnasium and its distractions, and the lure of new customs such as the Greek hat. Surprisingly, 2 Maccabees neglects to mention that some Jews removed the marks of their circumcision (1 Mac 1:15), a rather more significant action than wearing the Greek hat. Yet both the marks of circumcision and the Greek hat were symbols which suggested a whole way of life, and the same shift of values is indicated in either case. The young men "disdained the honors prized by their fathers" and put "the highest value on Greek forms of prestige." When 2 Maccabees speaks, then, of irreverence for the divine laws, the main point at issue is departure from tradition. It is somewhat ironic that 2 Maccabees should appear so resolutely opposed to Greek culture, since the book itself is written in Greek according to the principles of Greek history writing. Strict consistency is not always maintained in times of cultural crisis. It must be said, however, that 2 Maccabees is far more conservative in its attitude towards the tradition than was the case with Jason and his followers.

Some of the problems inherent in the Hellenistic reform are illustrated in the episode concerning the games at Tyre. Athletic contests, in the Greek world, took place under the patronage of pagan deities—hence the sacrifice to Hercules. Jason may have regarded this sacrifice as a mere formality —just as some "enlightened" Christians at Corinth would later see no problem in eating meat sacrificed to idols, since an idol has no real existence (1 Cor 8). The people who carried the gift, however, were more scrupulous, and diverted the money. Yet these people too were supporters of the reform. It is important to recognize that the Hellenizers did not renounce Judaism, but tried to distinguish between the essentials which could not change and the less important elements which could. Any religious tradition must make some such distinction, but it is often difficult to make in practice.

Menelaus and the murder of Onias

Jason was still a member of the high priestly family. Menelaus, by contrast had no qualification for the position, and his rise greatly worsened the situation. Menelaus is depicted as a thoroughly unscrupulous individual, who is dishonorable even in his dealings with the king. His greatest outrage was the murder of the legitimate high priest Onias. This murder is also noted briefly in Daniel 9:26.

Menelaus did not murder Onias himself. He arranged to

have Andronicus do it. This Andronicus is otherwise known as the murderer of the young son of Seleucus IV in 175 BCE (on behalf of Antiochus Epiphanes). Some critics suspect that 2 Maccabees has confused the two murders, but there is no reason why Andronicus could not have committed both. Andronicus was evidently an active and dangerous figure in Seleucid politics. Antiochus probably had other reasons for executing him than the murder of Onias, but 2 Maccabees misses no opportunity to suggest that providence arranges the punishment of criminals. (This theme is also present in 2 Mac 4:26, in the observation that Jason, who supplanted Onias, was himself supplanted in turn.)

Perhaps the most striking aspect of the murder of Onias III is the setting in which it occurs. Onias has withdrawn to a place of sanctuary at Daphne. Some scholars have suggested that this sanctuary was a Jewish synagogue, but it is not certain whether there was a synagogue at Daphne at this time. Moreover, we should expect that 2 Maccabees would make it quite clear if a synagogue were meant. The more obvious place of sanctuary at Daphne was a famous temple of Apollo and Artemis. Onias presumably thought that the pagan temple would be respected by the pagans. The displeasure of the gentiles, noted in 2 Mac 4:35, might then be explained by the violation of the place of sanctuary. It is remarkable, however, that a Jewish high priest, praised for his devotion to the law, could seek shelter in a pagan temple. In fact there is no evidence that Onias was opposed to Hellenistic culture, any more than he was opposed to foreign rule. He opposed the profanation of the temple and priesthood by Jason and Menelaus, but prior to these developments there was no real conflict or antithesis between Greek and Jewish ways. We should note also that 2 Maccabees does not presume hostility between Jews and gentiles. The Greeks too hated this crime and even Antiochus Epiphanes was grieved. Undoubtedly, 2 Maccabees exaggerates here,

with the purpose of showing the universal respect for Onias.
Yet the moral is that a good Jew, who is faithful to his
ancestral laws, will win the respect of the gentiles too.

We can scarcely say that the course of events confirms this
moral. Antiochus disposed of the high priesthood to the
highest bidder, despite his alleged respect for Onias. No
charge was brought against Menelaus for the murder of
Onias. When charges were brought against him because of
the incident involving Lysimachus (2 Mac 4:39-42), bribery
again prevailed. Menelaus was acquitted and his accusers
were put to death, although even the Tyrians are said to have
been shocked by the injustice. Evidently, then, the veneration for the law-abiding Jew, suggested by the mourning for
Onias, is highly idealized. 2 Maccabees affirms that some
gentiles could be sympathetic and just, but their reaction
was not reliable. At best, Jewish piety *could* win the approval of the gentiles, and so was not incompatible with
good relations. The approval of the gentiles is only a minor
consideration in 2 Maccabees, and is not a primary motivation for keeping the law.

2 MAC 5: THE INTERVENTION OF ANTIOCHUS

5 About this time Antiochus made his second invasion of
Egypt. [2]And it happened that over all the city, for almost
forty days, there appeared golden-clad horsemen charging through the air, in companies fully armed with lances
and drawn swords—[3]troops of horsemen drawn up, attacks and counterattacks made on this side and on that,
brandishing of shields, massing of spears, hurling of
missiles, the flash of golden trappings, and armor of all
sorts. [4]Therefore all men prayed that the apparition
might prove to have been a good omen.

[5]When a false rumor arose that Antiochus was dead,
Jason took no less than a thousand men and suddenly

made an assault upon the city. When the troops upon the wall had been forced back and at last the city was being taken, Menelaus took refuge in the citadel. ⁶But Jason kept relentlessly slaughtering his fellow citizens, not realizing that success at the cost of one's kindred is the greatest misfortune, but imagining that he was setting up trophies of victory over enemies and not over fellow countrymen. ⁷He did not gain control of the government, however; and in the end got only disgrace from his conspiracy, and fled again into the country of the Ammonites. ⁸Finally, he met a miserable end. Accused before Aretas the ruler of the Arabs, fleeing from city to city, pursued by all men, hated as a rebel against the laws, and abhorred as the executioner of his country and his fellow citizens, he was cast ashore in Egypt; ⁹and he who had driven many from their own country into exile died in exile, having embarked to go to the Lacedaemonians in hope of finding protection because of their kinship. ¹⁰He who had cast out many to lie unburied had no one to mourn for him; he had no funeral of any sort and no place in the tomb of his fathers.

¹¹When news of what had happened reached the king, he took it to mean that Judea was in revolt. So, raging inwardly, he left Egypt and took the city by storm. ¹²And he commanded his soldiers to cut down relentlessly every one they met and to slay those who went into the houses. ¹³Then there was killing of young and old, destruction of boys, women, and children, and slaughter of virgins and infants. ¹⁴Within the total of three days eighty thousand were destroyed, forty thousand in hand-to-hand fighting; and as many were sold into slavery as were slain.

¹⁵Not content with this, Antiochus dared to enter the most holy temple in all the world, guided by Menelaus, who had become a traitor both to the laws and to his country. ¹⁶He took the holy vessels with his polluted

hands, and swept away with profane hands the votive offerings which other kings had made to enhance the glory and honor of the place. [17]Antiochus was elated in spirit, and did not perceive that the Lord was angered for a little while because of the sins of those who dwelt in the city, and that therefore he was disregarding the holy place. [18]But if it had not happened that they were involved in many sins, this man would have been scourged and turned back from his rash act as soon as he came forward, just as Heliodorus was, whom Seleucus the king sent to inspect the treasury. [19]But the Lord did not choose the nation for the sake of the holy place, but the place for the sake of the nation. [20]Therefore the place itself shared in the misfortunes that befell the nation and afterward participated in its benefits; and what was forsaken in the wrath of the Almighty was restored again in all its glory when the great Lord became reconciled.

[21]So Antiochus carried off eighteen hundred talents from the temple, and hurried away to Antioch, thinking in his arrogance that he could sail on the land and walk on the sea, because his mind was elated. [22]And he left governors to afflict the people: at Jerusalem, Philip, by birth a Phrygian and in character more barbarous than the man who appointed him; [23]and at Gerizim, Andronicus; and besides these Menelaus, who lorded it over his fellow citizens worse than the others did. In his malice toward the Jewish citizens [24]Antiochus sent Apollonius, the captain of the Mysians with an army of twenty-two thousand, and commanded him to slay all the grown men and to sell the women and boys as slaves. [25]When this man arrived in Jerusalem, he pretended to be peaceably disposed and waited until the holy sabbath day; then, finding the Jews not at work, he ordered his men to parade under arms. [26]He put to the sword all those who came out to see them, then rushed into the city with his armed men and killed great numbers of people.

²⁷But Judas Maccabeus, with about nine others, got away to the wilderness, and kept himself and his companions alive in the mountains as wild animals do; they continued to live on what grew wild, so that they might not share in the defilement.

2 Maccabees 5 makes quite clear that the intervention of the king came as a result of internal Jewish conflict.

The narrative begins with apparitions of horsemen in the air. Such ominous happenings are common in Greek and Roman literature in the centuries around the turn of the era. The function of the episode here is to build suspense and suggest that what is about to happen is already determined by heavenly powers.

The intervention of the king is provoked by the attempt of Jason to recapture the city. 2 Maccabees duly notes the miserable end of one who had caused so much misery. It is not clear whether the attack of the king in 2 Mac 5:11-14 was directed against Jason's forces, or against a distinct group such as the Hasideans who rejected both Jason and Menelaus. If Jason has already fled, as suggested by 2 Mac 5:7, we must assume that the city had fallen into the hands of the Hasideans or some group of traditional Jews, since Antiochus had no reason to attack Menelaus. Again in 2 Mac 5:24-26, the sudden attack of Apollonius seems to presuppose that there was a revolt, since otherwise there is no apparent reason for the slaughter.

The centerpiece of the chapter is the profanation of the temple by Antiochus Epiphanes. The abuse of the temple vessels recalls Daniel 1 and 5, and puts Antiochus on a par with Nebuchadnezzar and Belshazzar. 2 Maccabees is careful to explain that God only let the temple be profaned because of the sins of the people. Important though the temple is, it is subordinated to the nation and shares in its misfortunes. It receives no automatic divine protection.

The narrative twice emphasizes the elation of Antiochus. He thought he could sail on land and walk on sea. We are reminded of Daniel 8 and 11, where Antiochus tries to rise above the stars and magnify himself over every god. The pattern is familiar. Isaiah 14 provides the classic biblical prototype (see also Ezekiel 27 and 28). Hellenistic readers might catch here the overtones of tragedy. The king who lifts himself up in arrogance is riding for a fall. The wisdom of many peoples agrees that it is not good for a mortal to aspire to more than human status. Sooner or later, the proud must be humbled and the aspiration end in failure. This is already the lesson of Genesis 2-3. Antiochus Epiphanes will conform to the pattern in chapter 9.

Up to this point, there has been no religious persecution. Religious issues have, of course, been involved in the Hellenistic reform, but there has been no attempt to compel the Jews to abandon their own practices. According to 2 Maccabees, Judas Maccabee had already withdrawn to the wilderness before the religious persecution (contrary to what we found in 1 Maccabees). It is possible that the reference to Judas is misplaced here, as he is said to have withdrawn so that he would not share in "the defilement"— an expression which would seem to refer to the religious persecution which begins in Chapter 6. The introduction of Judas at this point has its purpose, however. In the following chapters, which tell of the gruesome deaths of the martyrs, we are aware that Judas is waiting in the wings. Deliverance is not far off.

2 MAC 6:1-11: THE RELIGIOUS PERSECUTION

6 Not long after this, the king sent an Athenian senator to compel the Jews to forsake the laws of their fathers and cease to live by the laws of God, ²and also to pollute the temple in Jerusalem and call it the temple of Olympian

Zeus, and to call the one in Gerizim the temple of Zeus the
Friend of Strangers, as did the people who dwelt in that
place.

³Harsh and utterly grievous was the onslaught of evil.
⁴For the temple was filled with debauchery and reveling
by the Gentiles, who dallied with harlots and had inter-
course with women within the sacred precincts, and besides brought in things for sacrifice that were unfit. ⁵The
altar was covered with abominable offerings which were
forbidden by the laws. ⁶A man could neither keep the sabbath, nor observe the feasts of his fathers, nor so much as
confess himself to be a Jew.

⁷On the monthly celebration of the king's birthday, the
Jews were taken, under bitter constraint, to partake of
the sacrifices; and when the feast of Dionysus came, they
were compelled to walk in the procession in honor of
Dionysus, wearing wreaths of ivy. ⁸At the suggestion of
Ptolemy a decree was issued to the neighboring Greek
cities, that they should adopt the same policy toward the
Jews and make them partake of the sacrifices, ⁹and
should slay those who did not choose to change over to
Greek customs. One could see, therefore, the misery that
had come upon them. ¹⁰For example, two women were
brought in for having circumcised their children. These
women they publicly paraded about the city, with their
babies hung at their breasts, then hurled them down head-
long from the wall. ¹¹Others who had assembled in the
caves near by, to observe the seventh day secretly, were
betrayed to Philip and were all burned together, because
their piety kept them from defending themselves, in view
of their regard for that most holy day.

2 Maccabees does not explain why the king now attempted
to make the Jews abandon their ancestral laws but this development can hardly be unrelated to the conflicts recorded in

the preceding chapters. In 2 Mac 5:11 we were told that the king thought Judaea was in revolt. The action of Apollonius suggests that the revolt had not been entirely suppressed. The suppression of the Jewish law may now have been intended to destroy the basis of the opposition. It is not clear why an Athenian (in Greek, *Athenaios)* should be sent. Some authorities read "Antiochean." Alternatively, it has been suggested that Athenaios was a proper name.

2 Maccabees provides some information about the persecution over and above what we found in 1 Maccabees. The Samaritans, who were descended from the northern tribes and from Assyrian settlers (2 Kings 17:24) but worshipped the God of Israel, at this time renamed their temple in honor of the Greek god Zeus. We had been told in 2 Mac 6:23 that Antiochus had placed a governor at Gerizim (the holy mountain of the Samaritans). Apparently the demands of Antiochus were also applied to the Samaritans, even if they complied more readily. (The Jewish historian Josephus says that the Samaritans asked Antiochus for permission to change the name of the temple [*Antiquities* 12.5.5].) It may have been possible for Jews and Samaritans to regard Zeus as simply another name for God, not a different deity. We know that some Jews of the second century BCE were prepared to take such a liberal attitude. The Letter of Aristeas, a document from Egyptian Judaism roughly contemporary with 2 Maccabees, says that the God of the Jews is the God whom all peoples worship, though the Greeks call him Zeus. We need not assume that the Samaritans abandoned their traditional worship. The persecution in Jerusalem, however, involved the active suppression of Jewish customs. As in 1 Maccabees, it is clear that the distinct identity of the Jewish people was in jeopardy. One could not even confess to being a Jew.

2 Maccabees also informs us that the Jews were compelled to participate in the worship of Dionysus, the god of wine.

The Third Book of Maccabees also tells of an attempt to impose the worship of Dionysus on the Jews, this time in Egypt at the hands of Ptolemy Philopator (3 Mac 2:29). The historical basis of the episode in 3 Maccabees is uncertain, but we know that Philopator was devoted to the worship of Dionysus. The Ptolemy mentioned in 2 Mac 6:8 is not the Ptolemy of Egypt but probably Ptolemy the son of Dorymenes, who was also mentioned in 2 Mac 4:45 (also in 1 Mac 3:38 and 2 Mac 8:8-9).

2 Maccabees refers more briefly than 1 Maccabees to the slaughter of the pious Jews on the sabbath (2 Mac 6:11; 1 Mac 2:29-38). The vivid description of the deaths of the women in 2 Mac 6:10 provides a foretaste of the following stories of martyrdom.

2 MAC 6:12-17: THE THEOLOGY OF PERSECUTION

[12]Now I urge those who read this book not to be depressed by such calamities, but to recognize that these punishments were designed not to destroy but to discipline our people. [13]In fact, not to let the impious alone for long, but to punish them immediately, is a sign of great kindness. [14]For in the case of the other nations the Lord waits patiently to punish them until they have reached the full measure of their sins; but he does not deal in this way with us, [15]in order that he may not take vengeance on us afterward when our sins have reached their height. [16]Therefore he never withdraws his mercy from us. Though he disciplines us with calamities, he does not forsake his own people. [17]Let what we have said serve as a reminder; we must go on briefly with the story.

At this point the abbreviator inserts his theological perspective on the persecution. The sufferings are indeed punishment, for the collective sins of the people in the preceding years, but they also have a more constructive aspect. Their purpose is not to destroy, but to discipline, and so, paradoxically, they reflect the mercy of God. They are a means by which the balance can be restored and reconciliation brought about. A biblical basis for this idea can be found in Isa 54:7-8: "For a brief moment I forsook you, but with great compassion I will gather you." It is not assumed that those who suffer are entirely innocent. At least they belong to a sinful people. The deaths of the martyrs are not a vicarious sacrifice, whereby the innocent atone for the sins of others. The martyrs are part of the people, and they make up the sufferings of the people which are necessary if the time of wrath is to pass.

This treatment of the Jewish people is contrasted with the apparently more indulgent attitude towards the gentiles. They are not punished in the present, so their final punishment will be worse. This theology bears some resemblance to the apocalyptic theology of Daniel. Present appearances are deceptive. Those who prosper now may yet be destroyed and those who now suffer may be rewarded. We cannot claim that this theology is consistently verified by events, but it provides a constructive way of coping with the injustice of life. Suffering is made to yield a positive lesson, and the envy towards the prosperous wicked is controlled.

This theology was widespread in Judaism in the Hellenistic age. A close parallel is found in the Wisdom of Solomon, 12:22: "while chastening us thou scourgest our enemies ten times more." We may also catch a reflection of it in the Gospel beatitudes, where those who hunger will be satisfied but those who are full will hunger (see especially the Lukan version, Luke 6:20-26). Such a theology provides compensation, in the imagination, for the privations of the present, but by so doing it can help people cope with difficult situations.

2 MAC 6:18-31: THE MARTYRDOM OF ELEAZAR

[18]Eleazar, one of the scribes in high position, a man now advanced in age and of noble presence, was being forced to open his mouth to eat swine's flesh. [19]But he, welcoming death with honor rather than life with pollution, went up to the rack of his own accord, spitting out the flesh, [20]as men ought to go who have the courage to refuse things that it is not right to taste, even for the natural love of life.

[21]Those who were in charge of that unlawful sacrifice took the man aside, because of their long acquaintance with him, and privately urged him to bring meat of his own providing, proper for him to use, and pretend that he was eating the flesh of the sacrificial meal which had been commanded by the king, [22]so that by doing this he might be saved from death, and be treated kindly on account of his old friendship with them. [23]But making a high resolve, worthy of his years and the dignity of his old age and the gray hairs which he had reached with distinction and his excellent life even from childhood, and moreover according to the holy God-given law, he declared himself quickly, telling them to send him to Hades.

[24]"Such pretense is not worthy of our time of life," he said, "lest many of the young should suppose that Eleazar in his ninetieth year has gone over to an alien religion, [25]and through my pretense, for the sake of living a brief moment longer, they should be led astray because of me, while I defile and disgrace my old age. [26]For even if for the present I should avoid the punishment of men, yet whether I live or die I shall not escape the hands of the Almighty. [27]Therefore, by manfully giving up my life now, I will show myself worthy of my old age [28]and leave to the young a noble example of how to die a good death willingly and nobly for the revered and holy laws."

When he had said this, he went at once to the rack. [29]And those who a little before had acted toward him with good will now changed to ill will, because the words he had uttered were in their opinion sheer madness. [30]When he was about to die under the blows, he groaned aloud and said: "It is clear to the Lord in his holy knowledge that, though I might have been saved from death, I am enduring terrible sufferings in my body under this beating, but in my soul I am glad to suffer these things because I fear him."

[31]So in this way he died, leaving in his death an example of nobility and a memorial of courage, not only to the young but to the great body of his nation.

The point at issue in the martyrdom both of Eleazar and of the seven brothers is eating swine's flesh. (From 6:21 and 7:42 we may infer that the meat had been sacrificed to idols.) The law is not a matter of ethics but of symbolism. The importance of the swine's flesh is that it is a point of distinction between Jew and gentile. The distinctive identity of Judaism is at stake.

Eleazar's situation is peculiar because of his advanced age. He could not hope to avoid death for long in any case, but then, even a younger person could have no guarantee of the duration of life. The age of Eleazar simply makes the point that the choice is not between life and death but between death sooner and later. There is no mention of afterlife in this story, although it may be implied (e.g. in 6:26; "whether I live or die I shall not escape the hands of the Almighty"). Yet the story suggests that Eleazar's choice is independent of the hope of afterlife. He has had his life, and cannot now reject what he has always stood for. He is motivated by fear of God, which is not only fear of punishment but a general attitude of reverence. There is also his own honor. For him, as for the Greek epic hero Achilles, death with honor is preferable to a life of shame. The abbreviator affirms that he went as men ought to go who have the courage to refuse what they should not take. The main point here is not whether it is right to taste pork. Eleazar is asserting his freedom, his right to decide for himself and to say no to the king. Quite apart from the specific point at issue, these rights are crucial to human dignity.

The symbolism rather than the substance of the act determines Eleazar's decision. This is apparent when he refuses the offer to substitute kosher meat and only pretend to eat the pork. Not only would such pretence mislead the young. It would also pollute Eleazar's old age by shaming him. Instead he prefers to die, as an act of defiance, showing that no power could compel him to do what he did not want. There can be no doubt that such examples were a significant factor in galvanizing the spirit of the Jewish resistance. So, while 2 Maccabees 6 does not make explicit the hope of afterlife, Eleazar has values which transcend death, and which are unintelligible to his tormentors. Those values are not destroyed by his death.

2 MAC 7: THE SEVEN BROTHERS

7 It happened also that seven brothers and their mother were arrested and were being compelled by the king, under torture with whips and cords, to partake of unlawful swine's flesh. [2]One of them, acting as their spokesman, said, "What do you intend to ask and learn from us? For we are ready to die rather than transgress the laws of our fathers."

[3]The king fell into a rage, and gave orders that pans and caldrons be heated. [4]These were heated immediately, and he commanded that the tongue of their spokesman be cut out and that they scalp him and cut off his hands and feet,

while the rest of the brothers and the mother looked on. ⁵When he was utterly helpless, the king ordered them to take him to the fire, still breathing, and to fry him in a pan. The smoke from the pan spread widely, but the brothers and their mother encouraged one another to die nobly, saying, ⁶"The Lord God is watching over us and in truth has compassion on us, as Moses declared in his song which bore witness against the people to their faces, when he said, 'And he will have compassion on his servants.'"

⁷After the first brother had died in this way, they brought forward the second for their sport. They tore off the skin of his head with the hair, and asked him, "Will you eat rather than have your body punished limb by limb?" ⁸He replied in the language of his fathers, and said to them, "No." Therefore he in turn underwent tortures as his first brother had done. ⁹And when he was at his last breath, he said, "You accursed wretch, you dismiss us from this present life, but the King of the universe will raise us up to an everlasting renewal of life, because we have died for his laws."

¹⁰After him, the third was the victim of their sport. When it was demanded, he quickly put out his tongue and courageously stretched forth his hands, ¹¹and said nobly, "I got these from Heaven, and because of his laws I disdain them, and from him I hope to get them back again." ¹²As a result the king himself and those with him were astonished at the young man's spirit, for he regarded his sufferings as nothing.

¹³When he too had died, they maltreated and tortured the fourth in the same way. ¹⁴And when he was near death, he said, "One cannot but choose to die at the hands of men and to cherish the hope that God gives of being raised again by him. But for you there will be no resurrection to life!"

¹⁵Next they brought forward the fifth and maltreated

him. ¹⁶But he looked at the king, and said, "Because you have authority among men, mortal though you are, you do what you please. But do not think that God has forsaken our people. ¹⁷Keep on, and see how his mighty power will torture you and your descendants!"

¹⁸After him they brought forward the sixth. And when he was about to die, he said, "Do not deceive yourself in vain. For we are suffering these things on our own account, because of our sins against our own God. Therefore astounding things have happened. ¹⁹But do not think that you will go unpunished for having tried to fight against God!"

²⁰The mother was especially admirable and worthy of honorable memory. Though she saw her seven sons perish within a single day, she bore it with good courage because of her hope in the Lord. ²¹She encouraged each of them in the language of their fathers. Filled with a noble spirit, she fired her woman's reasoning with a man's courage, and said to them, ²²"I do not know how you came into being in my womb. It was not I who gave you life and breath, nor I who set in order the elements within each of you. ²³Therefore the Creator of the world, who shaped the beginning of man and devised the origin of all things, will in his mercy give life and breath back to you again, since you now forget yourselves for the sake of his laws."

²⁴Antiochus felt that he was being treated with contempt, and he was suspicious of her reproachful tone. The youngest brother being still alive, Antiochus not only appealed to him in words, but promised with oaths that he would make him rich and enviable if he would turn from the ways of his fathers, and that he would take him for his friend and entrust him with public affairs. ²⁵Since the young man would not listen to him at all, the king called the mother to him and urged her to advise the youth to

save himself. ²⁶After much urging on his part, she undertook to persuade her son. ²⁷But, leaning close to him, she spoke in their native tongue as follows, deriding the cruel tyrant: "My son, have pity on me. I carried you nine months in my womb, and nursed you for three years, and have reared you and brought you up to this point in your life, and have taken care of you. ²⁸I beseech you, my child, to look at the heaven and the earth and see everything that is in them, and recognize that God did not make them out of things that existed. Thus also mankind comes into being. ²⁹Do not fear this butcher, but prove worthy of your brothers. Accept death, so that in God's mercy I may get you back again with your brothers."

³⁰While she was still speaking, the young man said, "What are you waiting for? I will not obey the king's command, but I obey the command of the law that was given to our fathers through Moses. ³¹But you, who have contrived all sorts of evil against the Hebrews, will certainly not escape the hands of God. ³²For we are suffering because of our own sins. ³³And if our living Lord is angry for a little while, to rebuke and discipline us, he will again be reconciled with his own servants. ³⁴But you, unholy wretch, you most defiled of all men, do not be elated in vain and puffed up by uncertain hopes, when you raise your hand against the children of heaven. ³⁵You have not yet escaped the judgment of the almighty, all-seeing God. ³⁶For our brothers after enduring a brief suffering have drunk of everflowing life under God's covenant; but you, by the judgment of God, will receive just punishment for your arrogance. ³⁷I, like my brothers, give up body and life for the laws of our fathers, appealing to God to show mercy soon to our nation and by afflictions and plagues to make you confess that he alone is God, ³⁸and through me and my brothers to bring to an end the wrath of the Almighty which has justly fallen on our whole nation."

[39]The king fell into a rage, and handled him worse than the others, being exasperated at his scorn. [40]So he died in his integrity, putting his whole trust in the Lord.

[41]Last of all, the mother died, after her sons.

[42]Let this be enough, then, about the eating of sacrifices and the extreme tortures.

The centerpiece of the book, and undoubtedly the best known part of it, is the story of the seven brothers. This story probably circulated originally as an independent piece. Many scholars think the setting is Antioch rather than Jerusalem because of the presence of the king, and the fact that the tombs of the martyrs were subsequently honored in Antioch. Yet the confrontation with the king is a stock motif in this kind of story. The geographical setting is simply not specified, and it is futile to look for historical elements in a legend of this sort.

The legendary character of 2 Maccabees 7 is shown not only by the highly implausible presence of the king, but also by the stock number of seven sons. There are numerous stories about seven sons even within ancient Judaism. There is also an elaborate re-telling of 2 Maccabees 7 in 4 Maccabees. There are seven sons in the story of Taxo in the *Testament (Assumption) of Moses,* which we have discussed in connection with 1 Mac 2. Josephus, in *Antiquities* 14.15.5 (429) tells how Herod surrounded Galilean brigands in caves. These included a father, mother and seven sons. The father killed the sons and their mother rather than let them out to Herod. Before he killed himself he reviled Herod, who was a witness to the entire scene. Variants of the story of the mother and her seven sons are found in the rabbinic literature, set in Roman times. Seven is the number of perfection, and seven sons is the proverbially perfect family.

The story of the seven sons is used in 2 Maccabees 7 as a vehicle to elaborate the theology of martyrdom. The first principle is laid down by the spokesman in 7:2: they are ready to die rather than transgress the ancestral laws. Light is thrown on their motivation in 7:6, where they quote Deuteronomy 32. We have had occasion to refer to this paradigmatic biblical passage in our discussion of 1 Maccabees 2. The verse quoted here is Deut 32:36. Deut 32:43 is more immediately illuminating: "he avenges the blood of his servants and takes vengeance on his adversaries, and makes expiation for the land of his people." As in the *Testament of Moses,* the deaths of the martyrs will trigger divine vengeance.

A second motivating factor, thoroughly compatible with the first, is introduced by the second brother. This is the hope of resurrection. The resurrection is envisaged in very physical terms by the third brother, who hopes to recover the limbs he now loses. Such a physical idea of resurrection is unusual in the second century BCE Jewish texts, and only becomes dominant in the late first century CE. As we have seen in connection with Daniel 12, there was no one fixed way of imagining the resurrection. The emphasis here on the recovery of limbs is not due to any set dogma that the resurrection must be physical, but is suggested by the physical nature of the martyr's sufferings. A physical resurrection is required here to make satisfaction for the tortures endured.

The function of resurrection here is similar to what it was in Daniel and the apocalyptic literature. It is a hope which gives freedom. It enables the martyrs to give up everything in this world, so that they cannot be blackmailed into violating their integrity. Of course there is no proof that the hope will be fulfilled, but it is vindicated by the triumph of human dignity which it makes possible in the present.

The hope for resurrection adds a significant dimension over against the piety of 1 Maccabees, and allows for greater concern with the fulfillment of the individual.

The fourth son not only expresses the hope of resurrection

but also introduces the expectation that the tyrant will be punished. The first consideration is that the king will not be resurrected. Oddly enough, punishment after death is not envisaged. The fifth son adds the note that God will torture the king and his descendents. Whether Antiochus and his line were in fact appropriately punished is, of course, a matter of opinion. The king and his son met abrupt deaths, but they certainly were not tortured after the manner of the martyrs in 2 Maccabees 7. The real force of the fifth son's remarks lies in the uncertainty of anyone's future, even that of a king. In presuming to torture his fellow men, Antiochus takes no thought of the possibility that he may one day be at the mercy of others. The possibility that we will at some time depend on others is one of the great motivations for charity. "As you would that men should do to you. . ." is not so much an exhortation to altruism as a matter of enlightened self-interest.

The sixth brother throws light on another side of the theology of martyrdom. The martyrs are suffering for their sins against their own God. This statement must be seen in the context of the remarks in 6:12-17. It is better to be punished speedily by God. The sins are not so much the personal sins of the brothers, but the sins of the Jewish people. Antiochus is thus the instrument of God's punishment against the Jews. Yet he is also "fighting against God." We may recall Isaiah 10, where Assyria is the rod of God's anger, but will nonetheless be punished for his haughty pride.

The mother introduces yet another consideration for the theology of martyrdom. They owe their lives in the first case to the creator. Therefore they can hope to get their lives back from him again. She returns to the creation motif in 7:28, in what is perhaps the earliest Jewish formulation of the doctrine of creation out of nothing. Since God is creator, humanity is absolutely dependent on him. Therefore there is no reason to fear a human tyrant. The doctrine of creation puts human life in perspective. The brothers must forget, or overlook, their own interests for the sake of the creator's laws. Death must be accepted if the afterlife is to follow.

The final speech of the youngest brother rehearses the major themes of the chapter, except for the theme of creation. The determination to die for the law is presupposed from the outset. The doctrine of divine discipline is repeated and also the conviction that the king will be punished. The hope for resurrection is now explicitly linked to the covenant, and therefore placed in the context of the experience of the whole people. The final emphasis, however, does not fall on the resurrection of the individuals, but on the restoration of the nation. The deaths of the brothers will be instrumental in bringing to an end the age of wrath. The punishment of the nation was just, but the sufferings of the martyrs absorb the punishment and so bring it to an end. The martyr even suggests that Antiochus himself will have to confess the one true God. In the context this is a taunt, but 2 Maccabees takes care to have it fulfilled in chap. 9 in defiance of historical truth.

The impact of the chapter

The story of the seven brothers is recorded in greater detail than any other episode in 2 Maccabees. It is designed not only to provide reasons for fidelity to the law in the face of death, but above all to influence the emotions. The torture of the first brother is described in lurid detail, and the sufferings of the others are amply clear. The appeal of the mother to her youngest child to accept death as an act of pity for her motherhood is designed to excite the pity of the reader too. The total impact is one of admiration. Whatever we may think of their cause, the martyrs have persisted in face of the ultimate human challenge, death. The example of martyrs like these surely did much to inspire the Jews against Antiochus (granted that this story is fictional). Even in terms of human causality we must grant some truth to the claim that their deaths were a turning point in the crisis.

2 MAC 8: THE MACCABEAN REVOLT

8 But Judas, who was also called Maccabeus, and his companions secretly entered the villages and summoned their kinsmen and enlisted those who had continued in the Jewish faith, and so they gathered about six thousand men. ²They besought the Lord to look upon the people who were oppressed by all, and to have pity on the temple which had been profaned by ungodly men, ³and to have mercy on the city which was being destroyed and about to be leveled to the ground, and to hearken to the blood that cried out to him, ⁴and to remember also the lawless destruction of the innocent babies and the blasphemies committed against his name, and to show his hatred of evil.

⁵As soon as Maccabeus got his army organized, the Gentiles could not withstand him, for the wrath of the Lord had turned to mercy. ⁶Coming without warning, he would set fire to towns and villages. He captured strategic positions and put to flight not a few of the enemy. ⁷He found the nights most advantageous for such attacks. And talk of his valor spread everywhere.

⁸When Philip saw that the man was gaining ground little by little, and that he was pushing ahead with more frequent successes, he wrote to Ptolemy, the governor of Coelesyria and Phoenicia, for aid to the king's government. ⁹And Ptolemy promptly appointed Nicanor the son of Patroclus, one of the king's chief friends, and sent him, in command of no fewer than twenty thousand Gentiles of all nations, to wipe out the whole race of Judea. He associated with him Gorgias, a general and a man of

experience in military service. ¹⁰Nicanor determined to make up for the king the tribute due to the Romans, two thousand talents, by selling the captured Jews into slavery. ¹¹And he immediately sent to the cities on the seacoast, inviting them to buy Jewish slaves and promising to hand over ninety slaves for a talent, not expecting the judgment from the Almighty that was about to overtake him.

¹²Word came to Judas concerning Nicanor's invasion; and when he told his companions of the arrival of the army, ¹³those who were cowardly and distrustful of God's justice ran off and got away. ¹⁴Others sold all their remaining property, and at the same time besought the Lord to rescue those who had been sold by the ungodly Nicanor before he ever met them, ¹⁵if not for their own sake, yet for the sake of the covenants made with their fathers, and because he had called them by his holy and glorious name. ¹⁶But Maccabeus gathered his men together, to the number of six thousand, and exhorted them not to be frightened by the enemy and not to fear the great multitude of Gentiles who were wickedly coming against them, but to fight nobly, ¹⁷keeping before their eyes the lawless outrage which the Gentiles had committed against the holy place, and the torture of the derided city, and besides, the overthrow of their ancestral way of life. ¹⁸"For they trust to arms and acts of daring," he said, "but we trust in the Almighty God, who is able with a single nod to strike down those who are coming against us and even the whole world."

¹⁹Moreover, he told them of the times when help came to their ancestors; both the time of Sennacherib, when one hundred and eighty-five thousand perished, ²⁰and the time of the battle with the Galatians that took place in Babylonia, when eight thousand in all went into the affair, with four thousand Macedonians; and when the

Macedonians were hard pressed, the eight thousand, by the help that came to them from heaven, destroyed one hundred and twenty thousand and took much booty.

²¹With these words he filled them with good courage and made them ready to die for their laws and their country; then he divided his army into four parts. ²²He appointed his brothers also, Simon and Joseph and Jonathan, each to command a division, putting fifteen hundred men under each. ²³Besides, he appointed Eleazar to read aloud from the holy book, and gave the watchword, "God's help"; then, leading the first division himself, he joined battle with Nicanor.

²⁴With the Almighty as their ally, they slew more than nine thousand of the enemy, and wounded and disabled most of Nicanor's army, and forced them all to flee. ²⁵They captured the money of those who had come to buy them as slaves. After pursuing them for some distance, they were obliged to return because the hour was late. ²⁶For it was the day before the sabbath, and for that reason they did not continue their pursuit. ²⁷And when they had collected the arms of the enemy and stripped them of their spoils, they kept the sabbath, giving great praise and thanks to the Lord, who had preserved them for that day and allotted it to them as the beginning of mercy. ²⁸After the sabbath they gave some of the spoils to those who had been tortured and to the widows and orphans, and distributed the rest among themselves and their children. ²⁹When they had done this, they made common supplication and besought the merciful Lord to be wholly reconciled with his servants.

³⁰In encounters with the forces of Timothy and Bacchides they killed more than twenty thousand of them and got possession of some exceedingly high strongholds, and they divided very much plunder, giving to those who had been tortured and to the orphans and widows, and also to

the aged, shares equal to their own. [31]Collecting the arms of the enemy, they stored them all carefully in strategic places, and carried the rest of the spoils to Jerusalem. [32]They killed the commander of Timothy's forces, a most unholy man, and one who had greatly troubled the Jews. [33]While they were celebrating the victory in the city of their fathers, they burned those who had set fire to the sacred gates, Callisthenes and some others, who had fled into one little house; so these received the proper recompense for their impiety.

[34]The thrice-accursed Nicanor, who had brought the thousand merchants to buy the Jews, [35]having been humbled with the help of the Lord by opponents whom he regarded as of the least account, took off his splendid uniform and made his way alone like a runaway slave across the country till he reached Antioch, having succeeded chiefly in the destruction of his own army! [36]Thus he who had undertaken to secure tribute for the Romans by the capture of the people of Jerusalem proclaimed that the Jews had a Defender, and that therefore the Jews were invulnerable, because they followed the laws ordained by him.

The revolt of Judas Maccabee is only introduced half way through the narrative of 2 Maccabees. In a sense, the decisive action has already taken place, since we are told in 2 Maccabees 8:5 that the wrath of God had turned to mercy. Before the military campaign begins, Judas and his followers pray, and their prayer may give an indication of what it is that turns the tide. In part, it is simply that the oppression and profanation have gone far enough. The city has been adequately punished by the persecution, and God will endure no more insult. Note is also taken, however, of the blood that cries out to God for vengeance, in accordance with Deuteronomy 32. This includes both the innocent babies and the martyrs of chaps. 6 and 7. Judas, then, is the instrument of God's deliverance, but the stage has been set before he enters.

The account of the campaign differs from that of 1 Maccabees in a few respects. 2 Maccabees passes quickly over the initial skirmishes to the first major battle, the one described in 1 Mac 3:38-4:25. In 2 Maccabees, Nicanor is singled out as commander-in-chief of the Syrian forces and Gorgias is subordinated to him. In this way the campaigns recorded in 2 Maccabees both begin and end with defeats of Nicanor, (see below, 2 Mac 15). 2 Maccabees explains more clearly than 1 Maccabees the reason for Nicanor's intention to sell the Jews as slaves. He wished to make up the money for the Syrian tribute to Rome. With typical irony, 2 Maccabees notes that Nicanor, who had attempted to enslave the Jews, fled from the battle like a runaway slave (8:35).

The exhortation of Judas before the battle is of special interest. 2 Mac 3:19 had confessed that victory does not depend on the size of the army but on the strength that comes from heaven. 2 Mac 8:18 is more extreme: "they trust to arms and acts of daring, but we trust in the Almighty God." This God could even strike down the whole world, by his power as creator. The Maccabean army is scarcely necessary at all.

The power of heaven in battle is illustrated not only by the destruction of Sennacherib (2 Kings 19:35; Isa 37:36) but also by the victory of the Macedonians over the Galatians. It is difficult to see how the latter concerns the ancestors of the Jews. Evidently the point is that a smaller force can be victorious, whether it is Jewish or not. The unexpected can happen on the field of battle, and that is the role of "heaven." Accordingly, an inferior army need not despair. It is possible that some Jews had fought with the Macedonians (who are possibly to be identified here as the Seleucid army).

The division of the army lists the brothers of Judas as

Simon, Joseph and Jonathan. Joseph may be a mistake for John (compare 1 Mac 1:2). Eleazar, the reader, was also a brother of the Maccabees. The watchword "God's help" is a pun on the Hebrew meaning of Eleazar's name.

After the victory over Nicanor, 2 Maccabees is careful to note the observance of the sabbath and the charitable use of some of the spoils.

The victory over Timothy is placed earlier here than in 1 Maccabees (compare 1 Mac 5: 37-44). According to 1 Maccabees, however, Judas had no victory over Bacchides. It was in battle against Bacchides that he lost his life (1 Mac 9:18). The passing reference to him here may be intended to compensate for the embarrassment of the later defeat, which is not mentioned at all in 2 Maccabees.

The chapter ends with the due punishment of some tormentors of the Jews. Nicanor is implausibly said to confess that the Jews were protected by God. There is little sign of this confession when he appears later in the story. The other punishments mentioned are more realistic. Those who had burned the sacred gates were now burned in a house. Apart from the poetic justice of this death, we cannot fail to notice its cruelty. For all its emphasis on piety, 2 Maccabees is the account of a war between deadly enemies. It is not a time for forgiveness and compassion. The security of the people required the destruction of some of its enemies, and the note of vengeance is surely understandable in view of what the Jews had endured. 2 Maccabees is not idealistic in its attitude towards the enemies of the Jews. It does not preach the loftiest form of charity, but then the heights of charity may not always be accessible to the human emotions.

2 MAC 9: THE DEATH OF ANTIOCHUS EPIPHANES

9 About that time, as it happened, Antiochus had retreated in disorder from the region of Persia. ²For he

had entered the city called Persepolis and attempted to
rob the temples and control the city. Therefore the people
rushed to the rescue with arms, and Antiochus and his
men were defeated, with the result that Antiochus was put
to flight by the inhabitants and beat a shameful retreat.
³While he was in Ecbatana, news came to him of what had
happened to Nicanor and the forces of Timothy. ⁴Trans-
ported with rage, he conceived the idea of turning upon
the Jews the injury done by those who had put him to
flight; so he ordered his charioteer to drive without stop-
ping until he completed the journey. But the judgment
of heaven rode with him! For in his arrogance he said,
"When I get there I will make Jerusalem a cemetery of
Jews."

⁵But the all-seeing Lord, the God of Israel, struck him
an incurable and unseen blow. As soon as he ceased
speaking he was seized with a pain in his bowels for which
there was no relief and with sharp internal tortures
— ⁶and that very justly, for he had tortured the bowels of
others with many and strange inflictions. ⁷Yet he did not
in any way stop his insolence, but was even more filled
with arrogance, breathing fire in his rage against the
Jews, and giving orders to hasten the journey. And so it
came about that he fell out of his chariot as it was rushing
along, and the fall was so hard as to torture every limb of
his body. ⁸Thus he who had just been thinking that he
could command the waves of the sea, in his superhuman
arrogance, and imagining that he could weigh the high
mountains in a balance, was brought down to earth and
carried in a litter, making the power of God manifest to
all. ⁹And so the ungodly man's body swarmed with
worms, and while he was still living in anguish and pain,
his flesh rotted away, and because of his stench the whole
army felt revulsion at his decay. ¹⁰Because of his in-
tolerable stench no one was able to carry the man who a

little while before had thought that he could touch the stars of heaven. [11]Then it was that, broken in spirit, he began to lose much of his arrogance and to come to his senses under the scourge of God, for he was tortured with pain every moment. [12]And when he could not endure his own stench, he uttered these words: "It is right to be subject to God, and no mortal should think that he is equal to God."

[13]Then the abominable fellow made a vow to the Lord, who would no longer have mercy on him, stating [14]that the holy city, which he was hastening to level to the ground and to make a cemetery, he was now declaring to be free; [15]and the Jews, whom he had not considered worth burying but had planned to throw out with their children to the beasts, for the birds to pick, he would make, all of them, equal to citizens of Athens; [16]and the holy sanctuary, which he had formerly plundered, he would adorn with the finest offerings; and the holy vessels he would give back, all of them, many times over; and the expenses incurred for the sacrifices he would provide from his own revenues; [17]and in addition to all this he also would become a Jew and would visit every inhabited place to proclaim the power of God. [18]But when his sufferings did not in any way abate, for the judgment of God had justly come upon him, he gave up all hope for himself and wrote to the Jews the following letter, in the form of a supplication. This was its content:

[19]"To his worthy Jewish citizens, Antiochus their king and general sends hearty greetings and good wishes for their health and prosperity. [20]If you and your children are well and your affairs are as you wish, I am glad. As my hope is in heaven, [21]I remember with affection your esteem and good will. On my way back from the region of Persia I suffered an annoying illness, and I have deemed it necessary to take thought for the general security of all.

²²I do not despair of my condition, for I have good hope of recovering from my illness, ²³but I observed that my father, on the occasions when he made expeditions into the upper country, appointed his successor, ²⁴so that, if anything unexpected happened or any unwelcome news came, the people throughout the realm would not be troubled, for they would know to whom the government was left. ²⁵Moreover, I understand how the princes along the borders and the neighbors to my kingdom keep watching for opportunities and waiting to see what will happen. So I have appointed my son Antiochus to be king, whom I have often entrusted and commended to most of you when I hastened off to the upper provinces; and I have written to him what is written here. ²⁶I therefore urge and beseech you to remember the public and private services rendered to you and to maintain your present good will, each of you, toward me and my son. ²⁷For I am sure that he will follow my policy and will treat you with moderation and kindness."

²⁸So the murderer and blasphemer, having endured the most intense suffering, such as he had inflicted on others, came to the end of his life by a most pitiable fate, among the mountains in a strange land. ²⁹And Philip, one of his courtiers, took his body home; then, fearing the son of Antiochus, he betook himself to Ptolemy Philometor in Egypt.

The account of the death of Antiochus Epiphanes is quite different from what was given in 2 Maccabees 1, and is closer to historical fact in so far as Antiochus IV was not killed raiding a temple (as Antiochus III had been). The main embellishment of the story in 2 Maccabees 9 concerns the king's alleged preoccupation with the Jews. 2 Maccabees seeks to give the impression that what happened to Antiochus was directly a punishment for his treatment of the Jews.

The painful and repulsive nature of Antiochus' illness is described with relish. Jewish tradition preserved a similar account of the death of Herod the Great. Whatever measure of historical truth there may be in this account, its purpose is evidently to provide imaginative satisfaction for those who suffered at his hands. Antiochus is shown to have deserved such a fate because of his arrogance. He thought that he could command the sea. This was a pretension to divine power by Greek as well as Jewish standards. The Persian king Xerxes was said to have shown his *hybris,* or arrogance in this way, according to the fifth century tragedian Aeschylus. The aspiration to touch the stars of heaven (9:10) recalls Daniel 8 and Isaiah 14. The pattern is inevitable. Pride goes before a fall. The greater the arrogance, the greater the humiliation.

The conversion of Antiochus

The account of Antiochus' death-bed repentance is of course legendary, although it may contain historical elements. The promise to subsidize the temple sacrifices would be consistent with earlier Seleucid policy. The promise to make Jews "equal to citizens of Athens" is surprising. Athens was not part of the Seleucid empire, so presumably the comparison is meant to convey a sense of status and freedom. Yet, in 2 Mac 6:1, we hear that an Athenian senator was sent to compel the Jews to forsake the laws of their fathers. The king's idea of equality with the citizens of Athens may not have been quite so acceptable to the Jews. This offer may be quite consistent with the policies which led to the persecution.

2 Maccabees abandons all historical verisimilitude with the claim that Antiochus would become a Jew and do a world tour to proclaim the power of God. This is surely wish fulfilment, reminiscent of the conversion of Nebuchadnezzar in Daniel 4. The story reflects the widespread fantasy of Jews in the Hellenistic world, that their rulers would convert

and so that they would be exalted. This fantasy is nationalistic in a sense, but it is not separatist. It envisages the conversion of the Gentiles, not their destruction. The ability to fantasize the conversion even of Antiochus Epiphanes testifies to a stubbornly optimistic attitude towards the gentile world, despite all that had transpired.

The letter of Antiochus in 2 Mac 9:19-27 makes no mention of his proposed conversion to Judaism and can scarcely be described as a supplication. The letter is essentially an authorization for his son to succeed to the throne. Antiochus repeatedly refers to his benevolent policy towards the Jews and their good will towards him. From a Jewish point of view, this attitude is highly ironic, and the letter can scarcely have been composed for its present context. Whether or not it is authentic, it is at least a plausible letter from the king's point of view. It involves no apology for his conduct towards the Jews, and seems to suppose that he has acted in their best interests.

In the end, the emphasis of 2 Maccabees falls neither on the king's conversion nor on his letter but on his punishment. As he had inflicted on others, so he suffered himself. The faith in such a law of retribution is more important to 2 Maccabees than political relations with the Seleucid kings. Historical experience may not have vindicated this faith as dramatically as 2 Maccabees suggests, but the very inevitability of the death of a tyrant like Antiochus lent it credibility. The conviction that retribution would come in some form lent a perspective to history, so that the changing fortunes of the moment could be viewed with equanimity.

2 MAC 10:1-9: THE PURIFICATION OF THE TEMPLE

10 Now Maccabeus and his followers, the Lord leading them on, recovered the temple and the city; ²and they tore down the altars which had been built in the public square by the foreigners, and also destroyed the sacred precincts.

³They purified the sanctuary, and made another altar of sacrifice; then, striking fire out of flint, they offered sacrifices, after a lapse of two years, and they burned incense and lighted lamps and set out the bread of the Presence. ⁴And when they had done this, they fell prostrate and besought the Lord that they might never again fall into such misfortunes, but that, if they should ever sin, they might be disciplined by him with forbearance and not be handed over to blasphemous and barbarous nations. ⁵It happened that on the same day on which the sanctuary had been profaned by the foreigners, the purification of the sanctuary took place, that is, on the twenty-fifth day of the same month, which was Chislev. ⁶And they celebrated it for eight days with rejoicing, in the manner of the feast of booths, remembering how not long before, during the feast of booths, they had been wandering in the mountains and caves like wild animals. ⁷Therefore bearing ivy-wreathed wands and beautiful branches and also fronds of palm, they offered hymns of thanksgiving to him who had given success to the purifying of his own holy place. ⁸They decreed by public ordinance and vote that the whole nation of the Jews should observe these days every year.

⁹Such then was the end of Antiochus, who was called Epiphanes.

The account of the re-dedication parallels 1 Mac 4:36-61. 2 Maccabees is far more emphatic than 1 Maccabees on the active participation of the Lord. It also emphasizes ironic, and providential, correspondences. So it claims that the reconsecration took place on the very same day as the profanation. The figure of two years is incorrect. Three years had elapsed since the installation of "the abomination that makes desolate." In another respect, however, the chronology of 2 Maccabees is correct. The purification took place after the death of Antiochus Epiphanes.

Three aspects of the celebration are worthy of note. First, the Jews pray that if they ever sin again they be punished directly by God, and not by the gentiles. The profanation of the temple is then acknowledged as a punishment. This is consistent with the theology of 2 Maccabees throughout. Second, the celebration is compared to the festival of Tabernacles (compare 2 Mac 1:9). The comparison concerns both the manner of celebration and the importance of the festival. Third, they celebrate bearing not only branches but also "ivy-wreathed wands" or *thyrsoi*. These were emblems of the festival of Dionysus. Since the worship of Dionysus had been enforced during the persecution (2 Mac 6:7) we are surprised that such emblems were used in the purification of the temple. Perhaps the *thyrsoi* had already become traditional in the celebration of Tabernacles prior to the persecution. In any case it is interesting that even in their reaction against the Hellenization of Judaism, the Maccabees could not avoid some cultural influence of their environment.

The purification restores the temple to its central place in the narrative. The remaining episodes in 2 Maccabees resume the pattern of the assault of the gentiles and the miraculous protection of the temple—the pattern which was illustrated earlier, in the story of Heliodorus. The purification also marks the end of one phase of the story. Only now does 2 Maccabees pronounce the definitive end of Antiochus Epiphanes.

Part Three: The Successors of Epiphanes

A.   The Reign of Antiochus Eupator
2 MAC 10:10-38: GORGIAS AND TIMOTHY

[10]Now we will tell what took place under Antiochus Eupator, who was the son of that ungodly man, and will

give a brief summary of the principal calamities of the wars. . . .

[18]When no less than nine thousand took refuge in two very strong towers well equipped to withstand a siege, [19]Maccabeus left Simon and Joseph, and also Zacchaeus and his men, a force sufficient to besiege them; and he himself set off for places where he was more urgently needed. [20]But the men with Simon, who were money-hungry, were bribed by some of those who were in the towers, and on receiving seventy thousand drachmas let some of them slip away. [21]When word of what had happened came to Maccabeus, he gathered the leaders of the people, and accused these men of having sold their brethren for money by setting their enemies free to fight against them. [22]Then he slew these men who had turned traitor, and immediately captured the two towers. [23]Having success at arms in everything he undertook, he destroyed more than twenty thousand in the two strongholds.

[24]Now Timothy, who had been defeated by the Jews before, gathered a tremendous force of mercenaries and collected the cavalry from Asia in no small number. He came on, intending to take Judea by storm. [25]As he drew near, Maccabeus and his men sprinkled dust upon their heads and girded their loins with sackcloth, in supplication to God. [26]Falling upon the steps before the altar, they besought him to be gracious to them and to be an enemy to their enemies and an adversary to their adversaries, as the law declares. [27]And rising from their prayer they took up their arms and advanced a considerable distance from the city; and when they came near to the enemy they halted. [28]Just as dawn was breaking, the two armies joined battle, the one having as pledge of success and victory not only their valor but their reliance upon the Lord, while the other made rage their leader in the fight.

[29]When the battle became fierce, there appeared to the

enemy from heaven five resplendent men on horses with golden bridles, and they were leading the Jews. [30]Surrounding Maccabeus and protecting him with their own armor and weapons, they kept him from being wounded. And they showered arrows and thunderbolts upon the enemy, so that, confused and blinded, they were thrown into disorder and cut to pieces. [31]Twenty thousand five hundred were slaughtered, besides six hundred horsemen.

[32]Timothy himself fled to a stronghold called Gazara, especially well garrisoned, where Chaereas was commander. [33]Then Maccabeus and his men were glad, and they besieged the fort for four days. [34]The men within, relying on the strength of the place, blasphemed terribly and hurled out wicked words. [35]But at dawn of the fifth day, twenty young men in the army of Maccabeus, fired with anger because of the blasphemies, bravely stormed the wall and with savage fury cut down every one they met. [36]Others who came up in the same way wheeled around against the defenders and set fire to the towers; they kindled fires and burned the blasphemers alive. Others broke open the gates and let in the rest of the force, and they occupied the city. [37]They killed Timothy, who was hidden in a cistern, and his brother Chaereas, and Apollophanes. [38]When they had accomplished these things, with hymns and thanksgivings they blessed the Lord who shows great kindness to Israel and gives them the victory.

The details of the military escapades in 2 Maccabees do not conform to those in 1 Maccabees. In 1 Maccabees, the fellow officer of Joseph is Azarias, not Zacchaeus, and they encounter problems because they attempt to act independently of the Maccabees. In 2 Maccabees, they are apparently the ones involved in bribery. The battles involving Timothy are highly confused, especially since Timothy appears still active in 2 Mac 12: 10-25, although his death is reported in 10:37. The capture of Gazara, here ascribed to Judas, is attributed to Simon, at a later date, in 1 Mac 13:43. The difference may be due to a tendency in 2 Maccabees to maximize the glory of Judas.

More important for our purpose are the theological modifications in 2 Maccabees. In 2 Mac 10:22, Judas succeeds in capturing two towers after he executes the traitors within the Jewish ranks. A causal connection is clearly implied. We are reminded of Joshua 7, where Joshua fails to conquer Ai until he executes the Hebrews who violated the commandment through personal greed. In 2 Mac 10:16 and 10:25-26, the importance of prayer before battle is stressed. Most striking of all is the account of the battle in 2 Mac 10:29-31. Here the battle is effectively decided by the intervention of five angelic warriors. While 1 Maccabees held that Judas conquered by the power of God, it has no place for such explicit supernatural intervention. In this respect 2 Maccabees is closer to the world of Daniel, although it still preserves a role for the human warrior.

Supernatural manifestations of this sort were popular in the literature of the Hellenistic age. From a modern critical perspective they must be seen as symbolic narratives. What is symbolized by the repeated apparitions in 2 Maccabees is the lively faith that Judas' success was not due to his military prowess, but to factors beyond his control, and indirectly, to his fidelity to the law. For 2 Maccabees, piety is more important than pragmatic action. The narrative of 1 Maccabees is more realistic in this respect. 2 Maccabees must be viewed not so much as an account of what happened but as a way of looking at things designed to encourage fidelity to the law.

The piety of 2 Maccabees does not exclude vengeance. We cannot fail to note the cruelty with which the "blasphemers" are burned alive. There is also a touch of irony in praising the

Lord for such achievements. 2 Maccabees reflects sentiments which were natural enough in the context but it does
not always realize the highest human potential.

2 MAC 11:1-15: THE DEFEAT OF LYSIAS

11 Very soon after this, Lysias, the king's guardian and
kinsman, who was in charge of the government, being
vexed at what had happened, ²gathered about eighty
thousand men and all his cavalry and came against the
Jews. He intended to make the city a home for Greeks,
³and to levy tribute on the temple as he did on the sacred
places of the other nations, and to put up the high
priesthood for sale every year. ⁴He took no account
whatever of the power of God, but was elated with his ten
thousands of infantry, and his thousands of cavalry, and
his eighty elephants. ⁵Invading Judea, he approached
Beth-zur, which was a fortified place about five leagues
from Jerusalem, and pressed it hard.

⁶When Maccabeus and his men got word that Lysias
was besieging the strongholds, they and all the people,
with lamentations and tears, besought the Lord to send a
good angel to save Israel. ⁷Maccabeus himself was the
first to take up arms, and he urged the others to risk their
lives with him to aid their brethren. Then they eagerly
rushed off together. ⁸And there, while they were still near
Jerusalem, a horseman appeared at their head, clothed in
white and brandishing weapons of gold. ⁹And they all
together praised the merciful God, and were strengthened
in heart, ready to assail not only men but the wildest
beasts or walls of iron. ¹⁰They advanced in battle order,
having their heavenly ally, for the Lord had mercy on
them. ¹¹They hurled themselves like lions against the
enemy, and slew eleven thousand of them and sixteen
hundred horsemen, and forced all the rest to flee. ¹²Most

of them got away stripped and wounded, and Lysias himself escaped by disgraceful flight. [13]And as he was not without intelligence, he pondered over the defeat which had befallen him, and realized that the Hebrews were invincible because the mighty God fought on their side. So he sent to them [14]and persuaded them to settle everything on just terms, promising that he would persuade the king, constraining him to be their friend. [15]Maccabeus, having regard for the common good, agreed to all that Lysias urged. For the king granted every request in behalf of the Jews which Maccabeus delivered to Lysias in writing.

The defeat of Lysias at Beth-zur is misplaced here. In 1 Mac 4: 28-35 it is placed before the purification of the temple, and the letters cited later in 2 Mac 11 support the earlier date. In 2 Maccabees, this battle becomes a miniature for the entire conflict. Lysias is determined "to make the city a home for the Greeks" and his arrogance is comparable to that of Antiochus Epiphanes. He is also determined to put the priesthood up for sale, every year, thereby going beyond the corruption of Jason and Menelaus.

The highlight of the battle is the angel who is sent in response to Judas' prayer, and who leads them into battle. This episode is strikingly reminiscent of the so-called Animal Apocalypse in 1 Enoch 85-91, a document written in support of Judas Maccabee at the time of the revolt. There we read in 1 Enoch 90:14 that an angelic "man" came and helped the "ram," Judas Maccabee, after it had cried out for help. It is possible that the apocalypse is referring to the same legend preserved in 2 Maccabees 11. The Animal Apocalypse differs from 2 Maccabees in its expectation that the revolt will culminate in a general judgment.

2 Maccabees goes far beyond 1 Maccabees in claiming that Lysias "realized that the Hebrews were invincible because the mighty God fought on their side" (2 Mac 11:13).

Yet Lysias will return undaunted in 2 Maccabees 13. 2 Maccabees can project a belief in the invincibility of the Jews because it never acknowledges their defeats—the one at Beth-zechariah (1 Mac 6:32-47) or the more embarrassing one at the hands of Bacchides in which Judas was killed (1 Mac 9:1-22). This refusal to face up to the fact that even the pious Judas was defeated is surely a significant deficiency in 2 Maccabees. Evidently the author was concerned with effect rather than with objective truth. He wished to maximize the reader's respect for the Jews rather than to give a complete and accurate account of what happened.

The negotiations between Judas and Lysias are not reported in 1 Maccabees, but are corroborated by the documents cited. 2 Maccabees is very careful to point out that the treaty was in no way compromising, but was entirely favorable to the Jews. The peace was short-lived. In all probability it was broken by Judas' seizure and purification of the Jerusalem temple.

2 MAC 11:16-38: FOUR LETTERS

[16]The letter written to the Jews by Lysias was to this effect: "Lysias to the people of the Jews, greeting. [17]John and Absalom, who were sent by you, have delivered your signed communication and have asked about the matters indicated therein. [18]I have informed the king of everything that needed to be brought before him, and he has agreed to what was possible. [19]If you will maintain your good will toward the government, I will endeavor for the future to help promote your welfare. [20]And concerning these matters and their details, I have ordered these men and my representatives to confer with you. [21]Farewell. The one hundred and forty-eighth year, Dioscorinthius twenty-fourth."

[22]The king's letter ran thus:

"King Antiochus to his brother Lysias, greeting. ²³Now that our father has gone on to the gods, we desire that the subjects of the kingdom be undisturbed in caring for their own affairs. ²⁴We have heard that the Jews do not consent to our father's change to Greek customs but prefer their own way of living and ask that their own customs be allowed them. ²⁵Accordingly, since we choose that this nation also be free from disturbance, our decision is that their temple be restored to them and that they live according to the customs of their ancestors. ²⁶You will do well, therefore, to send word to them and give them pledges of friendship, so that they may know our policy and be of good cheer and go on happily in the conduct of their own affairs."

²⁷To the nation the king's letter was as follows:

"King Antiochus to the senate of the Jews and to the other Jews, greeting. ²⁸If you are well, it is as we desire. We also are in good health. ²⁹Menelaus has informed us that you wish to return home and look after your own affairs. ³⁰Therefore those who go home by the thirtieth day of Xanthicus will have our pledge of friendship and full permission ³¹for the Jews to enjoy their own food and laws, just as formerly, and none of them shall be molested in any way for what he may have done in ignorance. ³²And I have also sent Menelaus to encourage you. ³³Farewell. The one hundred and forty-eighth year, Xanthicus fifteenth."

³⁴The Romans also sent them a letter, which read thus:

"Quintus Memmius and Titus Manius, envoys of the Romans, to the people of the Jews, greeting. ³⁵With regard to what Lysias the kinsman of the king has granted you, we also give consent. ³⁶But as to the matters which he decided are to be referred to the king, as soon as you have considered them, send some one promptly, so that we may make proposals appropriate for you. For we are on

our way to Antioch. ³⁷Therefore make haste and send
some men, so that we may have your judgment.
³⁸Farewell. The one hundred and forty-eighth year, Xan-
thicus fifteenth.''

The documents appended here are authentic letters, but
their chronological setting is confused. The first, third and
fourth letters are dated to the year 148 of the Seleucid era,
that is, late 165 or early 164 BCE. This was before the death
of Antiochus Epiphanes. This date is compatible with 1
Maccabees where the battle with Lysias is placed before the
purification of the temple. The second letter is clearly later
than the death of Epiphanes, and is a letter of Antiochus V
Eupator.

The first letter merely confirms the arrangements made
with Lysias. The third letter, by Antiochus Epiphanes, is an
interesting attempt to drain Judas' support by repealing the
prohibition of the Jewish food laws. Significantly,
Epiphanes makes no apology for what he has done. He
merely pardons the Jews who have resisted him. This con-
cession by Epiphanes was not, however, enough to defuse
the situation, as we can see from the more extensive concessions granted by Antiochus V.

The letter from the Romans is of interest as the earliest
contact between the Maccabees and Rome. It shows that the
Romans had an active interest in the internal affairs of the
Seleucid empire. When Judas later sent an embassy to
Rome, he was not making the first initiative.

Finally, the second letter, which presupposes the death of
Epiphanes, cuts to the heart of the problem between Greeks
and Jews. Incomprehensible as it may have been to Antiochus Epiphanes, the Jews preferred their own traditional
customs, and the simplest way to have peace was to let them
observe them. The Hellenizers would doubtless be displeased
with this letter, but its effect was short-lived in any case,
since Antiochus Eupator too was short-lived when Demetri-

us II arrived on the scene.

Taken together these letters represent a triumph for the Jews, but the war was not yet over. The conflict is resumed in chapter 12.

2 MAC 12:1-9: THE MASSACRE AT JOPPA

12 When this agreement had been reached, Lysias returned to the king, and the Jews went about their farming.

²But some of the governors in various places, Timothy and Apollonius the son of Gennaeus, as well as Hieronymus and Demophon, and in addition to these Nicanor the governor of Cyprus, would not let them live quietly and in peace. ³And some men of Joppa did so ungodly a deed as this: they invited the Jews who lived among them to embark, with their wives and children, on boats which they had provided, as though there were no ill will to the Jews; ⁴and this was done by public vote of the city. And when they accepted, because they wished to live peaceably and suspected nothing, the men of Joppa took them out to sea and drowned them, not less than two hundred. ⁵When Judas heard of the cruelty visited on his countrymen, he gave orders to his men ⁶and, calling upon God the righteous Judge, attacked the murderers of his brethren. He set fire to the harbor by night, and burned the boats, and massacred those who had taken refuge there. ⁷Then, because the city's gates were closed, he withdrew, intending to come again and root out the whole community of Joppa. ⁸But learning that the men in Jamnia meant in the same way to wipe out the Jews who were living among them, ⁹he attacked the people of Jamnia by night and set fire to the harbor and the fleet, so that the glow of the light was seen in Jerusalem, thirty miles distant.

2 Maccabees is careful to point out that the Jews were willing to live quietly and at peace, but were not allowed to do

so. Whether this was entirely true is doubtful, but it is probable that many of Judas' followers were eager to get back
to their farming. 1 Mac 5:15 claims that the gentiles were attempting to annihilate the Jews in the coastal areas and
Galilee, although Joppa and Jamnia are not explicitly mentioned. Presumably the Greeks in those regions were afraid
that the Maccabean rebellion would spread. In any case, the
episode at Joppa (modern Tel-Aviv), if it is historical, is one
of the earliest outright attacks on a Jewish community in a
Greek city, and sets an ominous precedent for the pogroms
in Alexandria and elsewhere in the first century CE, not to
mention those of later times.

The Maccabean response to such outrages, according to
both Books of Maccabees, is to meet violence with violence,
"calling upon God the righteous Judge" (2 Mac 12:6).
Whether this was the most effective response in the long
term, or the most appropriate for religious reasons, may be
disputed. There is little doubt that violence breeds more
violence. We saw in 1 Maccabees that all the Maccabean
brothers met violent deaths. Yet it is by no means certain
that a pacifist response would have prevented further
violence. In the immediate context of the Maccabean revolt,
the violence won for the Jews the respect that had been
denied them, and eventually for a time also security. No one
who recalls the disastrous submission of the Jews under
Hitler can blame the Maccabees for adopting the methods of
their enemies.

2 MAC 12: 10-31: THE CAMPAIGN AGAINST TIMOTHY

> [10]When they had gone more than a mile from there,
> on their march against Timothy, not less than five thou-
> sand Arabs with five hundred horsemen attacked them.
> [11]After a hard fight Judas and his men won the victory,

by the help of God. The defeated nomads besought
Judas to grant them pledges of friendship, promising to
give him cattle and to help his people in all other ways.
¹²Judas, thinking that they might really be useful in
many ways, agreed to make peace with them; and after
receiving his pledges they departed to their tents.

¹³He also attacked a certain city which was strongly
fortified with earthworks and walls, and inhabited by all
sorts of Gentiles. Its name was Caspin. ¹⁴And those who
were within, relying on the strength of the walls and on
their supply of provisions, behaved most insolently
toward Judas and his men, railing at them and even
blaspheming and saying unholy things. ¹⁵But Judas and
his men, calling upon the great Sovereign of the world,
who without battering-rams or engines of war overthrew Jericho in the days of Joshua, rushed furiously
upon the walls. ¹⁶They took the city by the will of God,
and slaughtered untold numbers, so that the adjoining
lake, a quarter of a mile wide, appeared to be running
over with blood.

¹⁷When they had gone ninety-five miles from there,
they came to Charax, to the Jews who are called Tou-
biani. ¹⁸They did not find Timothy in that region, for he
had by then departed from the region without ac-
complishing anything, though in one place he had left a
very strong garrison. ¹⁹Dositheus and Sosipater, who
were captains under Maccabeus, marched out and
destroyed those whom Timothy had left in the
stronghold, more than ten thousand men. ²⁰But Maccabeus arranged his army in divisions, set men in command
of the divisions, and hastened after Timothy, who had with
him a hundred and twenty thousand infantry and two thousand five hundred cavalry. ²¹When Timothy learned of the approach of Judas, he sent off the women and the children and
also the baggage to a place called Carnaim; for that place

was hard to besiege and difficult of access because of
the narrowness of all the approaches. ²²But when Judas'
first division appeared, terror and fear came over the
enemy at the manifestation to them of him who sees all
things; and they rushed off in flight and were swept on,
this way and that, so that often they were injured by
their own men and pierced by the points of their swords.
²³And Judas pressed the pursuit with the utmost vigor,
putting the sinners to the sword, and destroyed as many
as thirty thousand men.

²⁴Timothy himself fell into the hands of Dositheus
and Sosipater and their men. With great guile he
besought them to let him go in safety, because he held
the parents of most of them and the brothers of some
and no consideration would be shown them. ²⁵And
when with many words he had confirmed his solemn
promise to restore them unharmed, they let him go, for
the sake of saving their brethren.

²⁶Then Judas marched against Carnaim and the temple of Atargatis, and slaughtered twenty-five thousand
people. ²⁷After the rout and destruction of these, he
marched also against Ephron, a fortified city where
Lysias dwelt with multitudes of people of all na-
tionalities. Stalwart young men took their stand before
the walls and made a vigorous defense; and great stores
of war engines and missiles were there. ²⁸But the Jews
called upon the Sovereign who with power shatters the
might of his enemies, and they got the city into their
hands, and killed as many as twenty-five thousand of
those who were within it.

²⁹Setting out from there, they hastened to Scythopolis, which is seventy-five miles from Jerusalem. ³⁰But
when the Jews who dwelt there bore witness to the
good will which the people of Scythopolis had shown
them and their kind treatment of them in times of mis-

fortune, ³¹they thanked them and exhorted them to be well disposed to their race in the future also. Then they went up to Jerusalem, as the feasts of weeks was close at hand.

The campaign in Transjordan is parallel to 1 Mac 5:24-54. The Toubian Jews (12:17) are presumably the men of Tob (1 Mac 5:13, compare Judges 11:3,5). There are evident historical and geographical problems with the way this material is arranged in 2 Maccabees. Timothy had already been killed in 2 Mac 10:37. In 12:10 the Jews implausibly encounter Arab nomads when they are only a mile from Jamnia. Presumably, this incident has been misplaced too.

2 Maccabees emphatically ascribes Judas' success to supernatural aid, and attaches little importance to the human contribution. In 2 Mac 12:15 the destruction of Jericho is invoked as a paradigm. God threw down the walls of Jericho without battering rams or engines. When the Jews attack, terror falls on the enemy (12:22). We are reminded not only of 1 Mac 3:25 but also of Exod 15:16, where terror fell on the Canaanites and other peoples at the approach of the Israelites. The Jews pray before the battle (12:28) and are careful to return to Jerusalem for the festival of Tabernacles. Piety, more than military prowess, is required for success.

Success takes the form of bloody slaughter. In 12:16 a whole lake is left running over with blood. 2 Maccabees has no qualms about violence. Yet the slaughter is not indiscriminate. The Greeks in Scythopolis (biblical Bethshan) had been good neighbors to the Jews, and are thanked accordingly. 2 Maccabees is not simplistic in its distinction between Jews and gentiles. The significant distinction is between lawful and peaceful people, on the one hand, and sinners on the other.

2 MAC 12:39-45: AFTER THE BATTLE

[39]On the next day, as by that time it had become necessary, Judas and his men went to take up the bodies of the fallen and to bring them back to lie with their kinsmen in the sepulchres of their fathers. [40]Then under the tunic of every one of the dead they found sacred tokens of the idols of Jamnia, which the law forbids the Jews to wear. And it became clear to all that this was why these men had fallen. [41]So they all blessed the ways of the Lord, the righteous Judge, who reveals the things that are hidden; [42]and they turned to prayer, beseeching that the sin which had been committed might be wholly blotted out. And the noble Judas exhorted the people to keep themselves free from sin, for they had seen with their own eyes what had happened because of the sin of those who had fallen. [43]He also took up a collection, man by man, to the amount of two thousand drachmas of silver, and sent it to Jerusalem to provide for a sin offering. In doing this he acted very well and honorably, taking account of the resurrection. [44]For if he were not expecting that those who had fallen would rise again, it would have been superfluous and foolish to pray for the dead. [45]But if he was looking to the splendid reward that is laid up for those who fall asleep in godliness, it was a holy and pious thought. Therefore he made atonement for the dead, that they might be delivered from their sin.

The relation between virtue and success in battle is underlined in the conclusion to this chapter. The Jews who had fallen were killed because they carried sacred tokens of the idols of Jamnia. We are reminded again of the story of Ai in Joshua 7, where the first attack fails because Achan had violated the laws of holy war. 2 Maccabees is straining here to convey the sense that human affairs are regulated by a strict law of retribution. We may appreciate a certain educational value in this claim: it surely encourages people to keep the law. We cannot, however, accept it as a true account of the way the world works. Indeed, the deaths of the martyrs in 2 Maccabees itself show that violent death can not be fully explained as a proper punishment for personal sin. The Book of Job, and some New Testament passages such as John 9, go further and dispute the dogma that suffering must be seen as a punishment for sin at all.

The final point in 2 Maccabees 12 concerns the resurrection of the dead. As we have seen, belief in resurrection is not apparent in 1 Maccabees. It is doubtful whether Judas himself had such a belief. Since resurrection is very important in 2 Maccabees (see especially 2 Maccabees 7), the author is anxious to show that Judas did so believe. In fact, the inference from the sacrifice is not warranted. The most obvious purpose of the sacrifice is to atone for the sins of the dead, so that the army, or the people, will not be punished for them. We have seen in 2 Maccabees 7 that the trials of the martyrs were part of the punishment for the general corruption of Jerusalem in the preceding years. To some degree, the guilt is collective. Accordingly, the sin offering would be necessary whether Judas believed in the resurrection or not. The interpretation of this action by the author is the earliest attestation of the idea that people could be delivered from their sins after death.

2 MAC 13:1-8: THE DEATH OF MENELAUS

13 In the one hundred and forty-ninth year word came to Judas and his men that Antiochus Eupator was coming with a great army against Judea, ²and with him Lysias, his guardian, who had charge of the government. Each of them had a Greek force of one hundred and ten thousand infantry, five thousand three hundred cavalry, twenty-two elephants, and three hundred chariots armed with scythes.

³Menelaus also joined them and with utter hypocrisy urged Antiochus on, not for the sake of his country's welfare, but because he thought that he would be established in office. ⁴But the King of kings aroused the anger of Antiochus against the scoundrel; and when Lysias informed him that this man was to blame for all the trouble, he ordered them to take him to Beroea and to put him to death by the method which is the custom in that place. ⁵For there is a tower in that place, fifty cubits high, full of ashes, and it has a rim running around it which on all sides inclines precipitously into the ashes. ⁶There they all push to destruction any man guilty of sacrilege or notorious for other crimes. ⁷By such a fate it came about that Menelaus the lawbreaker died, without even burial in the earth. ⁸And this was eminently just; because he had committed many sins against the altar whose fire and ashes were holy, he met his death in ashes.

The execution of Menelaus provides the author with a fine example of providential irony. The arch-Hellenizer meets his death at the hands of the Greeks. The defiler of the temple fire is smothered in ashes. The dispatch of Menelaus seems out of place here. It would more plausibly follow the decision of the king to make peace with the Jews. Only then would Menelaus have appeared as a hindrance to the king, and the cause of his troubles. The execution reflects the growing weariness of the Seleucids with the Jewish problem, and willingness to appease rather than overpower the resisters.

2 MAC 13:9-26: THE FAILURE OF EUPATOR'S ATTACK

⁹The king with barbarous arrogance was coming to show to the Jews things far worse than those that had

been done in his father's time. ¹⁰But when Judas heard of this, he ordered the people to call upon the Lord day and night, now if ever to help those who were on the point of being deprived of the law and their country and the holy temple, ¹¹and not to let the people who had just begun to revive fall into the hands of the blasphemous Gentiles. ¹²When they had all joined in the same petition and had besought the merciful Lord with weeping and fasting and lying prostrate for three days without ceasing, Judas exhorted them and ordered them to stand ready.

¹³After consulting privately with the elders, he determined to march out and decide the matter by the help of God before the king's army could enter Judea and get possession of the city. ¹⁴So, committing the decision to the Creator of the world and exhorting his men to fight nobly to the death for the laws, temple, city, country, and commonwealth, he pitched his camp near Modein. ¹⁵He gave his men the watchword, "God's victory," and with a picked force of the bravest young men, he attacked the king's pavilion at night and slew as many as two thousand men in the camp. He stabbed the leading elephant and its rider. ¹⁶In the end they filled the camp with terror and confusion and withdrew in triumph. ¹⁷This happened, just as day was dawning, because the Lord's help protected him.

¹⁸The king, having had a taste of the daring of the Jews, tried strategy in attacking their positions. ¹⁹He advanced against Beth-zur, a strong fortress of the Jews, was turned back, attacked again, and was defeated. ²⁰Judas sent in to the garrison whatever was necessary. ²¹But Rhodocus, a man from the ranks of the Jews, gave secret information to the enemy; he was sought for, caught, and put in prison. ²²The king negotiated a second time with the people in Beth-zur, gave pledges, received theirs, withdrew, attacked Judas and his men,

was defeated; [23]he got word that Philip, who had been left in charge of the government, had revolted in Antioch; he was dismayed, called in the Jews, yielded and swore to observe all their rights, settled with them and offered sacrifice, honored the sanctuary and showed generosity to the holy place. [24]He received Maccabeus, left Hegemonides as governor from Ptolemais to Gerar, [25]and went to Ptolemais. The people of Ptolemais were indignant over the treaty; in fact they were so angry that they wanted to annul its terms. [26]Lysias took the public platform, made the best possible defense, convinced them, appeased them, gained their good will, and set out for Antioch. This is how the king's attack and withdrawal turned out.

The campaign of Lysias and Antiochus Eupator is also described in 1 Mac 6:18-63. The differences are noteworthy for the perspective of 2 Maccabees. 1 Maccabees describes the defeat of the Jews at Beth-zechariah. 2 Maccabees admits no defeat, but concentrates on a night skirmish in which the Jews were victorious. 1 Maccabees tells how Beth-zur surrendered for lack of supplies. 2 Maccabees claims that Judas managed to supply the city and that the king was defeated, but admits that he reached an agreement with the defenders. 1 Maccabees stresses the weakness of the Jews who were defending the temple (1 Mac 6:53-54) and suggests that they were on the verge of capitulation. 2 Maccabees admits no weakness and says that the king was defeated (13:22). Both accounts agree that the cause of Eupator's withdrawal was the revolt of Philip in Antioch, and that concessions were made to the Jews. 1 Mac 6:62, however, says that the king broke his oath and tore down the wall around Mt. Zion. Besides these points, all designed to obscure any suggestion that the Jews could be defeated, one other modification is noteworthy. 2 Mac 13:15 neglects to mention that it was

Eleazar, brother of Judas, who brought down the leading elephant, and that he met his death in the process. The mention of the watchword in this context, and the correlation of Eleazar's name with the watchword in 2 Mac 8:23, suggests that the source of 2 Maccabees (perhaps even the work of Jason) mentioned Eleazar. The omission indicates 2 Maccabees lack of interest in the Maccabean family, which was a major focus of attention in 1 Maccabees.

This chapter shows clearly a tendency in 2 Maccabees to gloss over the facts of history which are not easily reconciled with a clear theological doctrine. Evidently the author was concerned to put across his theological message rather than to report what happened accurately. (This tendency may be due to the abbreviator rather than to Jason.) Yet any theology must be able to account for the data of experience, for the defeat of the Jews when they were keeping the law and defending the temple, as well as for their success. The failure of 2 Maccabees to deal with the defeats of Judas must be considered a major defect.

B. The Reign of Demetrius

2 MAC 14:1-10: THE COMPLAINT OF ALCIMUS

14 Three years later, word came to Judas and his men that Demetrius, the son of Seleucus, had sailed into the harbor of Tripolis with a strong army and a fleet, ²and had taken possession of the country, having made away with Antiochus and his guardian Lysias.

³Now a certain Alcimus, who had formerly been high priest but had wilfully defiled himself in the times of separation, realized that there was no way for him to be safe or to have access again to the holy altar, ⁴and went to King Demetrius in about the one hundred and fifty-first year, presenting to him a crown of gold and a palm, and besides these some of the customary olive branches

from the temple. During that day he kept quiet. ⁵But he found an opportunity that furthered his mad purpose when he was invited by Demetrius to a meeting of the council and was asked about the disposition and intentions of the Jews. He answered:

⁶"Those of the Jews who are called Hasideans, whose leader is Judas Maccabeus, are keeping up war and stirring up sedition, and will not let the kingdom attain tranquillity. ⁷Therefore I have laid aside my ancestral glory—I mean the high priesthood—and have now come here, ⁸first because I am genuinely concerned for the interests of the king, and second because I have regard also for my fellow citizens. For through the folly of those whom I have mentioned our whole nation is now in no small misfortune. ⁹Since you are acquainted, O king, with the details of this matter, deign to take thought for our country and our hard-pressed nation with the gracious kindness which you show to all. ¹⁰For as long as Judas lives, it is impossible for the government to find peace."

The final episode in 2 Maccabees is set in the reign of Demetrius I. In accordance with the consistent viewpoint of 2 Maccabees, the real instigator of the trouble is once more a Jew, in this case Alcimus, a member of the high priestly family. As in the case of Menelaus, Alcimus is interested only in his own advancement. It is somewhat surprising that 2 Maccabees passes over in silence the treacherous slaughter of the Hasideans by Alcimus (1 Mac 7:12-18) but this may be due to the tendency to ignore Jewish setbacks after the point where God's wrath had turned to mercy (8:5).

Alcimus is used in the narrative of 2 Maccabees to pronounce the Hellenizing Jews' view of the situation. From their perspective, the cause of the trouble lies with "the

Hasideans, whose leader is Judas Maccabee." In 1 Maccabees, the link between Judas and the Hasideans is not so close. They join after the revolt has been initiated and are the first to make peace. In 2 Maccabees, Judas does not figure as the representative of his family but as the leader of the Hasideans, and it is assumed that he shares their piety. A Hellenizer like Alcimus may well have overlooked differences within the resistance movement. On the other hand, the close linkage of Judas with the Hasideans may reflect the views of the author of 2 Maccabees, or of Jason of Cyrene.

2 MAC 14:11-36: JUDAS AND NICANOR

[11]When he had said this, the rest of the king's friends, who were hostile to Judas, quickly inflamed Demetrius still more. [12]And he immediately chose Nicanor, who had been in command of the elephants, appointed him governor of Judea, and sent him off [13]with orders to kill Judas and scatter his men, and to set up Alcimus as high priest of the greatest temple. [14]And the Gentiles throughout Judea, who had fled before Judas, flocked to join Nicanor, thinking that the misfortunes and calamities of the Jews would mean prosperity for themselves.

[15]When the Jews heard of Nicanor's coming and the gathering of the Gentiles, they sprinkled dust upon their heads and prayed to him who established his own people for ever and always upholds his own heritage by manifesting himself. [16]At the command of the leader, they set out from there immediately and engaged them in battle at a village called Dessau. [17]Simon, the brother of Judas, had encountered Nicanor, but had been temporarily checked because of the sudden consternation created by the enemy.

¹⁸Nevertheless Nicanor, hearing of the valor of Judas and his men and their courage in battle for their country, shrank from deciding the issue by bloodshed. ¹⁹Therefore he sent Posidonius and Theodotus and Mattathias to give and receive pledges of friendship. ²⁰When the terms had been fully considered, and the leader had informed the people, and it appeared that they were of one mind, they agreed to the covenant. ²¹And the leaders set a day on which to meet by themselves. A chariot came forward from each army; seats of honor were set in place; ²²Judas posted armed men in readiness at key places to prevent sudden treachery on the part of the enemy; they held the proper conference.

²³Nicanor stayed on in Jerusalem and did nothing out of the way, but dismissed the flocks of people that had gathered.²⁴And he kept Judas always in his presence; he was warmly attached to the man. ²⁵And he urged him to marry and have children; so he married, settled down, and shared the common life.

²⁶But when Alcimus noticed their good will for one another, he took the covenant that had been made and went to Demetrius. He told him that Nicanor was disloyal to the government, for he had appointed that conspirator against the kingdom, Judas, to be his successor. ²⁷The king became excited and, provoked by the false accusations of that depraved man, wrote to Nicanor, stating that he was displeased with the covenant and commanding him to send Maccabeus to Antioch as a prisoner without delay.

²⁸When this message came to Nicanor, he was troubled and grieved that he had to annul their agreement when the man had done no wrong. ²⁹Since it was not possible to oppose the king, he watched for an opportunity to accomplish this by a stratagem.

³⁰But Maccabeus, noticing that Nicanor was more

austere in his dealings with him and was meeting him more rudely than had been his custom, concluded that this austerity did not spring from the best motives. So he gathered not a few of his men, and went into hiding from Nicanor.

³¹When the latter became aware that he had been cleverly outwitted by the man, he went to the great and holy temple while the priests were offering the customary sacrifices, and commanded them to hand the man over. ³²And when they declared on oath that they did not know where the man was whom he sought, ³³he stretched out his right hand toward the sanctuary, and swore this oath: "If you do not hand Judas over to me as a prisoner, I will level this precinct of God to the ground and tear down the altar, and I will build here a splendid temple to Dionysus."

³⁴Having said this, he went away. Then the priests stretched forth their hands toward heaven and called upon the constant Defender of our nation, in these words: ³⁵"O Lord of all, who hast need of nothing, thou wast pleased that there be a temple for thy habitation among us; ³⁶so now, O holy One, Lord of all holiness, keep undefiled for ever this house that has been so recently purified."

The campaign of Nicanor is paralleled in 1 Mac 7:26-50. The most striking difference between the two accounts is that in 2 Maccabees Nicanor genuinely seeks peace and conceives an affection for Judas. He moves against Judas reluctantly, and only because of the scheming of Alcimus. In 1 Maccabees, by contrast, Nicanor is presumed to be hypocritical in his offer of peace. It is difficult to say which of these accounts is more correct. Both 1 Maccabees and 2 Maccabees elsewhere depict Nicanor as an especially arrogant individual, very hostile to the Jews. This portrayal could be polemical in intent, to make the account of his defeat more satisfying. On the other hand, 2 Maccabees' account of his friendship for Judas may be due to the desire to show how even a gentile found Judas attractive. We may compare how Antiochus Epiphanes was said to grieve over the murder of the high priest Onias (2 Mac 4:37). If Judas did indeed marry at this time, the peace must have lasted somewhat longer than 1 Maccabees suggested.

2 Maccabees omits the first defeat of Nicanor by Judas (1 Mac 7:31-32) perhaps to sharpen the focus on the final battle with which the book concludes. Both books emphasize the threat against the temple. (2 Maccabees adds the threat to build a temple of Dionysus.) This threat was made despite the loyalty of the high priest Alcimus. Nicanor knew that the supporters of Judas were passionately devoted to the temple.

The threat against the temple provides an appropriate backdrop for the final episode of the book. Just as the narrative began with the successful defence of the temple against Heliodorus, it ends with the successful repulse of Nicanor.

2 MAC 14: 37-46: THE SUICIDE OF RAZIS

[37]A certain Razis, one of the elders of Jerusalem, was denounced to Nicanor as a man who loved his fellow citizens and was very well thought of and for his good will was called father of the Jews. [38]For in former times, when there was no mingling with the Gentiles, he had been accused of Judaism, and for Judaism he had with all zeal risked body and life. [39]Nicanor, wishing to exhibit the enmity which he had for the Jews, sent more than five hundred soldiers to arrest him; [40]for he thought that by arresting him he would do them an in-

jury. [41]When the troops were about to capture the tower
and were forcing the door of the courtyard, they
ordered that fire be brought and the doors burned. Being surrounded Razis fell upon his own sword, [42]prefer-
ring to die nobly rather than to fall into the hands of sinners and suffer outrages unworthy of his noble birth.
[43]But in the heat of the struggle he did not hit exactly,
and the crowd was now rushing in through the doors.
He bravely ran up on the wall, and manfully threw
himself down into the crowd. [44]But as they quickly drew
back, a space opened and he fell in the middle of the
empty space. [45]Still alive and aflame with anger, he rose,
and though his blood gushed forth and his wounds were
severe he ran through the crowd; and standing upon a
steep rock, [46]with his blood now completely drained
from him, he tore out his entrails, took them with both
hands and hurled them at the crowd, calling upon the
Lord of life and spirit to give them back to him again.
This was the manner of his death.

The story of Razis has obvious affinities with that of the
martyrs in 2 Maccabees 6 and 7. The story is a distinct unit
in itself, which is inserted here because the tyrant is identified as Nicanor. There are a few anomalies in the present
setting. In 14:41 we find that the soldiers are attacking a
tower, which had not hitherto been mentioned. The inclusion of such a determined traditionalist among the Elders,
during the high priesthood of Alcimus, is surprising, but
the office adds to the dignity of the hero. The "former
times when there was no mingling with the gentiles" probably means the persecution under Antiochus Epiphanes.
No explanation is given for how he survived that ordeal.
The claim that Nicanor took five hundred soldiers to arrest
one man reflects the hyperbolic character of a legend.
  The death of Razis differs from that of the martyrs in so

far as it is self-inflicted. Although apparently rare in earlier biblical times (only three cases are recorded: Saul and his arm bearer; Ahitophel, Zimri), suicide in desperate situations became a respected act of defiance in ancient Judaism. The most famous example is the mass suicide of the Zealots at Masada, rather than fall into the hands of the Romans. In the case of Razis, it is in part inspired by the hope of resurrection. The suicide was evidently not considered sinful in itself.

The story is told in very gory detail. A later Jewish source, Josippon (a Hebrew re-writing of Josephus' *Jewish War* from about the fourth century CE) suggests that Razis had lost his mind when he ripped out his entrails and threw them at the crowd. 2 Maccabees apparently presents the act as one of heroism, but it is difficult to read it without some revulsion. Razis is not only defiant. He is fanatical in an extreme degree. He is scarcely a model to be imitated!

2 MAC 15:1-5: THE THREATENED ATTACK ON THE SABBATH

15 When Nicanor heard that Judas and his men were in the region of Samaria, he made plans to attack them with complete safety on the day of rest. ²And when the Jews who were compelled to follow him said, "Do not destroy so savagely and barbarously, but show respect for the day which he who sees all things has honored and hallowed above other days," ³the thrice-accursed wretch asked if there were a sovereign in heaven who had commanded the keeping of the sabbath day. ⁴And when they declared, "It is the living Lord himself, the Sovereign in heaven, who ordered us to observe the seventh day," ⁵he replied, "And I am a sovereign also, on earth, and I command you to take up arms and finish the king's business." Nevertheless, he did not succeed in carrying out his abominable design.

Nicanor's threat to attack the Jews on the sabbath is of interest for two reasons.

First, it ignores the decision of the Maccabees to fight on the sabbath to defend themselves (1 Mac 2:41). It is typical of 2 Maccabees that it obscures the deviation of the Maccabees from strict observance of the law.

Second, Nicanor sets himself up as sovereign on earth, over against the sovereign in heaven. His arrogance, or hybris, points forward inevitably to his fall.

2 MAC 15:6-27: THE MOTIVATION OF THE JEWS

⁶This Nicanor in his utter boastfulness and arrogance had determined to erect a public monument of victory over Judas and his men. ⁷But Maccabeus did not cease to trust with all confidence that he would get help from the Lord. ⁸And he exhorted his men not to fear the attack of the Gentiles, but to keep in mind the former times when help had come to them from heaven, and now to look for the victory which the Almighty would give them. ⁹Encouraging them from the law and the prophets, and reminding them also of the struggles they had won, he made them the more eager. ¹⁰And when he had aroused their courage, he gave his orders, at the same time pointing out the perfidy of the Gentiles and their violation of oaths. ¹¹He armed each of them not so much with confidence in shields and spears as with the inspiration of brave words, and he cheered them all by relating a dream, a sort of vision, which was worthy of belief.

¹²What he saw was this: Onias, who had been high priest, a noble and good man, of modest bearing and gentle manner, one who spoke fittingly and had been trained from childhood in all that belongs to excellence, was praying with outstretched hands for the whole body of the Jews. ¹³Then likewise a man appeared, distinguished by his gray hair and dignity, and of

marvelous majesty and authority. ¹⁴And Onias spoke, saying, "This is a man who loves the brethren and prays much for the people and the holy city, Jeremiah, the prophet of God." ¹⁵Jeremiah stretched out his right hand and gave to Judas a golden sword, and as he gave it he addressed him thus: ¹⁶"Take this holy sword, a gift from God, with which you will strike down your adversaries."

¹⁷Encouraged by the words of Judas, so noble and so effective in arousing valor and awaking manliness in the souls of the young, they determined not to carry on a campaign but to attack bravely, and to decide the matter, by fighting hand to hand with all courage, because the city and the sanctuary and the temple were in danger. ¹⁸Their concern for wives and children, and also for brethren and relatives, lay upon them less heavily; their greatest and first fear was for the consecrated sanctuary. ¹⁹And those who had to remain in the city were in no little distress, being anxious over the encounter in the open country.

²⁰When all were now looking forward to the coming decision, and the enemy was already close at hand with their army drawn up for battle, the elephants strategically stationed and the cavalry deployed on the flanks, ²¹Maccabeus, perceiving the hosts that were before him and the varied supply of arms and the savagery of the elephants, stretched out his hands toward heaven and called upon the Lord who works wonders; for he knew that it is not by arms, but as the Lord decides, that he gains the victory for those who deserve it. ²²And he called upon him in these words: "O Lord, thou didst send thy angel in the time of Hezekiah king of Judea, and he slew fully a hundred and eighty-five thousand in the camp of Sennacherib. ²³So now, O Sovereign of the heavens, send a good angel to carry ter-

ror and trembling before us. ²⁴By the might of thy arm may these blasphemers who come against thy holy people be struck down." With these words he ended his prayer.

²⁵Nicanor and his men advanced with trumpets and battle songs; ²⁶and Judas and his men met the enemy in battle with invocation to God and prayers. ²⁷So, fighting with their hands and praying to God in their hearts, they laid low no less than thirty-five thousand men, and were greatly gladdened by God's manifestation.

Judas, in sharp contrast to Nicanor, places all his trust in the Lord. The prayer before battle, and specifically the recollection of the destruction of Sennacherib by the angel of the Lord, are by now familiar elements in the battles of 2 Maccabees. (Compare 8:19; 10:29-31; 11:6-8.) So also is the concern for the sanctuary in 15:18. The distinctive element in chap. 15 is Judas' dream.

The dream juxtaposes the slain high priest, Onias III, and the prophet Jeremiah, thereby greatly exalting Onias. Moreover, both Onias and Jeremiah now lend their authority to Judas. There is a cerain irony in the endorsement of Judas by Onias, which must have been evident in the time when 2 Maccabees, in its present form was written. Judas' brothers would later usurp the high priesthood, while the son of Onias would go into exile in Egypt and build a temple at Leontopolis, in violation of Jewish law. 2 Maccabees pays minimal attention to the other Maccabees, and the passage can not be taken as a legitimation of the transfer of the high priesthood. Rather, it suggests that Judas was a man of whom Onias would have approved. That could scarcely be said of his brothers.

The introduction of Jeremiah here has a touch of irony too, but one which is less likely to have been perceived by

the author. Jeremiah was the prophet who had counselled
surrender to the Babylonians, and was accused of
"weakening the hands of the soldiers who are left in this city" (Jer 38:1-6). No biblical figure would be less apt to endorse the Maccabees. The reason that Jeremiah is chosen is
that the sword appears as the dominant image in an oracle
attributed to him, Jer 50:35-38: "A sword upon the Chaldeans, says the Lord, and upon the inhabitants of Babylon
. . ." Even though Jeremiah has Yahweh fight against
Israel more often than not (e.g. Jer 21:3-7) the oracle provides a basis for linking Jeremiah with a sword against the
gentiles.

The "Animal Apocalypse" in 1 Enoch, to which we
have referred above in connection with 2 Maccabees 11,
also says that "a big sword was given to the sheep (1 En
90:19; the sheep are the faithful Jews). The apocalypse
may be referring to the same legend as 2 Mac 15:15-16. The
constant reliance on the supernatural is a major point of
contact between the theology of 2 Maccabees and that of
the apocalypses.

The dream evidently adds authority and stature to
Judas. It could inspire deeper confidence in his followers,
and that was surely an advantage on the eve of battle. Yet
we must be wary of the use of supernatural legends as a
device for bolstering authority. The legend says nothing of
the merits of the way in which the authority is used.

2 MAC 15:28-36: THE DEATH OF NICANOR

> [28]When the action was over and they were returning
> with joy, they recognized Nicanor, lying dead, in full ar-
> mor. [29]Then there was shouting and tumult, and they
> blessed the Sovereign Lord in the language of their
> fathers. [30]And the man who was ever in body and soul
> the defender of his fellow citizens, the man who main-
> tained his youthful good will toward his countrymen,

ordered them to cut off Nicanor's head and arm and carry them to Jerusalem. ³¹And when he arrived there and had called his countrymen together and stationed the priests before the altar, he sent for those who were in the citadel. ³²He showed them the vile Nicanor's head and that profane man's arm, which had been boastfully stretched out against the holy house of the Almighty; ³³and he cut out the tongue of the ungodly Nicanor and said that he would give it piecemeal to the birds and hang up these rewards of his folly opposite the sanctuary. ³⁴And they all, looking to heaven, blessed the Lord who had manifested himself, saying, "Blessed is he who has kept his own place undefiled." ³⁵And he hung Nicanor's head from the citadel, a clear and conspicuous sign to every one of the help of the Lord. ³⁶And they all decreed by public vote never to let this day go unobserved, but to celebrate the thirteenth day of the twelfth month—which is called Adar in the Syrian language—the day before Mordecai's day.

The defeat of Nicanor was a major event, subsequently celebrated in a festival. We cannot fail to be struck, however, by the vengeful gloating over the dead general. Not only was his head cut off and displayed, a common though gruesome practice in warfare. His tongue was cut out to be fed to the birds. The gloating over Nicanor is all the more striking if 2 Maccabees 14 is correct in saying that Judas and Nicanor had been genuine friends.

The fact that Nicanor had blasphemed against the temple should not obscure the vengeful character of this treatment. Christians should not, however, assume that vengeance is a Jewish trait. Despite the well-known Christian teaching on loving one's enemy, the sentiments in the closing chapters of the New Testament Apocalypse are as vengeful as anything in Jewish literature. Passages like 2 Mac 15:28-36, or Rev 19:17-21, are not morally edifying in any sense, but they are emotionally satisfying for anyone who has ever had a serious enemy at all. This emotional satisfaction should not be despised. Human nature must have its due.

2 MAC 15:37-39: THE EPILOGUE

[37]This, then, is how matters turned out with Nicanor. And from that time the city has been in the possession of the Hebrews. So I too will here end my story. [38]If it is well told and to the point, that is what I myself desired; if it is poorly done and mediocre, that was the best I could do. [39]For just as it is harmful to drink wine alone, or, again, to drink water alone, while wine mixed with water is sweet and delicious and enhances one's enjoyment, so also the style of the story delights the ears of those who read the work. And here will be the end.

Nicanor's severed head and tongue scarcely prepare us for the abbreviator's concluding reflection on his work. His task had been to enhance our enjoyment. Whether or not enjoyment is quite the right word, there is no doubt that he has told a vivid and memorable story.

The reason given for breaking off here is that "from that time the city has been in the possession of the Hebrews." It is also consistent with the aims of the author that the story should end on an up-beat, before it has to reckon with the death of Judas Maccabee.

Second Maccabees in Retrospect

THERE IS MUCH historical information to be gleaned from 2 Maccabees. Yet we have seen that the sequence of this material is often disrupted. Major episodes in the book are clearly legendary in character. Furthermore, history is simplified, so that the Maccabees suffer no setbacks once the revolt gets underway, and the narrative stops before the death of Judas. 2 Maccabees has the character of an historical novel, where the historical data are selected, modified and supplemented as necessary to convey the author's message.

We have seen how that message has various political and theological facets. At the heart of the book is the Jewish covenant, symbolized by the temple, but demanding primarily fidelity to the law. History is regulated in accordance with performance within the covenant. The narrative of 2 Maccabees is constructed to show that the course of events is governed by a providential principle of retribution. Repeatedly in the course of the book sinners meet with punishments appropriate to their crimes. The crisis which befalls the Jews is explained uncompromisingly as punishment for sins within the Jewish people. Even the deaths of the martyrs are punishments for sin, although it is for the collective sins of the people rather than for those of the individuals who suffer. When Jews are killed in battle, they are found to be guilty of sin. Prosperity and success are due to the protection of God, but that protection is ensured by prayer and pious conduct.

This theological system is not easily falsified. When the wicked prosper, we may assume that their time will come. When the righteous suffer, we are reminded that it is a sign of the clemency of God to discipline his children, rather than wait until their sins reach their height. While verification is not always possible, this theology has at least a constructive effect. It invites self-criticism when anything goes wrong (whereas 1 Maccabees tends to externalize the blame onto the gentiles). It makes suffering bearable and restrains envy. This is all the more true in view of the belief in an afterlife, where retribution is always possible.

Yet, despite its advantages, we must also recognize that the theology of 2 Maccabees strains credibility in its insistence that all suffering is a punishment for sin. Human experience can not be so systematically explained. Life has its areas of randomness or of mystery, which defy reduction to a law of cause and effect.

The enduring impact of 2 Maccabees derives, not from its theology of retribution, but from the examples of the martyrs. The ability to resist coercion even in the face of death is the ultimate expression of human freedom, and commands our admiration, irrespective of the issues at stake. The major contribution of 2 Maccabees to the Judeo-Christian tradition lies in its affirmation of the inalienable human right to say no to oppression, and the human ability to do so even at the cost of life itself. This affirmation is shared by both Daniel and 1 Maccabees in their different ways. It is ultimately more important than the diverse theological conceptions which are used to support it. It is the most valuable legacy of the Maccabean revolt.

FOR FURTHER READING

I. History of the Maccabean Period

Aharoni, Y. and Avi-Yonah, M. eds., *The Macmillan Bible Atlas* (New York: Macmillan, 1968). Detailed maps illustrating the events of 1 and 2 Maccabees.

Bickermann, Elias, *The God of the Maccabees* (Leiden: Brill, forthcoming). First published in German in 1937. A seminal work which has had great influence on all subsequent studies.

Hengel, Martin, *Judaism and Hellenism.* 2 vols. (Philadelphia: Fortress, 1974). Ground-breaking study of the religious and cultural climate immediately before the revolt.

Nickelsburg, G.W. *Jewish Literature Between the Bible and the Mishnah* (Philadelphia: Fortress, 1981). Introduction to the literature of the period.

Schäfer, Peter, "The Hellenistic and Maccabean Periods," in J.H. Hayes and M. Miller, eds., *Israelite and Judean History.* Old Testament Library. (Philadelphia: Westminster, 1977) 539-604. Concise scholarly treatment.

Schürer, Emil, *A History of the Jewish People in the Time of Jesus Christ.* Vol. 1; revised and edited by G. Vermes and F. Millar (Edinburgh: Clark, 1973). Detailed presentation of the sources for the period.

Tcherikover, Victor, *Hellenistic Civilization and the Jews* (New York: Atheneum, 1959). Well documented but lively. Brilliant reconstruction of the history of the second century BCE.

II. Daniel

Clifford, Richard J., *The Book of Daniel.* Herald Biblical Booklets (Chicago: Franciscan Herald Press, 1980). Excellent brief treatment.

Collins, John J., *The Apocalyptic Vision of the Book of Daniel.* Harvard Semitic Monographs 16 (Chico, California: Scholars Press, 1977). Full, documented presentation of the interpretation of Daniel given here.

Hammer, Raymond J., *The Book of Daniel.* The Cambridge Bible Commentary on the New English Bible (Cambridge: Cambridge University, 1976). Good presentation of the spirit of the book.

Hartman, L.F. and DiLella, A.A., *The Book of Daniel.* Anchor Bible 23 (Garden City, New York: Doubleday, 1978). An interpretation of Daniel sharply different from that presented here.

Lacocque, André, *The Book of Daniel* (Atlanta: John Knox Press, London: S.P.C.K., 1979. The best recent full-length commentary on Daniel.

McNamara, Martin, "Daniel," in *The New Catholic Commentary on Holy Scripture* (London: Nelson, 1969) 650-675. Concise, reliable commentary.

Montgomery, J.A. *Daniel.* International Critical Commentary. (New York: Scribners; Edinburgh: T. & T. Clarke, 1927). Classic scholarly treatment. Still indispensable on chapters 1 to 6.

III. Apocalyptic Literature

Collins, John J. ed., *Apocalypse: The Morphology of a Genre.* Semeia 14 (Chico, California: Scholars Press, 1979). Overview and bibliography of the corpus of apocalyptic writings.

Hellholm, David, ed., *Apocalypticism in the Mediterranean World and the Near East.* Proceedings of the International Colloquium on Apocalypticism at Uppsala, Sweden, in August 1979 (Tübingen: Mohr, forthcoming). Extensive collection of essays, broadly representative of contemporary scholarship.

Hengel, Martin, *Judaism and Hellenism.* 2 vols. (Philadelphia: Fortress, 1974) 1:175-218. Rich information on the early apocalyptic literature.

Koch, Klaus, *The Rediscovery of Apocalyptic* (Naperville, Ill.: Allenson, 1972). Critical review of recent scholarly and theological treatments of the apocalyptic literature.

Russell, D.S. *The Method and Message of Jewish Apocalyptic.* Old Testament Library (Philadelphia: Westminster; London: S.C.M. Press, 1964). Still the best comprehensive treatment.

Rowley, H.H., *The Relevance of Apocalyptic* (New and revised edition, London: Lutterworth Press, 1963). Simple, classic discussion.

Schmithals, W. *The Apocalyptic Movement* (Nashville: Abingdon, 1975). Lively account of apocalypticism as a kind of religion in Judaism, Christianity and Gnosticism, but it tends to sweeping generalisations and is not always reliable.

Stone, M.E., *Scriptures, Sects and Visions* (Philadelphia: Fortress, 1980). Brief but excellent treatment of apocalypticism and related phenomena.

The main texts may be found in:

Charles, R.H., *Apocrypha and Pseudepigrapha of the Old Testament* (Oxford: Clarendon, 1913). Vol. 2. The introductions in this volume are no longer reliable.

Vermes, Geza, *The Dead Sea Scrolls in English.* 2nd ed. (Harmondsworth: Penguin Books, 1975; Baltimore: Pelican, 1978). The main documents from Qumran (except for the Temple Scroll, which has not yet been translated into English).

A new translation of the Pseudepigrapha, with introductions and notes, edited by J.H. Charlesworth, is in press, with Doubleday (scheduled for publication in 1982).

IV.　First and Second Maccabees

Abel, F.M., *Les Livres des Maccabées.* 2nd ed. (Paris: Gabalda, 1949). Still the best full commentary, but never translated into English.

Bartlett, John R., *The First and Second Books of Maccabees.* The Cambridge Bible Commentary on the New English Bible (Cambridge: Cambridge University, 1973). Reliable annotations on the historical and geographical references.

Corbishley, T., "1 and 2 Maccabees," in *The New Catholic Commentary on Holy Scripture* (London: Nelson, 1969) 743-758. Useful short commentary.

Dancy, J.C., *A Commentary on 1 Maccabees* (Oxford: Blackwells, 1954). Terse but useful.

Doran, Robert, *Temple Propaganda: The Purpose and Character of 2 Maccabees.* Catholic Biblical Quarterly Monographs (Washington: Catholic Biblical Association, forthcoming). Excellent study of the style and purpose of 2 Maccabees.

Goldstein, Jonathan, *1 Maccabees.* Anchor Bible 41 (Garden City, New York: Doubleday, 1976). Vast store of historical information, but very speculative and not always reliable. (Goldstein's companion commentary on 2 Maccabees is forthcoming.)

McEleny, N. "1-2 Maccabees," in *The Jerome Biblical Commentary* (Englewood-Cliffs, New Jersey: Prentice Hall, 1968) 461-486. Useful short commentary.

Tedesche, Sidney and Zeitlin, Solomon. *The First Book of Maccabees.* Dropsie College Series (New York: Harper, 1950) and *The Second Book of Maccabees.* Dropsie College Series (New York: Harper, 1954). Greek text with facing translation. Extensive introductions and notes. Very useful, but Zeitlin's historical reconstructions are not always reliable.

CHRONOLOGICAL TABLES

I The Babylonian and Persian Periods

605/4-562	Reign of Nebuchadnezzar
597	First deportation from Jerusalem
587	Fall of Jerusalem. Second deportation
562-560	Amel-marduk, king of Babylon
560-556	Nergilissar, king of Babylon
556-539	Nabonidus, king of Babylon (Belshazzar, regent in Babylon, 549-539)
550	Cyrus of Persia defeats Astyages and conquers Media
539	Cyrus takes Babylon, and shortly afterwards releases the Jewish captives
530-522	Cambyses, king of Persia
522-486	Darius I Hystaspes
486-465	Xerxes
465-424	Artaxerxes I Careers of Ezra and Nehemiah
423	Xerxes II
423-404	Darius II
404-358	Artaxerxes II
358-338	Artaxerxes III
338-336	Arses
336-331	Darius III
331	Alexander the Great conquers the Persian empire

II   The Hellenistic Kingdoms

Egypt: the Ptolemies	*Syria: the Seleucids*
Ptolemy I Soter 323–285	Seleucus I 312/11-280
Ptolemy II Philadelphus	Antiochus I 280-261
285-246	Antiochus II 261-246

Philadelphus gave his daughter Berenice in marriage to Antiochus II. She was later put aside and murdered.

Ptolemy III Euergetes	Seleucus II 246-226
246-221	
Ptolemy IV Philopator	Seleucus III 226-223
221-203	
Ptolemy V Epiphanes	Antiochus III the Great
203-181	223-187

198   Palestine passed from the Ptolemies to the Seleucids
197   Antiochus gave his daughter Cleopatra in
        marriage to Ptolemy V

Ptolemy VI Philometor	Seleucus IV 187-175
181-146	Antiochus IV Epiphanes
	175-164

III   The Maccabean Period

175   Death of Seleucus IV. He is succeeded by
                his brother Antiochus IV Epiphanes.
175/74   Jason obtains the high priesthood by
                bribery and begins the Hellenistic
                Reform.

172	Menelaus outbids Jason for the priesthood.
170	Murder of Onias III, the legitimate high priest.
170/69	Antiochus Epiphanes' first invasion of Egypt.
169	Jason tries to recapture Jerusalem but fails to hold it, and again goes into exile. Antiochus plunders the temple in Jerusalem.
168	Antiochus' second invasion of Egypt. He is forced to withdraw by a Roman ultimatum.
167	Apollonius massacres Jews in Jerusalem. The citadel Akra is fortified. Antiochus bans the Jewish law. The persecution begins. The "abomination of desolation" is placed on the altar in the temple. The rebellion also gets underway.
165	Nicanor and Gorgias defeated at Emmaus.
164	Lysias, repulsed at Beth-zur, makes a settlement with the Jews. End of the persecution. Death of Antiochus Epiphanes. Purification of the temple.
163	Lysias, accompanied by Antiochus V, defeats Judas at Beth-zechariah.
163	Menelaus deposed and executed by Antiochus V. Alcimus is appointed high priest.
162	Demetrius I, son of Seleucus IV, claims to be king. Antiochus V and Lysias are murdered.

161	Defeat of Nicanor by Judas at Adasa. Embassy of the Jews to Rome.
160	Judas defeated and killed by Bacchides at Elasa.
152	Alexander Balas, son of Antiochus IV claims to be king. He appoints Jonathan Maccabee high priest.
150	Demetrius I is killed in battle against Alexander Balas.
147	Demetrius II claims the throne.
145	Deaths of Alexander Balas and Ptolemy VI Philometor of Egypt.
145	Antiochus VI, son of Alexander Balas, is proclaimed king by Trypho.
143	Jonathan sends envoys to Rome and Sparta. Jonathan is captured by Trypho and subsequently murdered.
142	Simon is declared high priest. Death of Antiochus VI.
141	The Akra garrison is disbanded.
139	Demetrius II captured by the Parthians.
138	Antiochus VII Sidetes becomes king. Simon's sons, John and Judas, defeat the king's general in battle.
134	Simon and two of his sons are murdered at Jericho by his son-in-law, Ptolemy. John Hyrcanus becomes leader of the Jews.

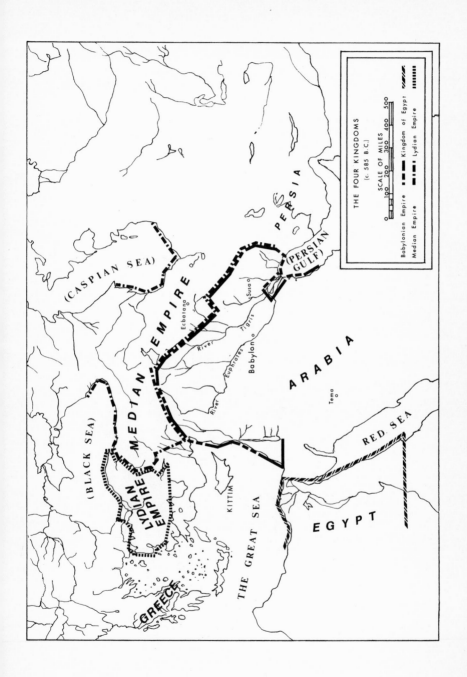

THE FOUR KINGDOMS
(c. 585 B.C.)

SCALE OF MILES
0   100 200 300 400 500

Babylonian Empire   Kingdom of Egypt
Median Empire   Lydian Empire

(CASPIAN SEA)

PERSIA

(PERSIAN GULF)

MEDIAN EMPIRE

Ecbatana

Susa

River Tigris

River Euphrates

Babylon

ARABIA

Tema

RED SEA

(BLACK SEA)

LYDIAN EMPIRE

KITTIM

THE GREAT SEA

EGYPT

GREECE

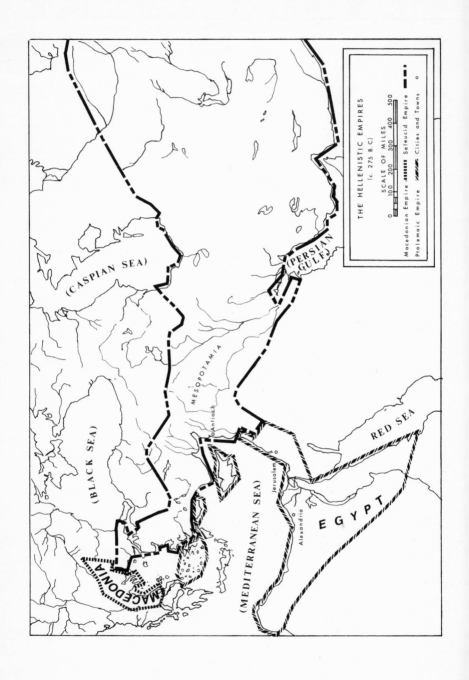

THE HELLENISTIC EMPIRES
(c. 275 B.C.)

SCALE OF MILES
0 100 200 300 400 500

Macedonian Empire ▓▓▓▓ Seleucid Empire ▓▓▓
Ptolemaic Empire ⁄⁄⁄⁄ Cities and Towns ○

(CASPIAN SEA)

(PERSIAN GULF)

(BLACK SEA)

MESOPOTAMIA

○Antioch

RED SEA

Jerusalem ○

(MEDITERRANEAN SEA)

Alexandria ○

E G Y P T

MACEDONIA

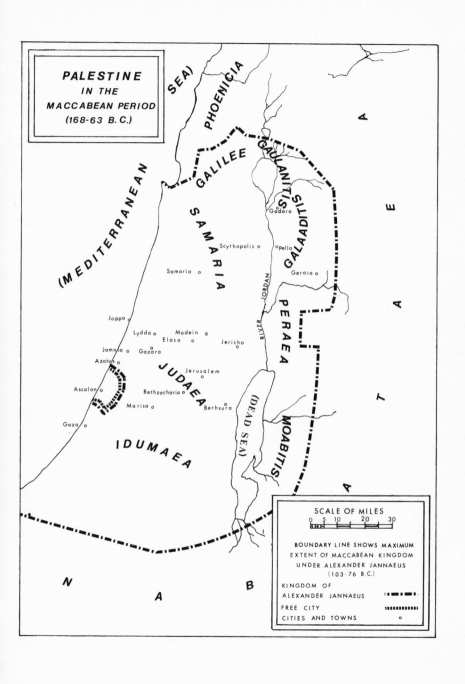

PALESTINE
IN THE
MACCABEAN PERIOD
(168-63 B.C.)

(MEDITERRANEAN SEA)

PHOENICIA

GALILEE

SAMARIA

GAULANITIS

GALAADITIS

o Gadara

Scythopolis o

o Pella

Samaria o

Gerasa o

JORDAN RIVER

PERAEA

Joppa o

Lydda o   Modein o

Elasa o   Jericho o

Jamnia o   Gazara o

Azotus o

JUDAEA

Jerusalem o

Ascalon o

Bethzacharia o

Marisa o   Bethsura o

Gaza o

(DEAD SEA)

MOABITIS

IDUMAEA

N   A   B   A   T   A   E

SCALE OF MILES

0 5 10   20   30

BOUNDARY LINE SHOWS MAXIMUM
EXTENT OF MACCABEAN KINGDOM
UNDER ALEXANDER JANNAEUS
(103-76 B.C.)

KINGDOM OF
ALEXANDER JANNAEUS

FREE CITY

CITIES AND TOWNS   o